THE DARK FOREVER

by
DAN BRERETON

lettered by
SEAN KONOT

introduction by
DAVE MANDEL

afterword & pin-ups by
ALEX ROSS

book design by
KEITH WOOD

edited by
JAMIE S. RICH

oni
PRESS

Published by Oni Press, Inc.

JOE NOZEMACK, publisher
JAMIE S. RICH, editor in chief
JAMES LUCAS JONES, associate editor

ONI PRESS, INC.
6336 SE Milwaukie Avenue, PMB30
Portland, OR 97202
USA

www.onipress.com
www.nocturnals.com

First Oni Press edition: May 2002
ISBN 1-929998-23-6

1 3 5 7 9 10 8 6 4 2

PRINTED IN CANADA.

xxxxxxxx INTRODUCTION xxxxxxxx

OK, before you read this *Nocturnals* trade paperback, there are just a couple of things I want to go over. Just a few ground rules and pieces of general information that I jotted down to help make your reading experience that much better. Or as they say in *Nocturnals*: "Mo' better!" Actually, nobody in *Nocturnals* has ever said that. I should really read the *Nocturnals* before I write this. Anyway, here we go:

1. The Nocturnals are from another dimension. If this is the first time you have ever heard of the Nocturnals, and you just picked this book up in Barnes and Noble, then the first thing I must tell you is that you can probably find it for a lot cheaper on Amazon.com. Barnes and Noble had really low prices when they first opened their superstores, but that was so they could drive out all the small independent booksellers. After all the competition was gone, Barnes and Noble raised all the prices again. They are to blame for the destruction of the independent bookstore in America with their fancy magazine racks and coffee bars. I hate them. I hate them. I hate them. The Nocturnals come from a dimension where there is no Barnes and there was only one Noble, but he was killed by Barnes. Actually, there isn't much of anything because their dimension was basically destroyed. That's why they are here on Earth: to save us from what destroyed their home. And that's why they look so darn scary.

2. Dan Brereton loves monsters. Dan is the biggest Godzilla fan in the world. He has three kids, but Dan has more Godzilla toys than the three kids put together. His past work has included *Giantkiller*, which had monsters in it, and a Justice League story where they all turned into monsters. I'm no psychiatrist, but maybe deep down, Dan thinks he is a monster. Boy, that's kind of sad. Why don't you buy two copies of this book to help pay for his therapy.

3. If you are a film producer or own a large film studio or are the son of a man who owns a large film studio or you are the seventeen-year-old girl secretly sleeping with the man who owns his own large film studio, then please, for the love of God, turn *Nocturnals* into a movie. What's the big deal? Every other crappy comic book in the world has been turned into a movie. What the hell was *Barb Wire*? Or that *X-Men* thing with the big climactic fight in the Statue of Liberty gift shop? "Look out, Wolverine, you'll knock over the snow globes and postcard racks!" There are no gift shops in *Nocturnals*. And if there was a gift shop in *Nocturnals*, it would be a really cool and spooky gift shop. A gift shop that would help to defend the people of earth from the forces of evil. A gift shop that people would see and shout out to the heavens, "That gift shop should be in the movies!" C'mon, people, this thing is a no-brainer. Doc Horror...Tommy Lee Jones. Halloween Girl...Tommy Lee Jones. You must put Tommy Lee Jones in this film. And check out that Gunwitch guy. I bet the guy who played Jaws in *Spy Who Loved Me* could play him. Plus, I happen to know that Dan is not the strongest businessman in the world—he *does* do most of his work for Oni. So I am willing to bet you could get him to sign a really bad deal for him and his adorable family. You could probably own these Nocturnals characters outright and make all the Raccoon action figures and Gunwitch hats and never have to pay Dan a cent. Hell, you could probably get rid of Dan and bring in a couple of young kids from Korea to pound this thing out, and then sit back and count your moolah. So, before you read the rest of this trade

paperback, call your lawyer and get them to buy the movie rights to *Nocturnals*. And, if you act now, I will write that movie for you for a million dollars.

4. Don't become a painter. I don't care how long you have been attending art school or how good you have gotten, just give it up. There's no point. I don't have the words to describe Dan's work, but I know someone who does. In the words of Bell Biv Devoe, Dan Brereton's paintings are "smoothed out on the R&B tip with a pop appeal to it." Take a look at the pages in this book. Look at the cover. How are you ever going to do something that good? You're not. You'll never amount to anything. You're a waste of space, just like your stupid father. Seriously, though, I have sat there at 2 a.m. and watched Dan paint. And what gets me is the emotion that comes through the work. This isn't photo-realism. These are powerful, almost garish colors, and characters that are sometimes as hideous as they are beautiful. Gunwitch is both frightening and cool at the same time. Starfish is sexy but monstrous. I am crazy about Dan's style, in general, but when he paints these characters that mean so much to him, you can feel it. You feel it the same way when Bell Biv Devoe sings "Poison" or "Do Me Baby."

5. Don't reference Bell Biv Devoe in your introductions. At first, I thought it would be funny to mention BBD, but now I think it was a mistake.

And finally, and most important of all…

6. Never, and I mean never, agree to write an introduction for Dan Brereton. The man is a pest. He is like a starving dog with a juicy bone, and once you tell him you will write a "funny intro" for his silly characters, he will hound you to your grave. And even worse than the hounding is the passive-aggressive hounding. We would talk on the phone about the intro, and then hang up. And then five seconds later the phone would ring, and it would be Dan again, just to tell me about some great intro Brian Bendis wrote, and could mine be like that? And then he would call again ten minutes later, just to say that I shouldn't do one exactly like Brian Bendis did, but that I should make it my own, like Brian Bendis did. I don't even know who Brian Bendis is. And then I would get an e-mail, just to remind me that it was due on Friday, and how great he wanted it to be because this is his favorite creation and life's work. And on, and on, and on about putting food on his family's table. He would not shut up. I had to start screening my calls just to avoid him. Plus, he got really mad when I was four months late with this intro. And he claimed it read like I wrote it in five minutes, and that instead of writing on the nature of modern horror and how it relates to *Nocturnals*, I used the intro to make fun of Dan and complain about him. And then he didn't even pay me. Well screw him. The truth is that nobody reads these stupid introductions, and quite honestly Dan's work on *Nocturnals* speaks for itself. You don't need me to tell you it's good. But Dan is so nervous about his work that he makes himself crazy. So that's why you should never write an introduction for Dan Brereton.

Well, there you have it. Dan and I are no longer speaking to each other, but I remain a fan of both the Nocturnals and my beloved Bell Biv Devoe.

David Mandel

David Mandel is a TV and movie writer whose credits include Saturday Night Live, Seinfeld, Clerks: The Animated Series, *and* The Cat in the Hat. *He is co-host of* Dave and Steve's Video Game Explosion *on Burly TV.* *He can't believe he mentioned Burly TV.*

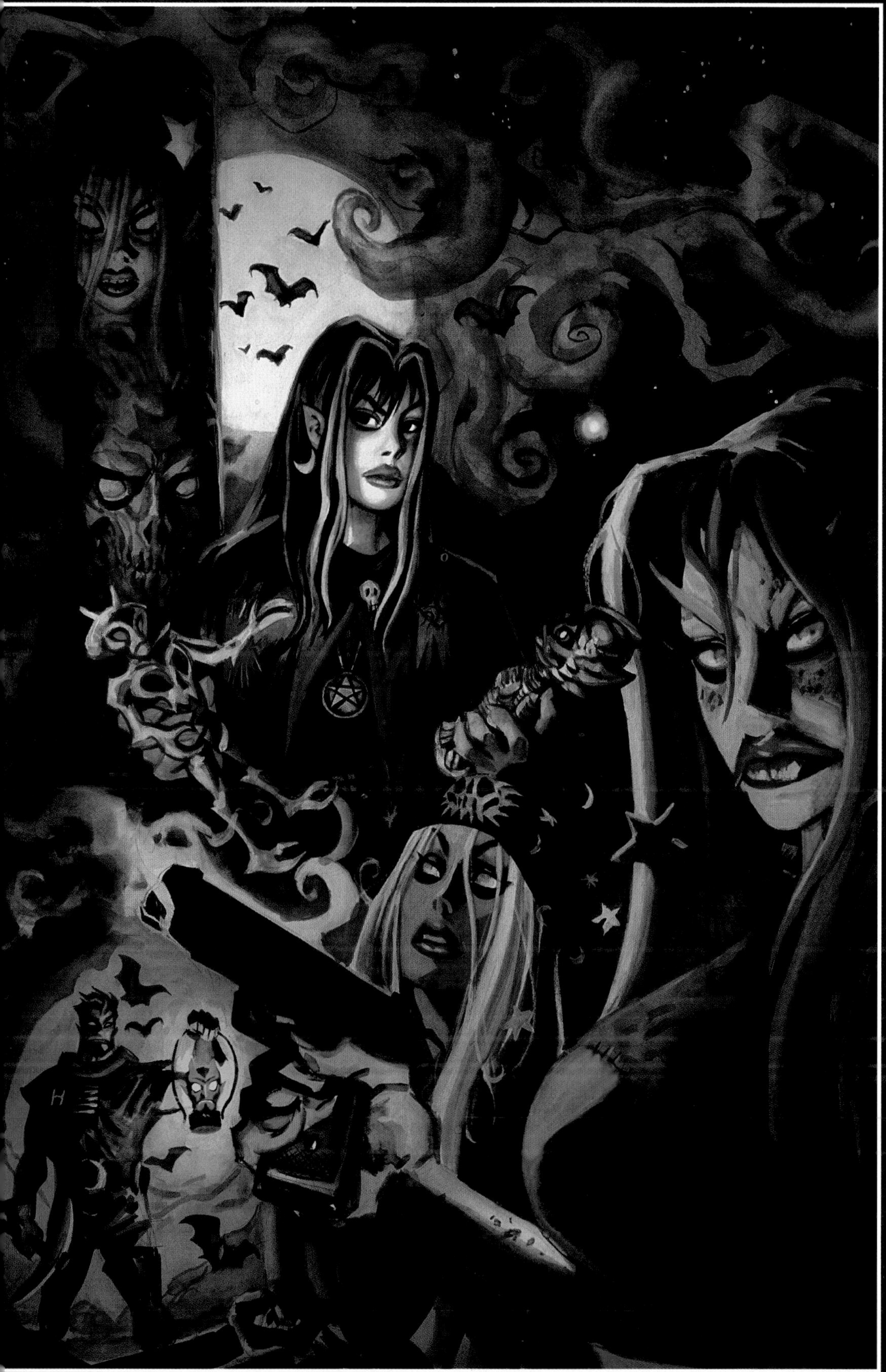

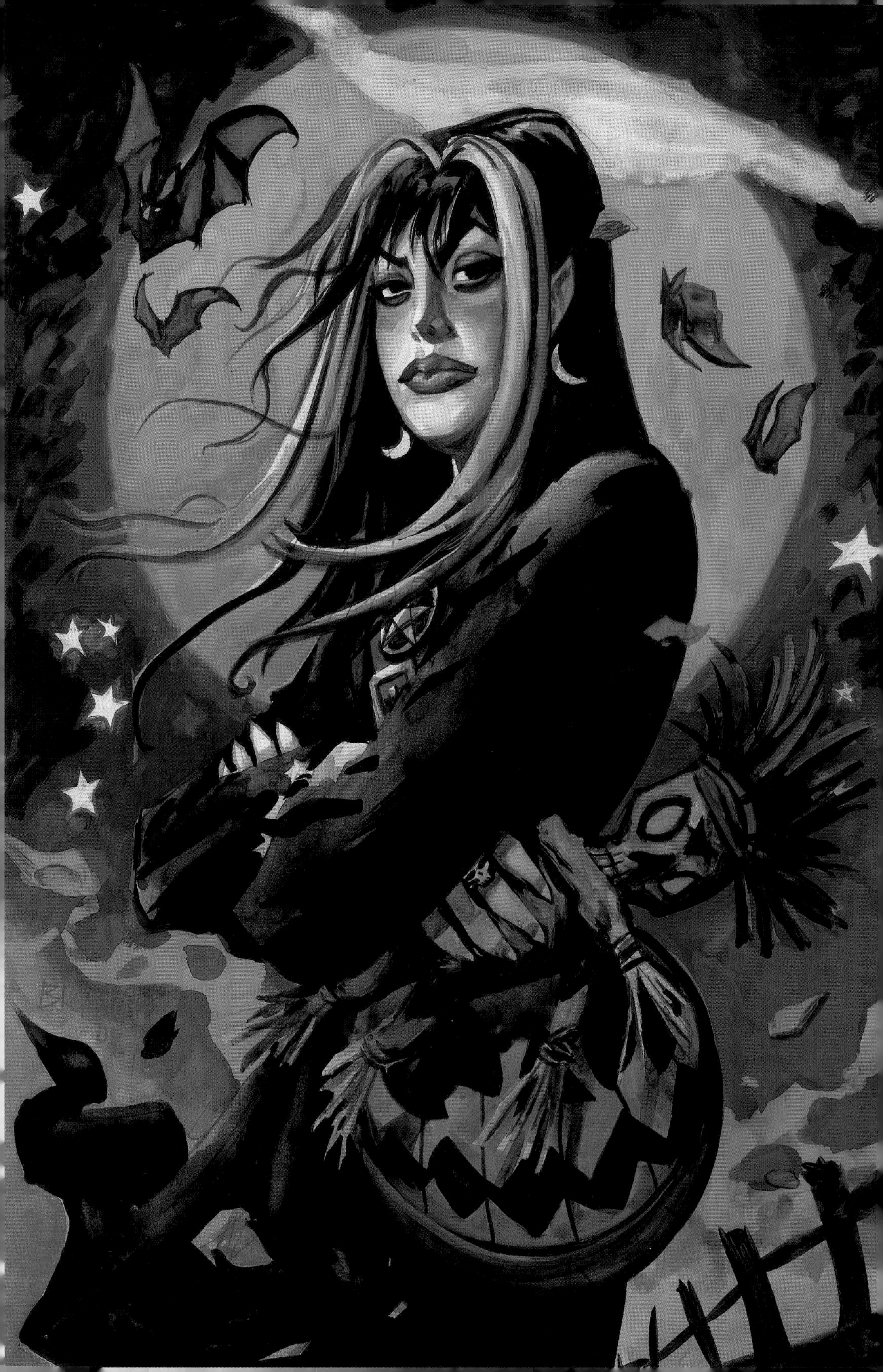

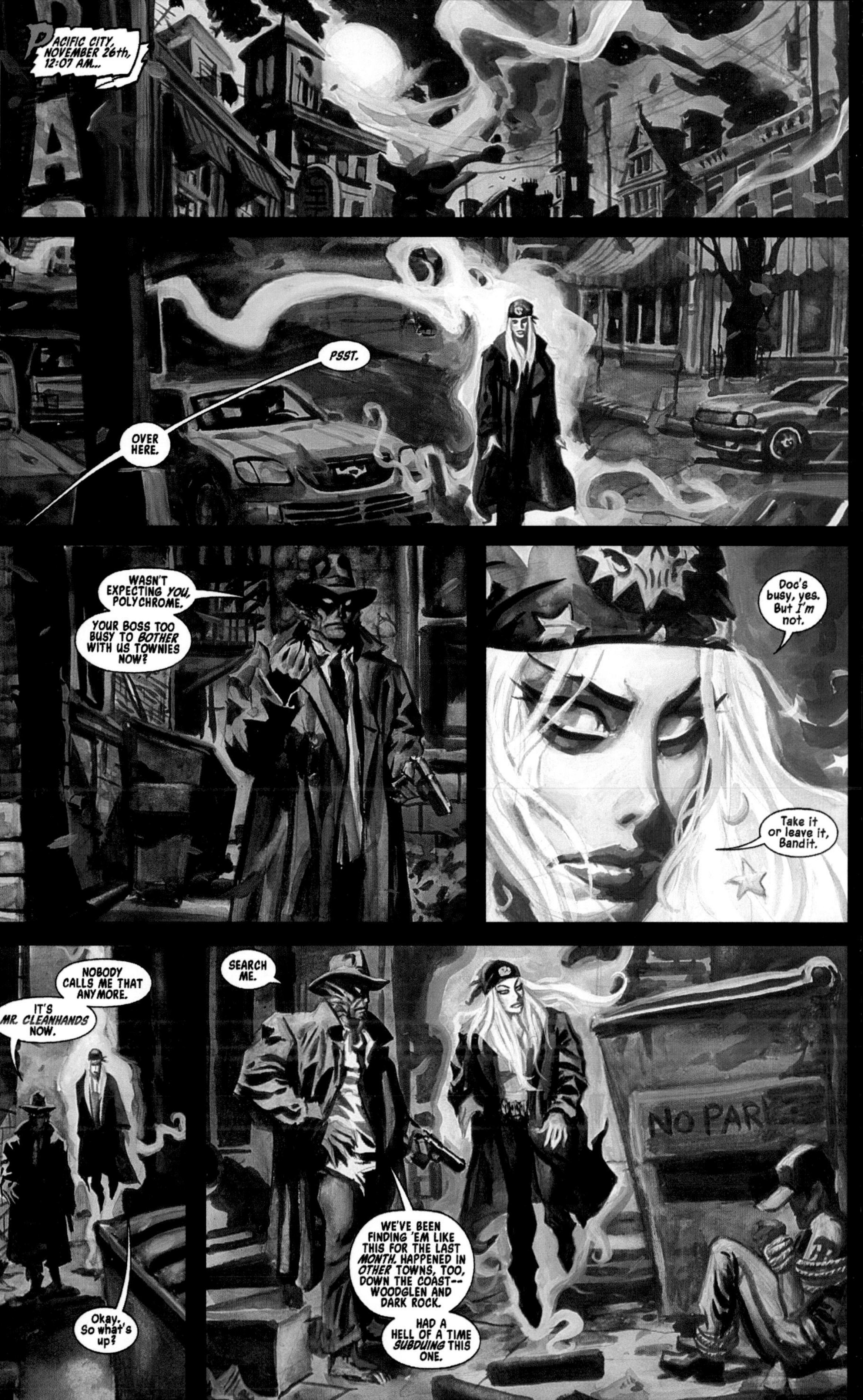
PACIFIC CITY, NOVEMBER 26th, 12:07 AM...
PSST.
OVER HERE.
WASN'T EXPECTING *YOU*, POLYCHROME.
YOUR BOSS TOO BUSY TO *BOTHER* WITH US TOWNIES NOW?
Doc's busy, yes. But *I'm* not.
Take it or leave it, Bandit.
NOBODY CALLS ME THAT ANYMORE.
IT'S *MR. CLEANHANDS* NOW.
Okay. So what's up?
SEARCH ME.
WE'VE BEEN FINDING 'EM LIKE THIS FOR THE LAST *MONTH*. HAPPENED IN *OTHER* TOWNS, TOO, DOWN THE COAST-- WOODGLEN AND DARK ROCK.
HAD A HELL OF A TIME *SUBDUING* THIS ONE.
NO PAR

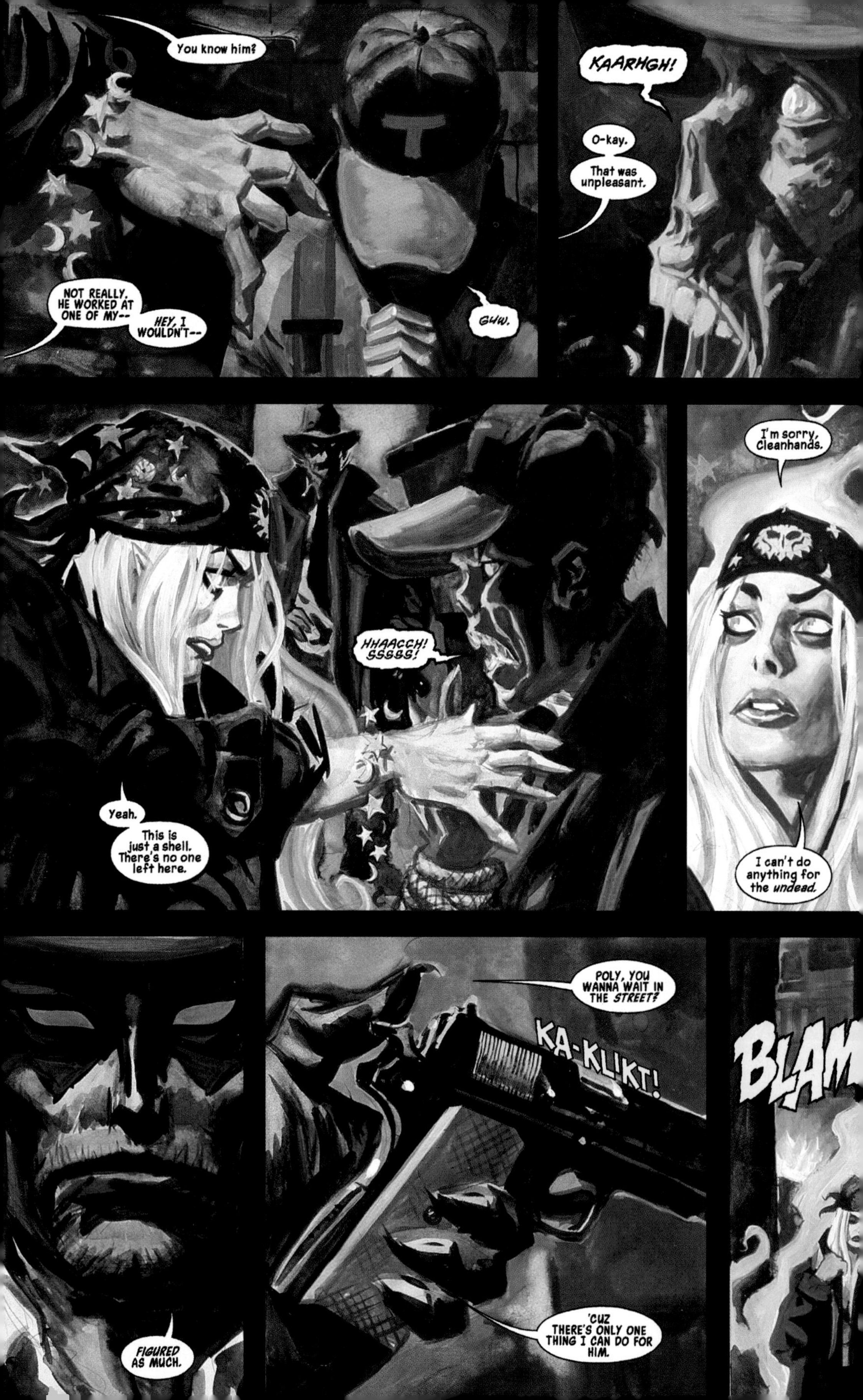
You know him?
NOT REALLY. HE WORKED AT ONE OF MY--
HEY, I WOULDN'T--
GUW.
KAARHGH!
O-kay.
That was unpleasant.
HHAACCH! SSSSS!
Yeah.
This is just a shell. There's no one left here.
I'm sorry, Cleanhands.
I can't do anything for the undead.
FIGURED AS MUCH.
POLY, YOU WANNA WAIT IN THE STREET?
KA-KLIKT!
'CUZ THERE'S ONLY ONE THING I CAN DO FOR HIM.
BLAM

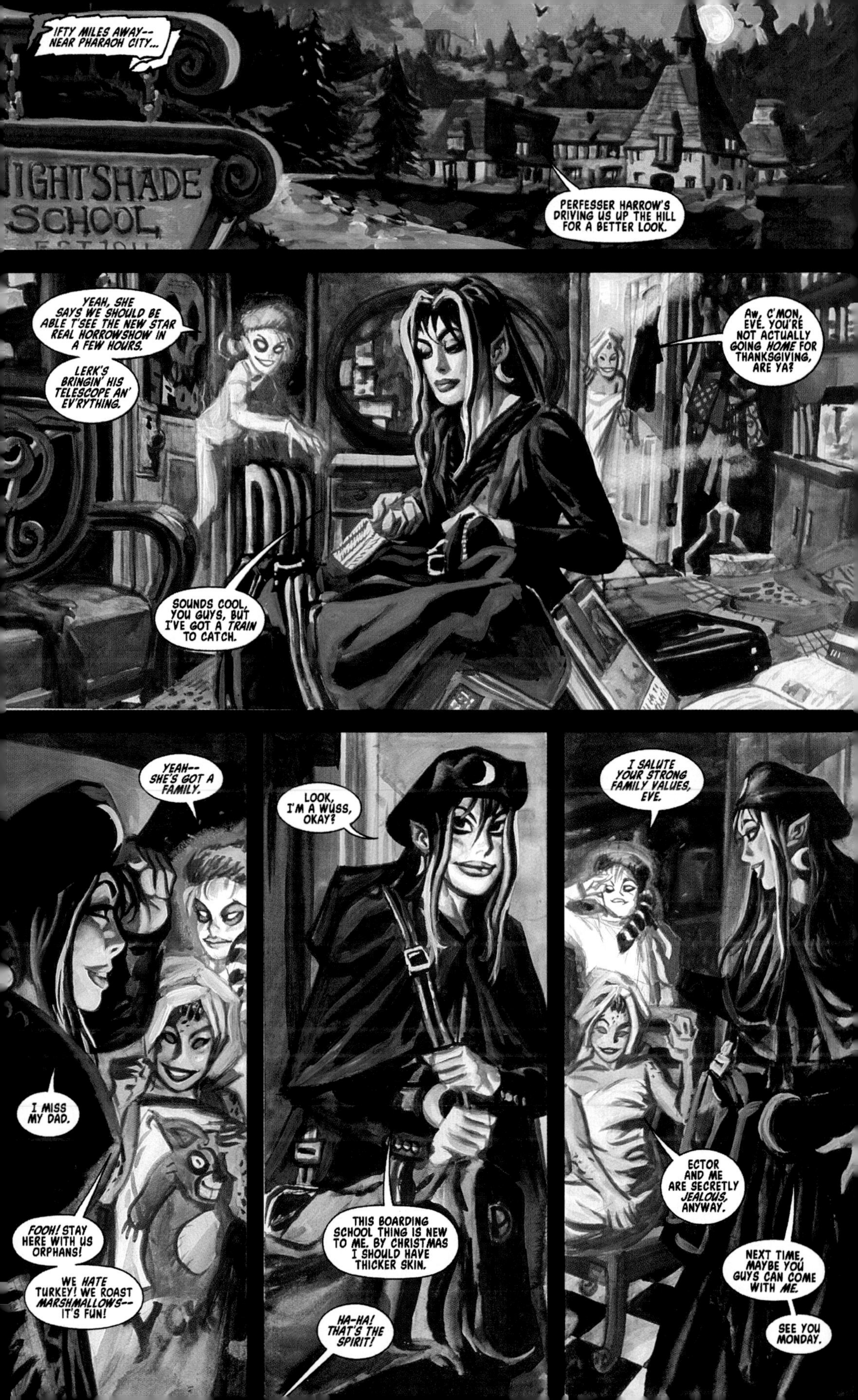
IFTY MILES AWAY--
NEAR PHARAOH CITY...
IGHTSHADE
SCHOOL
PERFESSER HARROW'S DRIVING US UP THE HILL FOR A BETTER LOOK.
YEAH, SHE SAYS WE SHOULD BE ABLE T'SEE THE NEW STAR REAL HORROWSHOW IN A FEW HOURS.
LERK'S BRINGIN' HIS TELESCOPE AN' EV'RYTHING.
AW, C'MON, EVE. YOU'RE NOT ACTUALLY GOING HOME FOR THANKSGIVING, ARE YA?
SOUNDS COOL, YOU GUYS, BUT I'VE GOT A TRAIN TO CATCH.
YEAH-- SHE'S GOT A FAMILY.
I MISS MY DAD.
FOOH! STAY HERE WITH US ORPHANS!
WE HATE TURKEY! WE ROAST MARSHMALLOWS-- IT'S FUN!
LOOK, I'M A WUSS, OKAY?
THIS BOARDING SCHOOL THING IS NEW TO ME. BY CHRISTMAS I SHOULD HAVE THICKER SKIN.
HA-HA! THAT'S THE SPIRIT!
I SALUTE YOUR STRONG FAMILY VALUES, EVE.
ECTOR AND ME ARE SECRETLY JEALOUS, ANYWAY.
NEXT TIME, MAYBE YOU GUYS CAN COME WITH ME.
SEE YOU MONDAY.

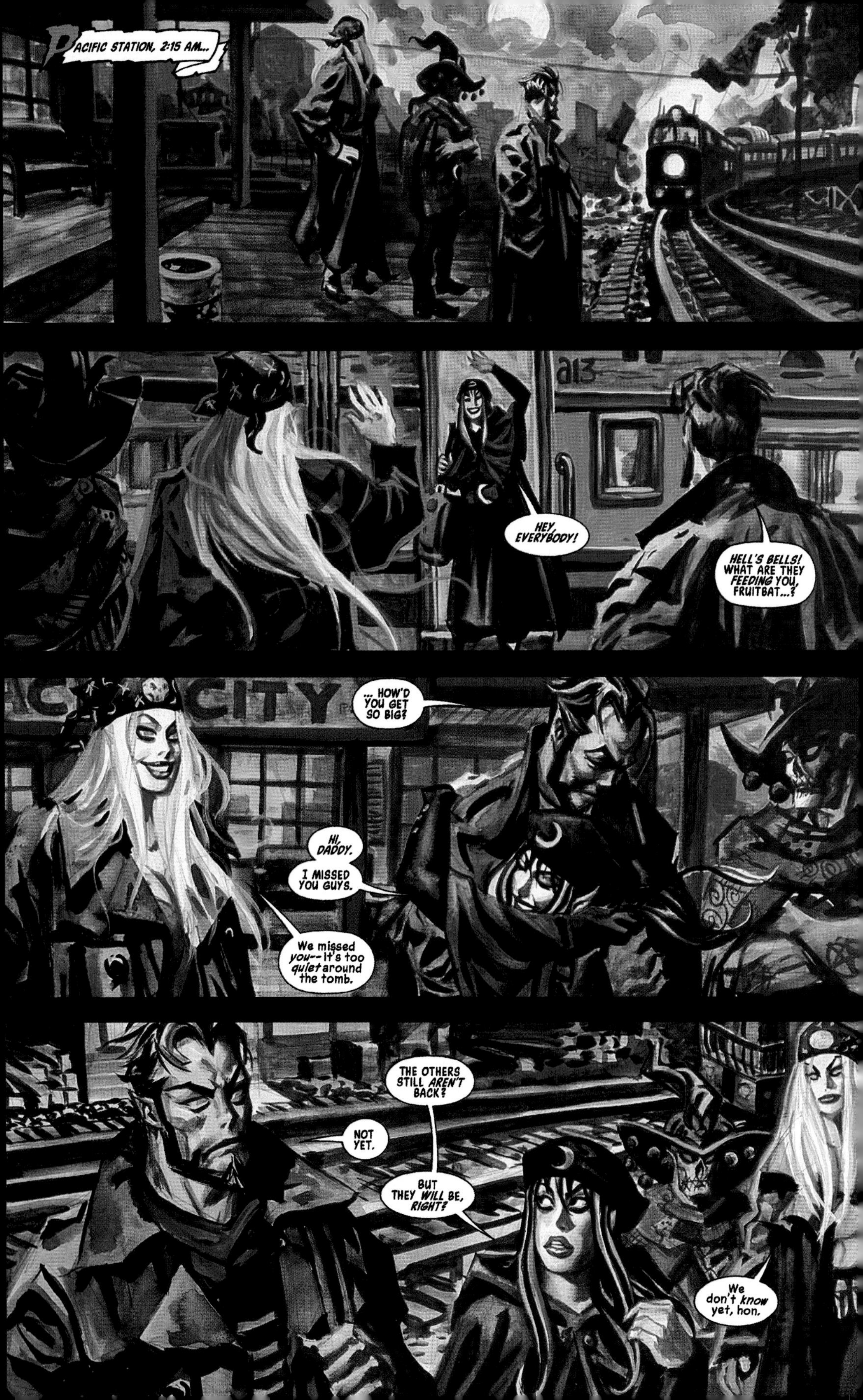
PACIFIC STATION, 2:15 AM...
a13
HEY, EVERYBODY!
HELL'S BELLS! WHAT ARE THEY FEEDING YOU, FRUITBAT...?
CITY
...HOW'D YOU GET SO BIG?
HI, DADDY.
I MISSED YOU GUYS.
We missed you--it's too quiet around the tomb.
THE OTHERS STILL AREN'T BACK?
NOT YET.
BUT THEY WILL BE, RIGHT?
We don't know yet, hon.

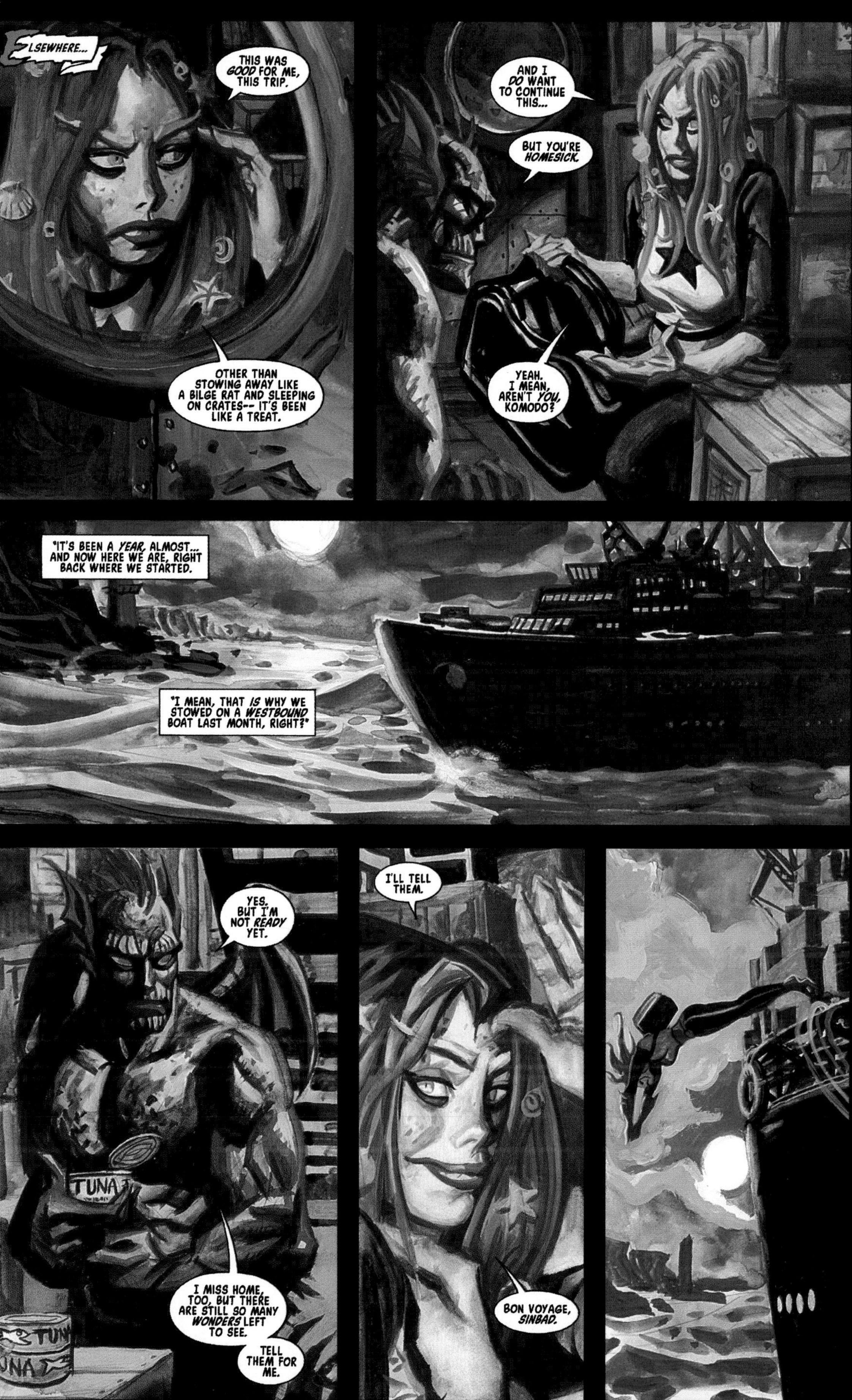
ELSEWHERE...
THIS WAS GOOD FOR ME, THIS TRIP.
OTHER THAN STOWING AWAY LIKE A BILGE RAT AND SLEEPING ON CRATES-- IT'S BEEN LIKE A TREAT.
AND I DO WANT TO CONTINUE THIS...
BUT YOU'RE HOMESICK.
YEAH. I MEAN, AREN'T YOU, KOMODO?
"IT'S BEEN A YEAR, ALMOST... AND NOW HERE WE ARE, RIGHT BACK WHERE WE STARTED.
"I MEAN, THAT IS WHY WE STOWED ON A WESTBOUND BOAT LAST MONTH, RIGHT?"
YES. BUT I'M NOT READY YET.
TUNA
I MISS HOME, TOO, BUT THERE ARE STILL SO MANY WONDERS LEFT TO SEE.
TELL THEM FOR ME.
I'LL TELL THEM.
BON VOYAGE, SINBAD.

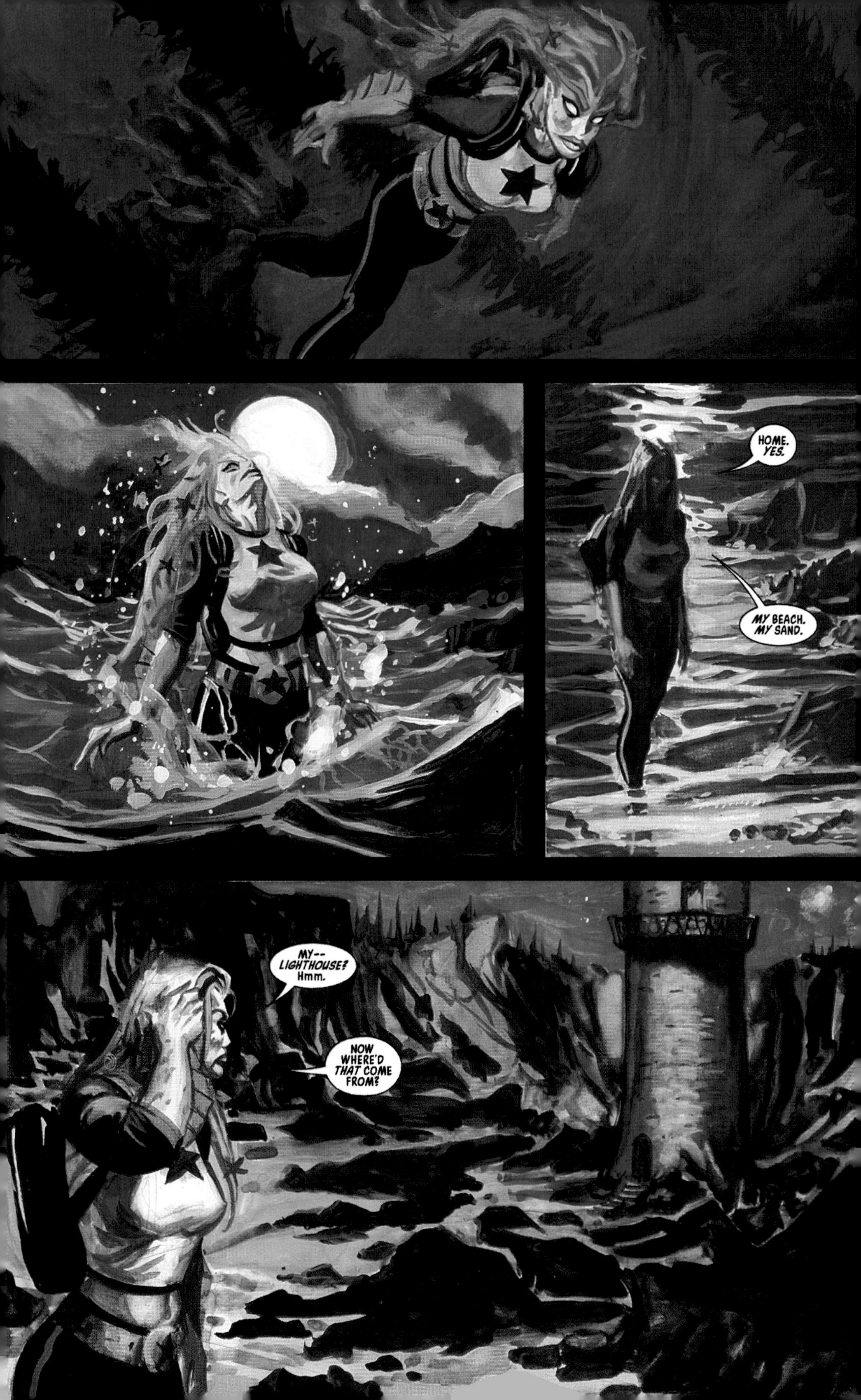
HOME. YES.
MY BEACH. MY SAND.
MY-- LIGHTHOUSE? Hmm.
NOW WHERE'D THAT COME FROM?

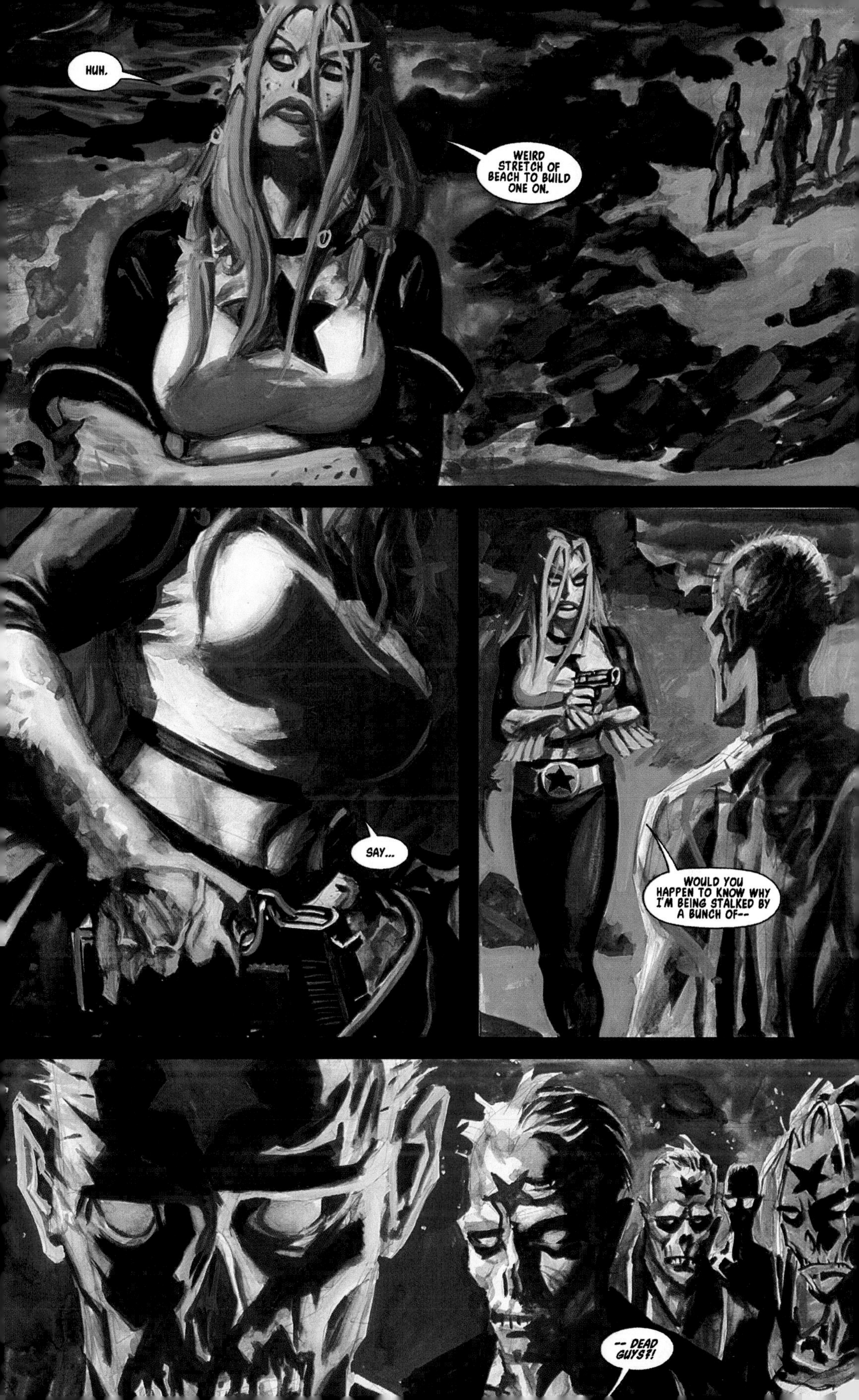
HUH.
WEIRD STRETCH OF BEACH TO BUILD ONE ON.
SAY...
WOULD YOU HAPPEN TO KNOW WHY I'M BEING STALKED BY A BUNCH OF--
-- DEAD GUYS?!

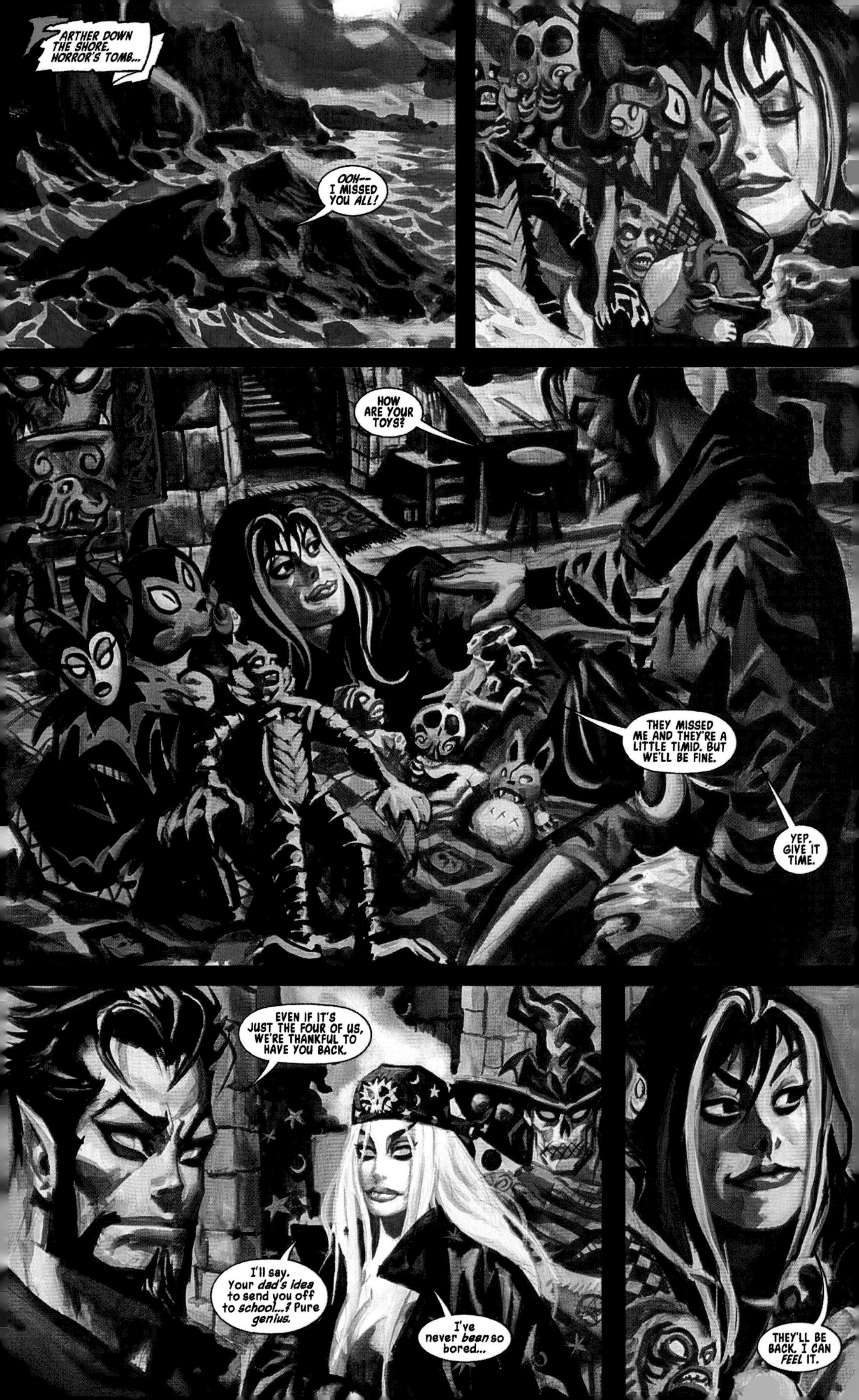

FARTHER DOWN THE SHORE. HORROR'S TOMB...
OOH-- I MISSED YOU ALL!
HOW ARE YOUR TOYS?
THEY MISSED ME AND THEY'RE A LITTLE TIMID. BUT WE'LL BE FINE.
YEP. GIVE IT TIME.
EVEN IF IT'S JUST THE FOUR OF US, WE'RE THANKFUL TO HAVE YOU BACK.
I'll say. Your dad's idea to send you off to school...? Pure genius.
I've never been so bored...
THEY'LL BE BACK. I CAN FEEL IT.

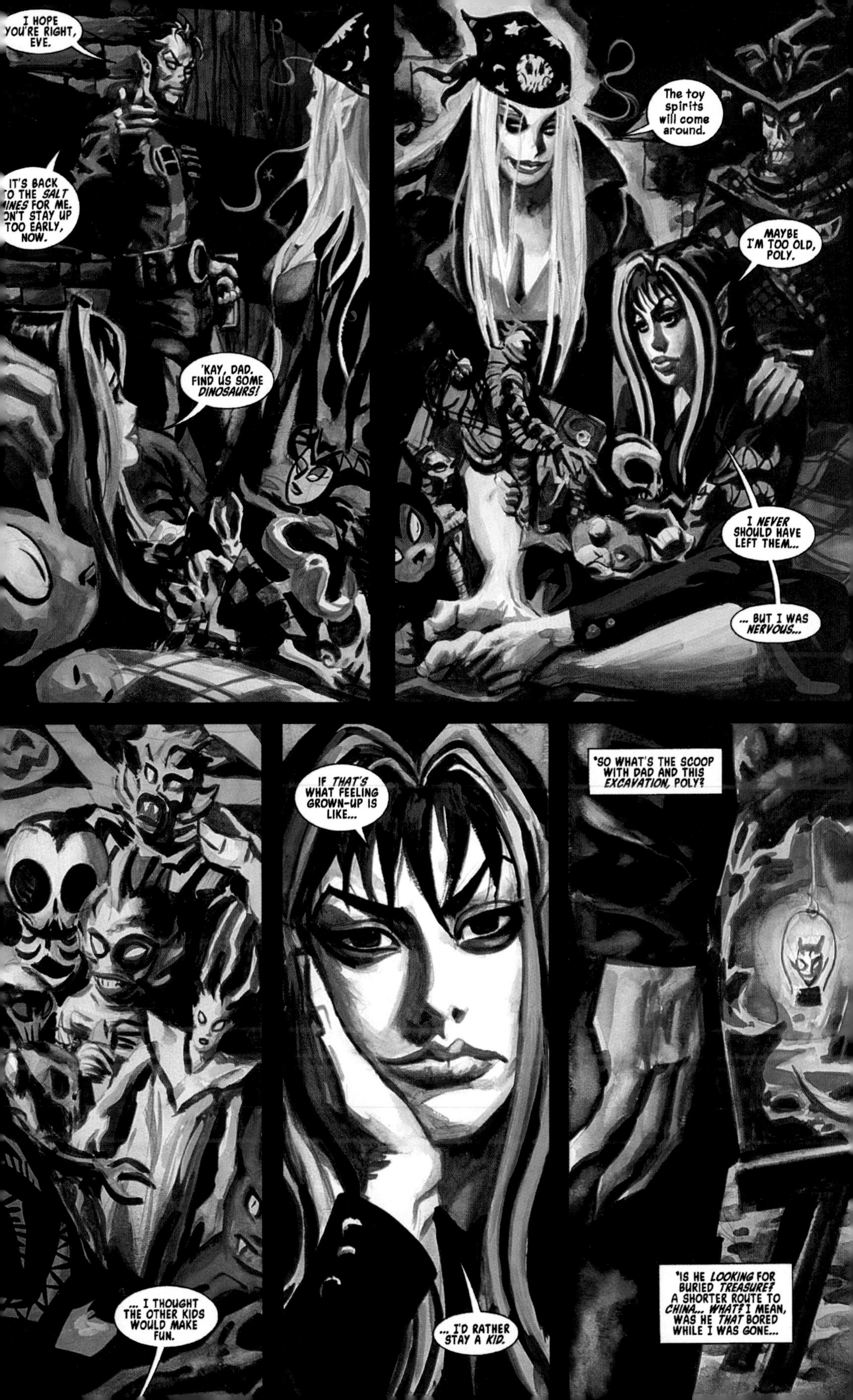
I HOPE YOU'RE RIGHT, EVE.
IT'S BACK TO THE SALT MINES FOR ME. ON'T STAY UP TOO EARLY, NOW.
'KAY, DAD. FIND US SOME DINOSAURS!
The toy spirits will come around.
MAYBE I'M TOO OLD, POLY.
I NEVER SHOULD HAVE LEFT THEM...
... BUT I WAS NERVOUS...
... I THOUGHT THE OTHER KIDS WOULD MAKE FUN.
IF THAT'S WHAT FEELING GROWN-UP IS LIKE...
... I'D RATHER STAY A KID.
"SO WHAT'S THE SCOOP WITH DAD AND THIS EXCAVATION, POLY?
"IS HE LOOKING FOR BURIED TREASURE? A SHORTER ROUTE TO CHINA... WHAT? I MEAN, WAS HE THAT BORED WHILE I WAS GONE...

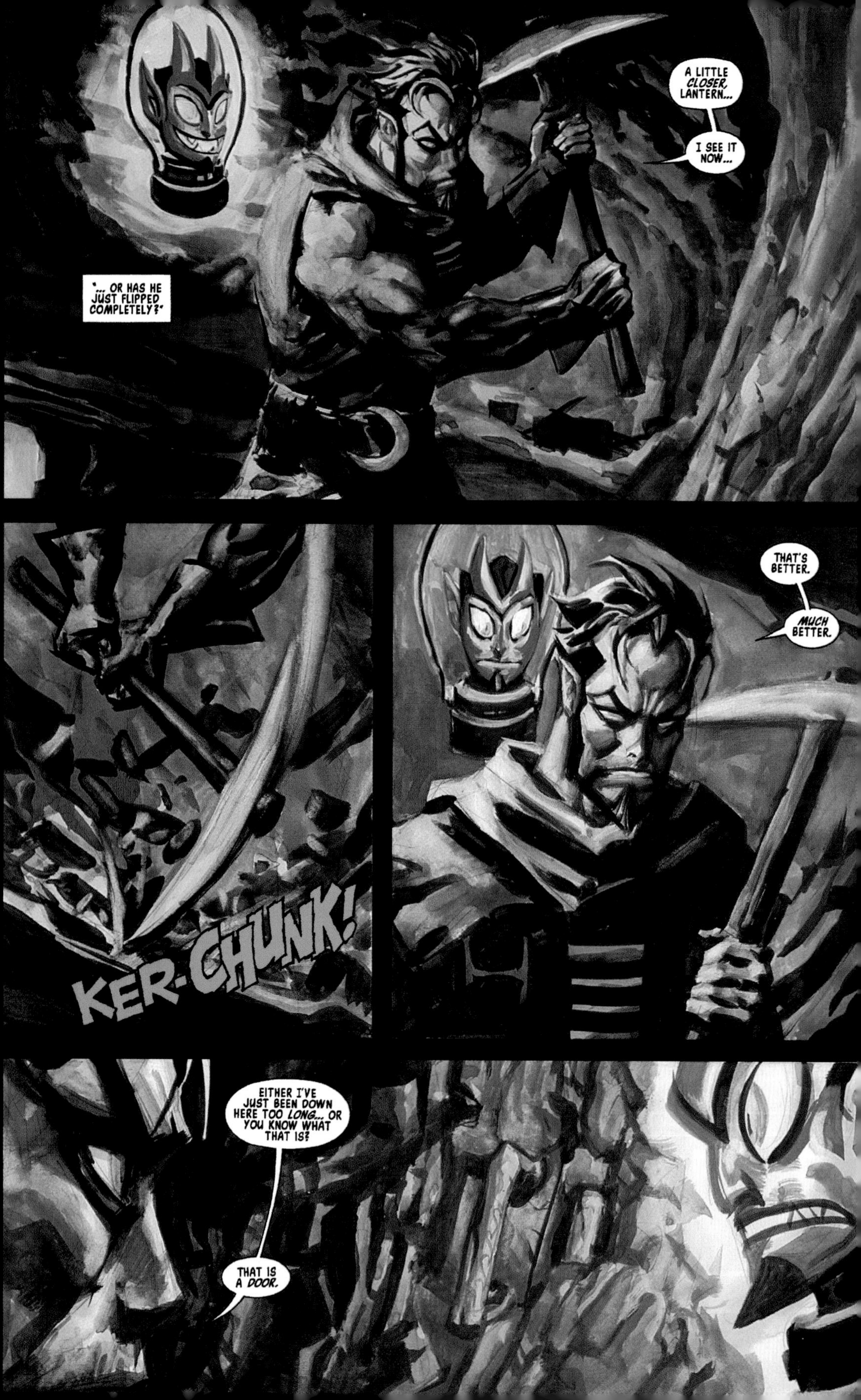
A LITTLE CLOSER, LANTERN...
I SEE IT NOW...
"... OR HAS HE JUST FLIPPED COMPLETELY?"
KER-CHUNK!
THAT'S BETTER.
MUCH BETTER.
EITHER I'VE JUST BEEN DOWN HERE TOO LONG... OR YOU KNOW WHAT THAT IS?
THAT IS A DOOR.

SIX WEEKS OF THIS...

... DIGGING...

... HAULING ROCK OUT OF THIS TUNNEL.

SWEAT!

CHTÄNK!

DIRT!

FKANK!

CHTÄNK!

TALKING TO MAGIC LANTERNS...!

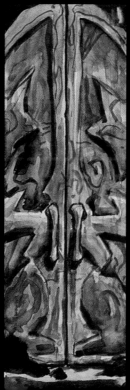

FOR WHAT?

FOR THIS.

IT'S OLD...

RRGGHHH!

OLDER THAN THE TOMB...

NNRRHH!

OLDER THAN THE GREAT WALL, THE SPHINX...

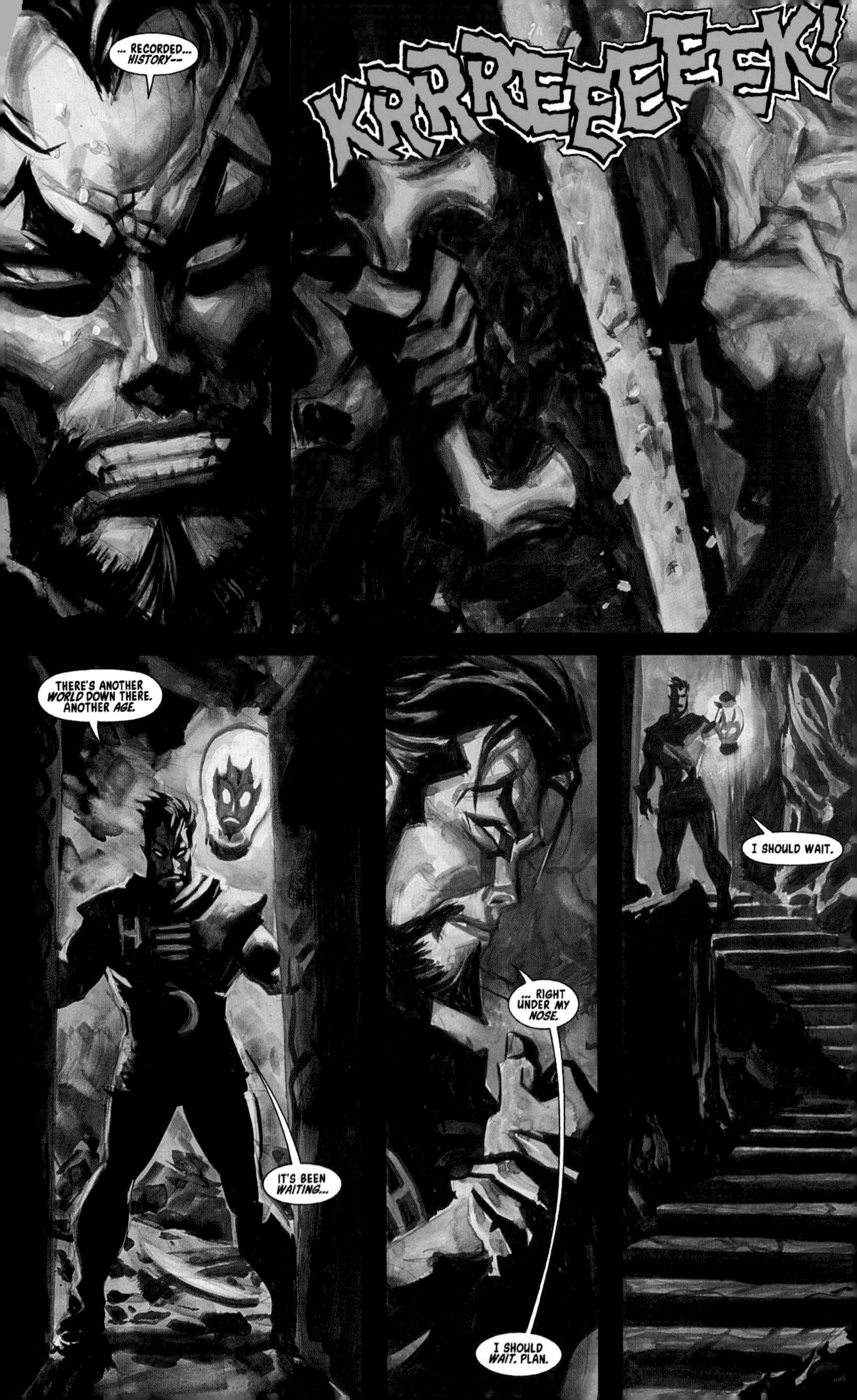

... RECORDED... HISTORY--
KRRREEEEEK!
THERE'S ANOTHER WORLD DOWN THERE. ANOTHER AGE.
IT'S BEEN WAITING...
... RIGHT UNDER MY NOSE.
I SHOULD WAIT. PLAN.
I SHOULD WAIT.

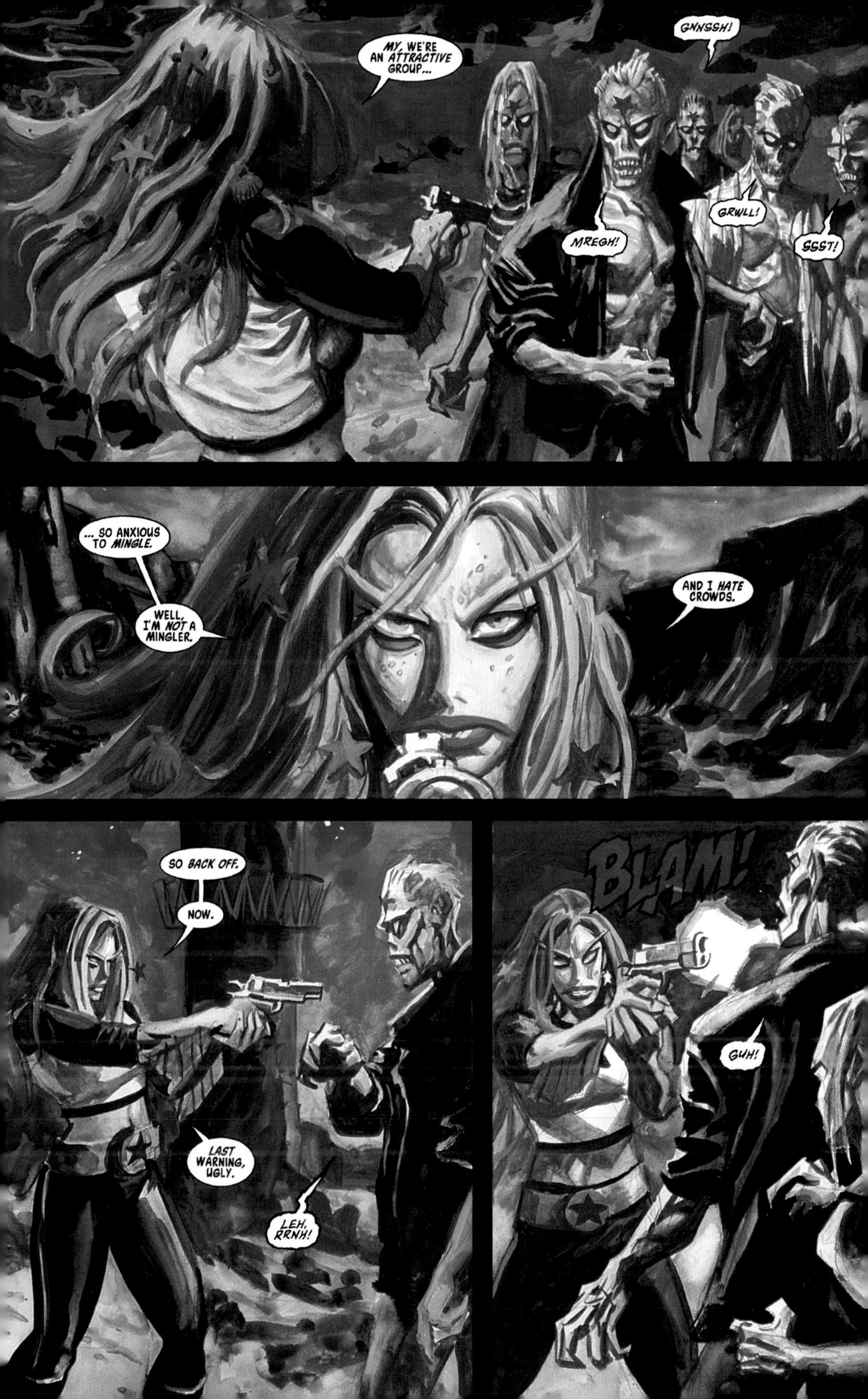
MY, WE'RE AN ATTRACTIVE GROUP...
GNNSSH!
MREGH!
GRWLL!
SSST!
... SO ANXIOUS TO MINGLE.
WELL, I'M NOT A MINGLER.
AND I HATE CROWDS.
SO BACK OFF.
NOW.
LAST WARNING, UGLY.
LEH, RRNH!
BLAM!
GUH!

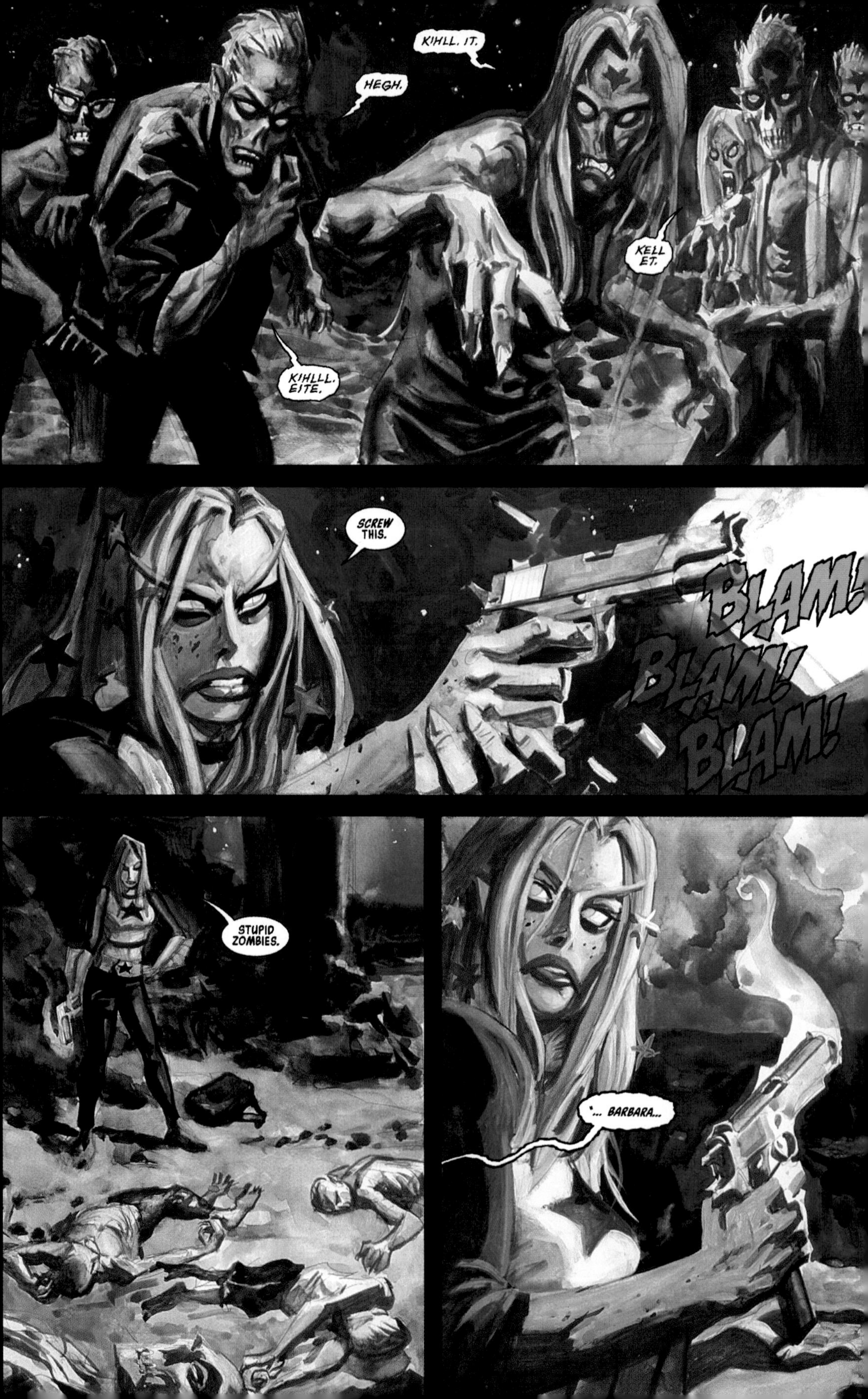
KIHLL. IT.
HEGH.
KELL ET.
KIHLLL. EITE.
SCREW THIS.
BLAM!
BLAM!
BLAM!
STUPID ZOMBIES.
"... BARBARA...

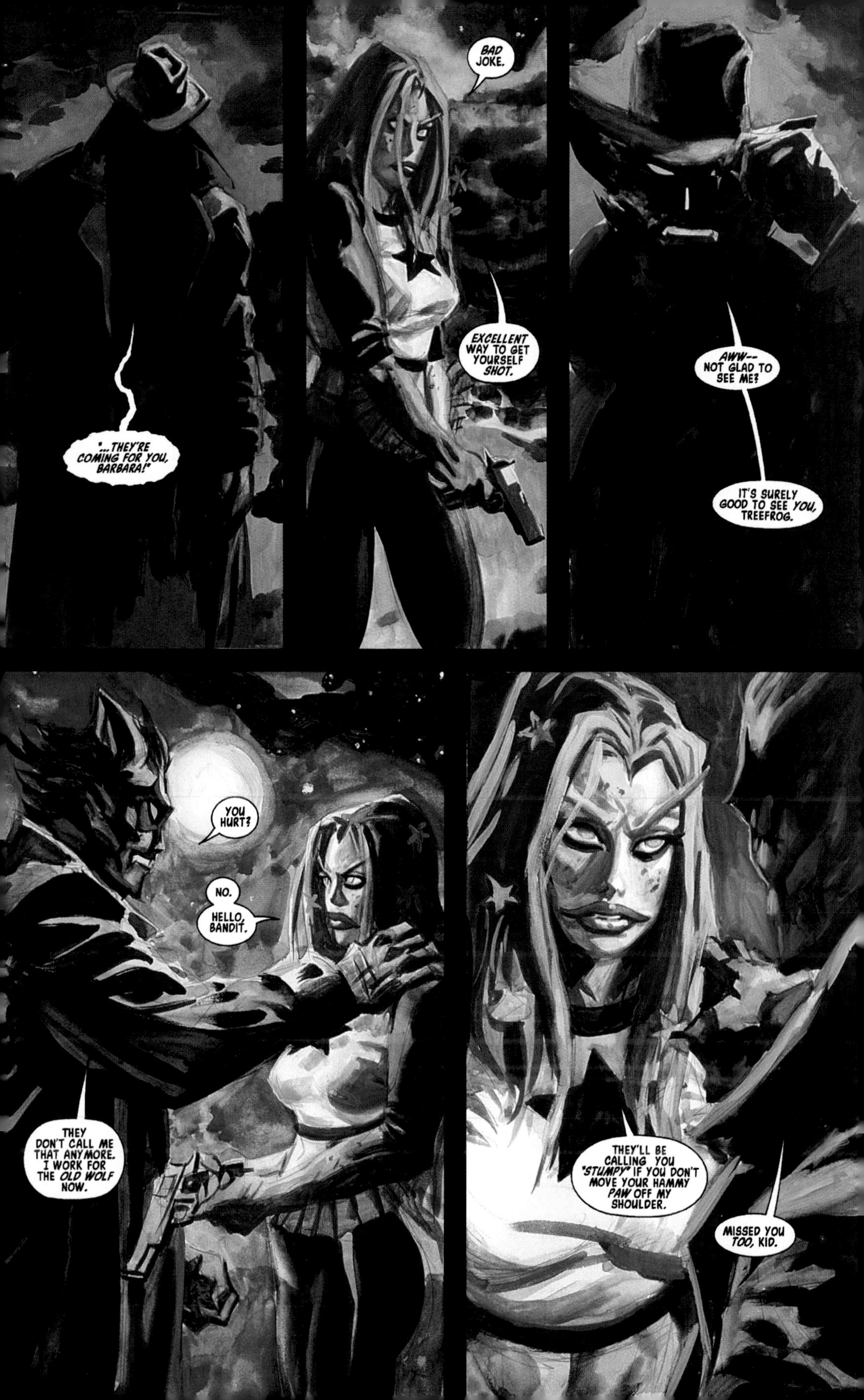
"...THEY'RE COMING FOR YOU, BARBARA!"
BAD JOKE.
EXCELLENT WAY TO GET YOURSELF SHOT.
AWW-- NOT GLAD TO SEE ME?
IT'S SURELY GOOD TO SEE YOU, TREEFROG.
YOU HURT?
NO.
HELLO, BANDIT.
THEY DON'T CALL ME THAT ANYMORE. I WORK FOR THE OLD WOLF NOW.
THEY'LL BE CALLING YOU "STUMPY" IF YOU DON'T MOVE YOUR HAMMY PAW OFF MY SHOULDER.
MISSED YOU TOO, KID.

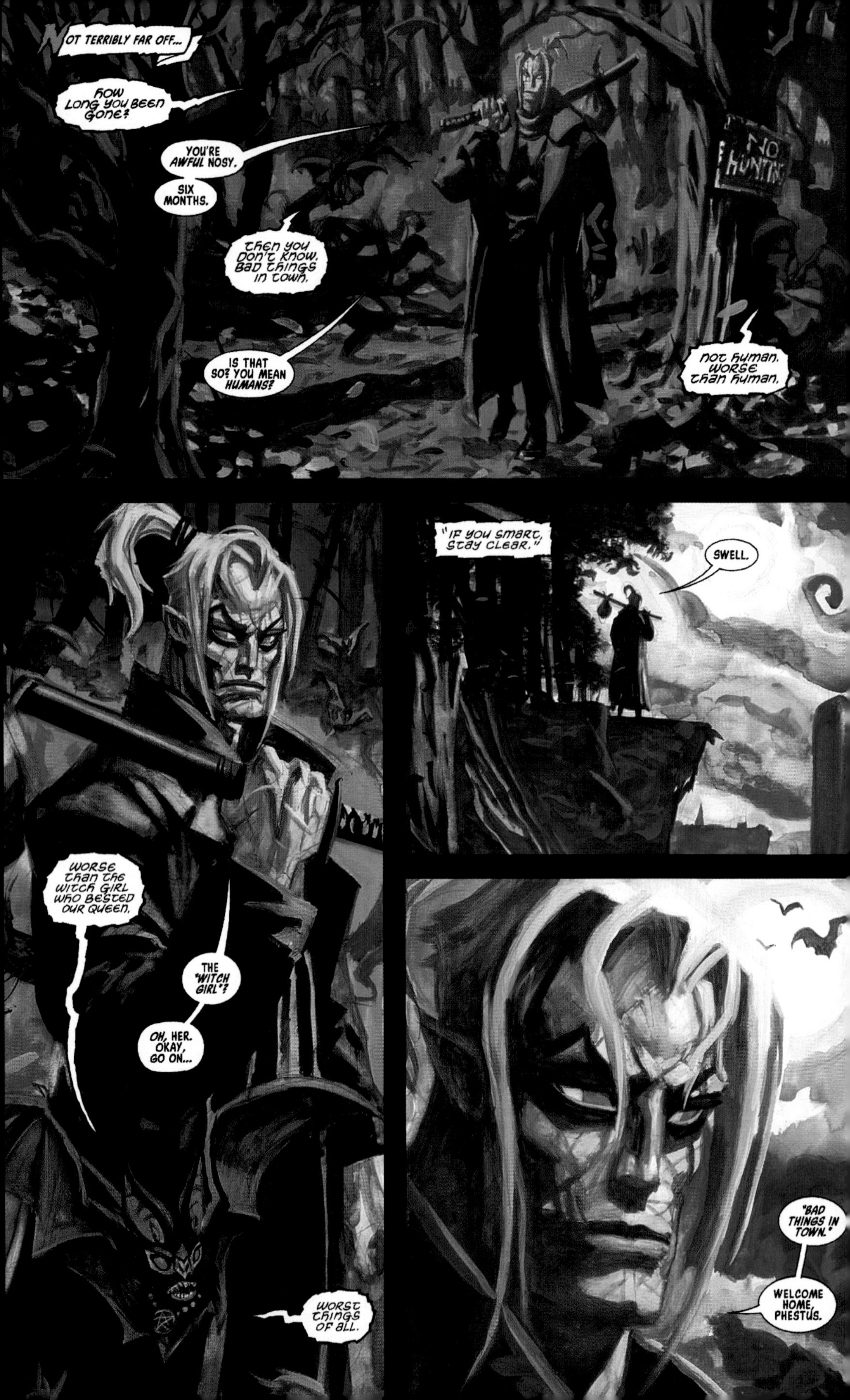
NOT TERRIBLY FAR OFF...
HOW LONG YOU BEEN GONE?
YOU'RE AWFUL NOSY.
SIX MONTHS.
THEN YOU DON'T KNOW. BAD THINGS IN TOWN.
IS THAT SO? YOU MEAN HUMANS?
NOT HUMAN. WORSE THAN HUMAN.
NO HUNTIN
WORSE THAN THE WITCH GIRL WHO BESTED OUR QUEEN.
THE "WITCH GIRL"?
OH, HER. OKAY, GO ON...
WORST THINGS OF ALL.
"IF YOU SMART, STAY CLEAR."
SWELL.
"BAD THINGS IN TOWN."
WELCOME HOME, PHESTUS.

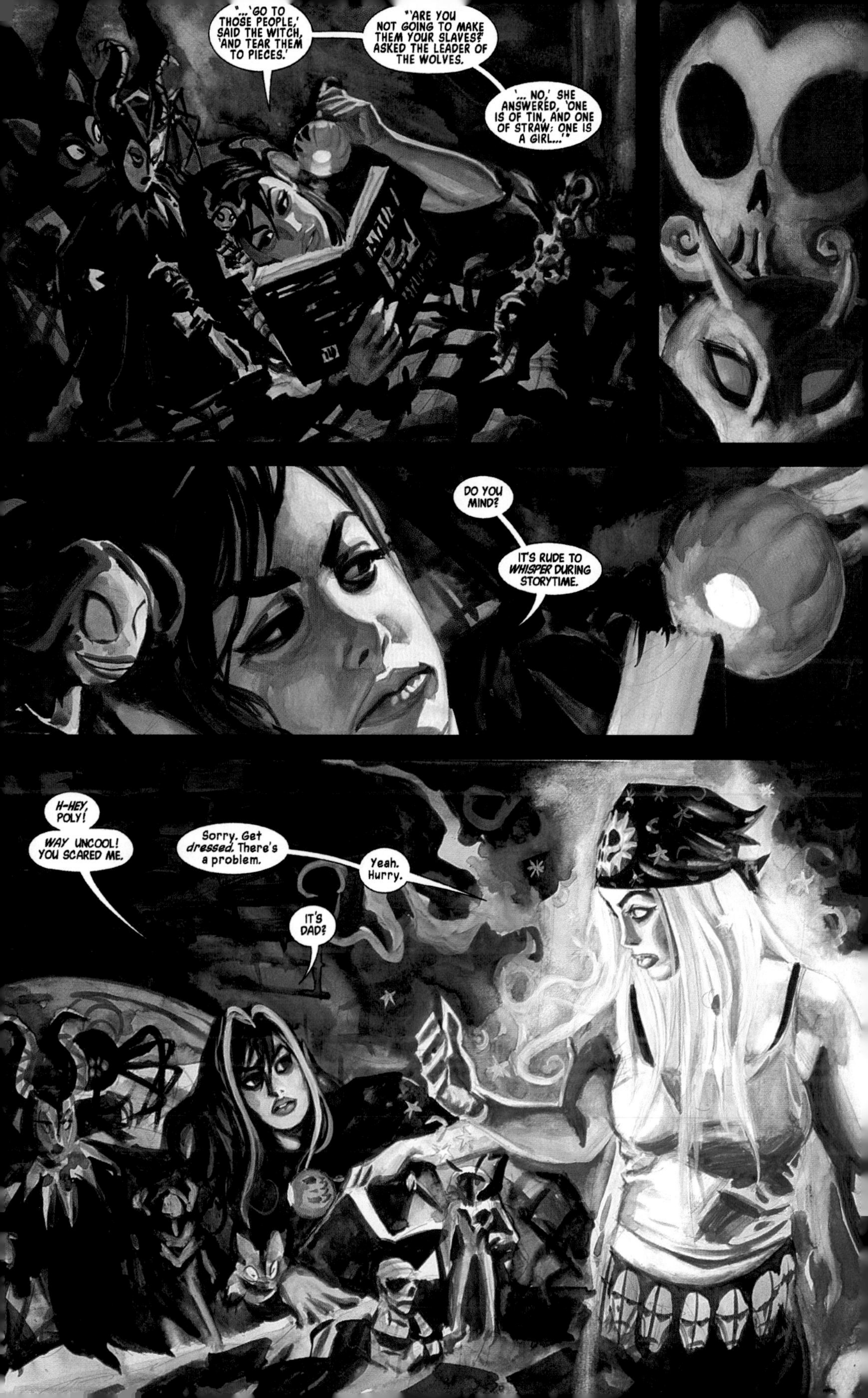
"...'GO TO THOSE PEOPLE,' SAID THE WITCH, 'AND TEAR THEM TO PIECES.'
"'ARE YOU NOT GOING TO MAKE THEM YOUR SLAVES?' ASKED THE LEADER OF THE WOLVES.
'... NO,' SHE ANSWERED, 'ONE IS OF TIN, AND ONE OF STRAW; ONE IS A GIRL...'"
DO YOU MIND?
IT'S RUDE TO *WHISPER* DURING STORYTIME.
H-HEY, POLY!
WAY UNCOOL! YOU SCARED ME.
Sorry. Get *dressed*. There's a problem.
Yeah. Hurry.
IT'S DAD?

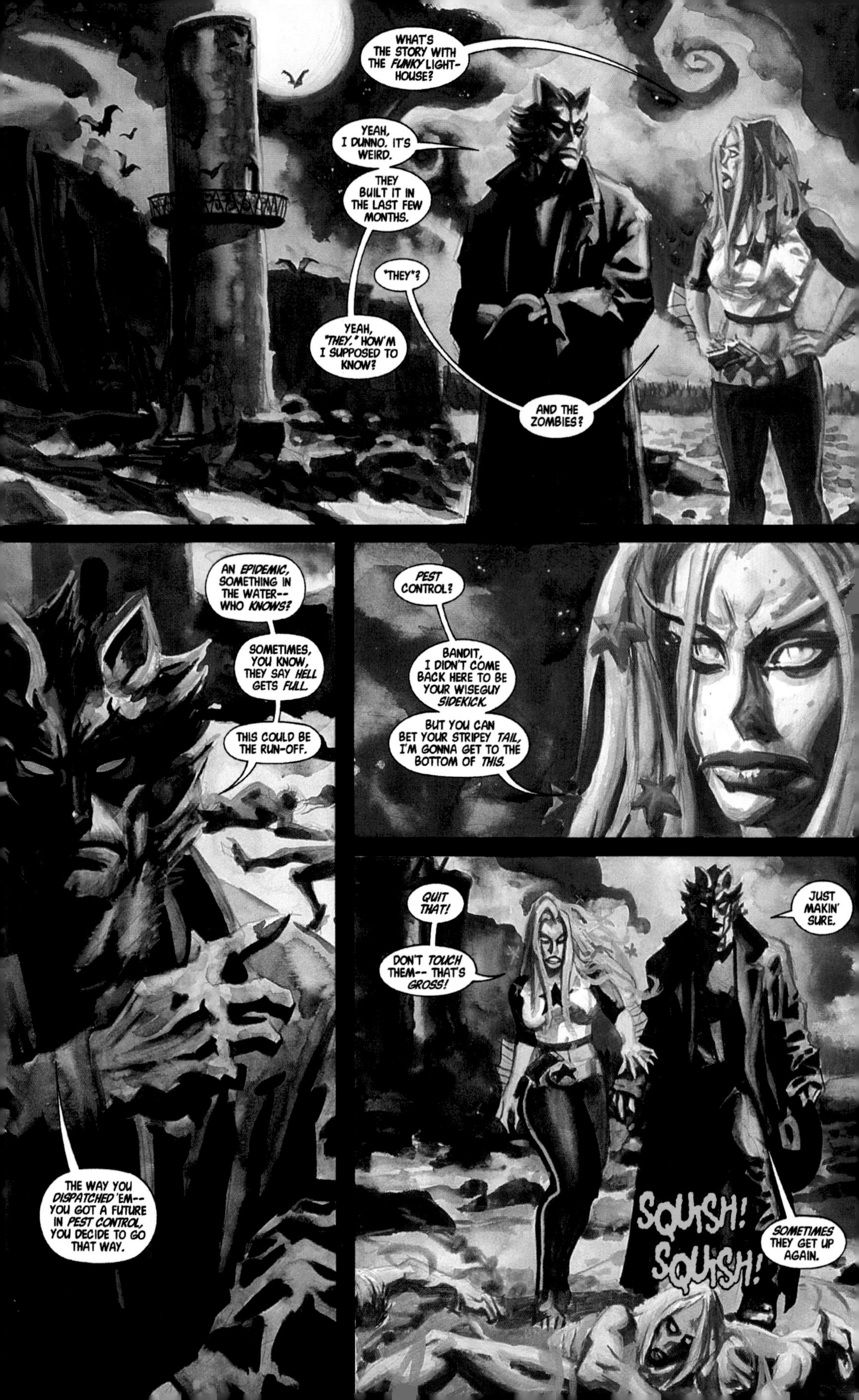
WHAT'S THE STORY WITH THE FUNKY LIGHT-HOUSE?
YEAH, I DUNNO. IT'S WEIRD.
THEY BUILT IT IN THE LAST FEW MONTHS.
"THEY"?
YEAH, "THEY." HOW'M I SUPPOSED TO KNOW?
AND THE ZOMBIES?
AN EPIDEMIC, SOMETHING IN THE WATER-- WHO KNOWS?
SOMETIMES, YOU KNOW, THEY SAY HELL GETS FULL.
THIS COULD BE THE RUN-OFF.
THE WAY YOU DISPATCHED 'EM-- YOU GOT A FUTURE IN PEST CONTROL, YOU DECIDE TO GO THAT WAY.
PEST CONTROL?
BANDIT, I DIDN'T COME BACK HERE TO BE YOUR WISEGUY SIDEKICK.
BUT YOU CAN BET YOUR STRIPEY TAIL, I'M GONNA GET TO THE BOTTOM OF THIS.
QUIT THAT!
DON'T TOUCH THEM-- THAT'S GROSS!
JUST MAKIN' SURE.
SQUISH! SQUISH!
SOMETIMES THEY GET UP AGAIN.

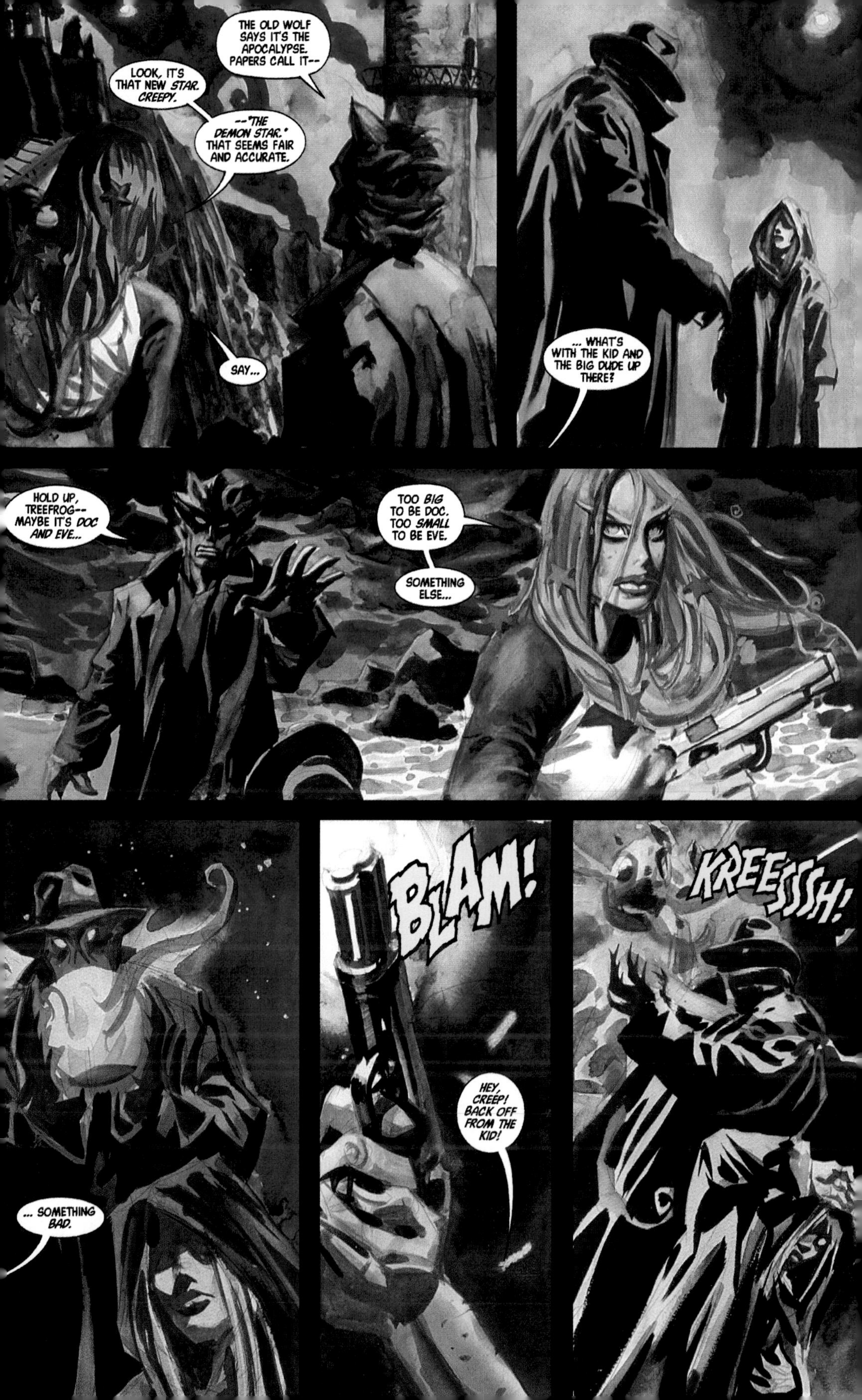
LOOK, IT'S THAT NEW STAR. CREEPY.
THE OLD WOLF SAYS IT'S THE APOCALYPSE. PAPERS CALL IT--
--"THE DEMON STAR." THAT SEEMS FAIR AND ACCURATE.
SAY...
... WHAT'S WITH THE KID AND THE BIG DUDE UP THERE?
HOLD UP, TREEFROG-- MAYBE IT'S DOC AND EVE...
TOO BIG TO BE DOC. TOO SMALL TO BE EVE.
SOMETHING ELSE...
... SOMETHING BAD.
BLAM!
HEY, CREEP! BACK OFF FROM THE KID!
KREESSSSH!

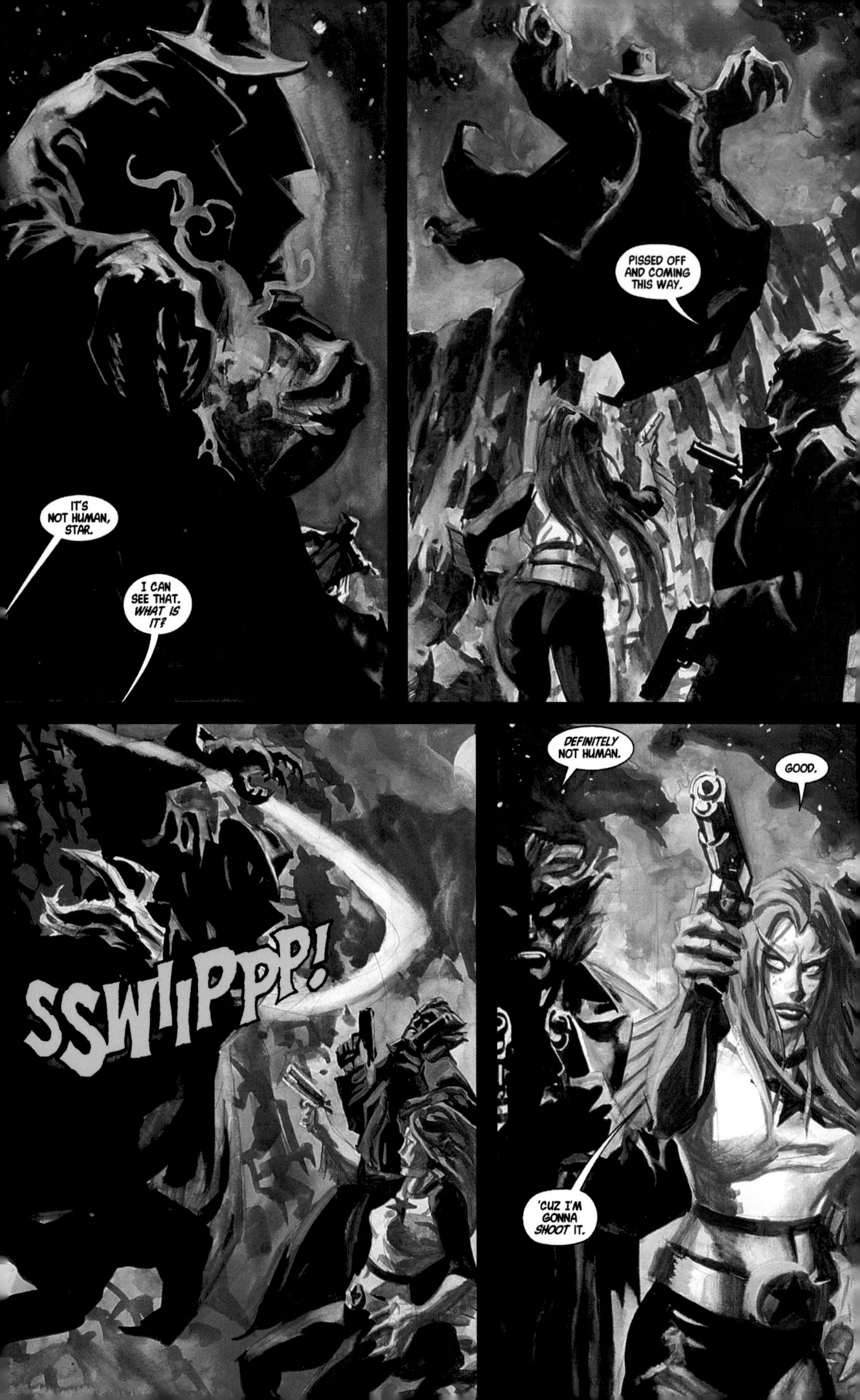
IT'S NOT HUMAN, STAR.
I CAN SEE THAT. *WHAT IS* IT?
PISSED OFF AND COMING THIS WAY.
SSWIIPPP!
DEFINITELY NOT HUMAN.
GOOD.
'CUZ I'M GONNA *SHOOT* IT.

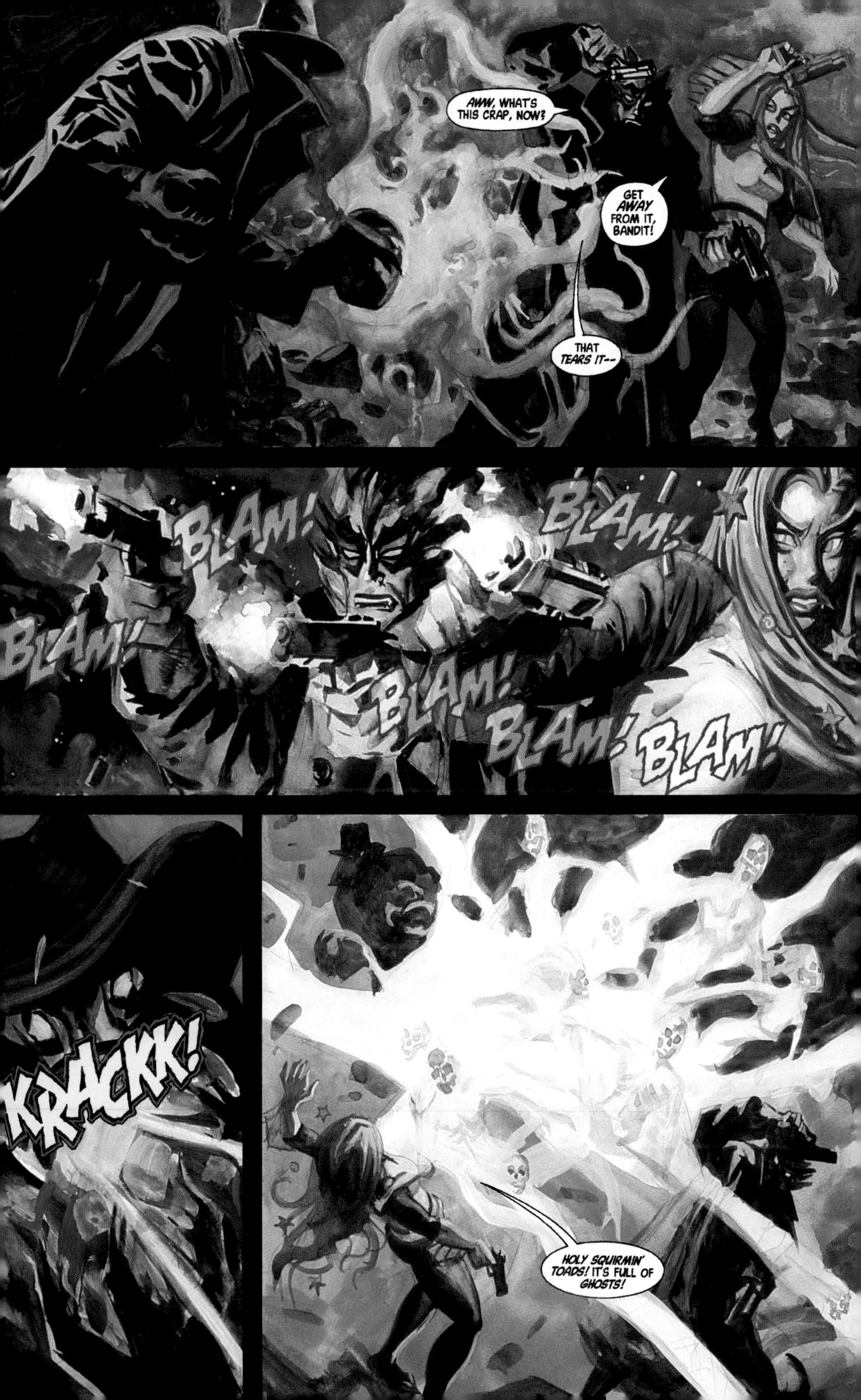
AWW, WHAT'S THIS CRAP, NOW?
GET AWAY FROM IT, BANDIT!
THAT TEARS IT--
BLAM!
BLAM!
BLAM!
BLAM!
BLAM!
BLAM!
KRACKK!
HOLY SQUIRMIN' TOADS! IT'S FULL OF GHOSTS!

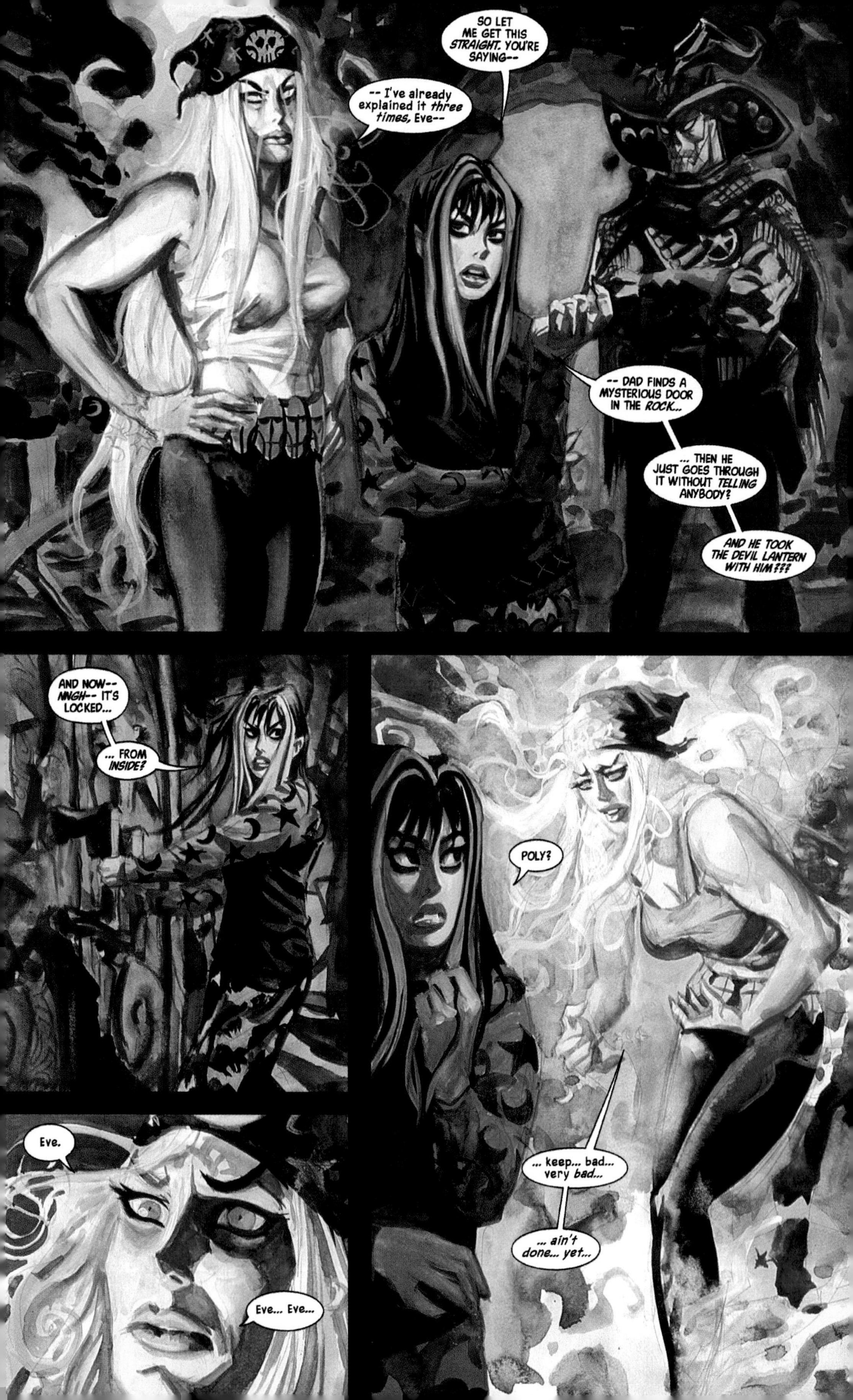

SO LET ME GET THIS STRAIGHT. YOU'RE SAYING--
-- I've already explained it three times, Eve--
-- DAD FINDS A MYSTERIOUS DOOR IN THE ROCK...
... THEN HE JUST GOES THROUGH IT WITHOUT TELLING ANYBODY?
AND HE TOOK THE DEVIL LANTERN WITH HIM???
AND NOW-- NNGH-- IT'S LOCKED...
... FROM INSIDE?
POLY?
Eve.
Eve... Eve...
... keep... bad... very bad...
... ain't done... yet...

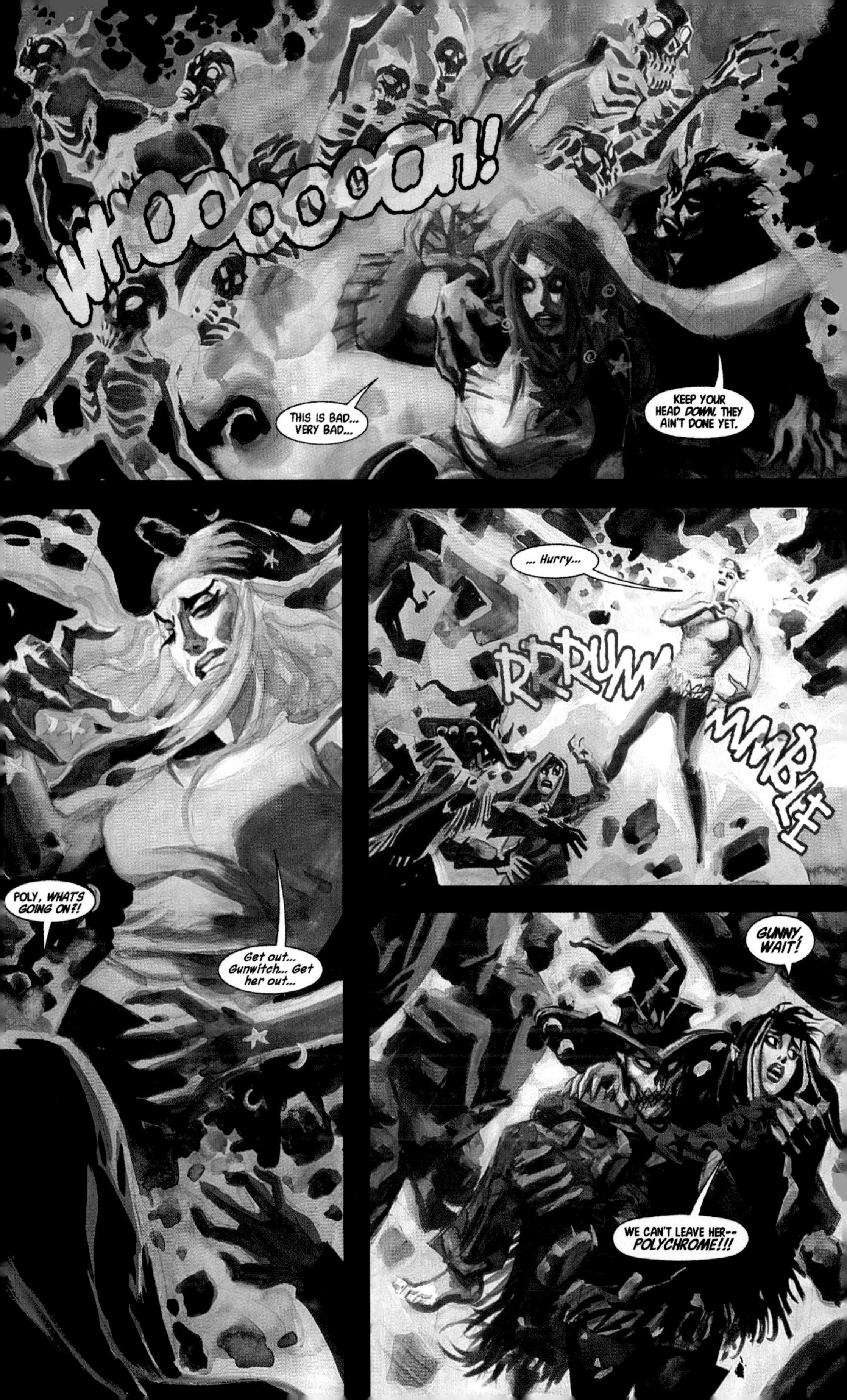
WHOOOOOOOH!
THIS IS BAD... VERY BAD...
KEEP YOUR HEAD DOWN. THEY AIN'T DONE YET.
POLY, WHAT'S GOING ON?!
Get out... Gunwitch... Get her out...
... Hurry...
RRRUMMMBLE
GUNNY, WAIT!
WE CAN'T LEAVE HER-- POLYCHROME!!!

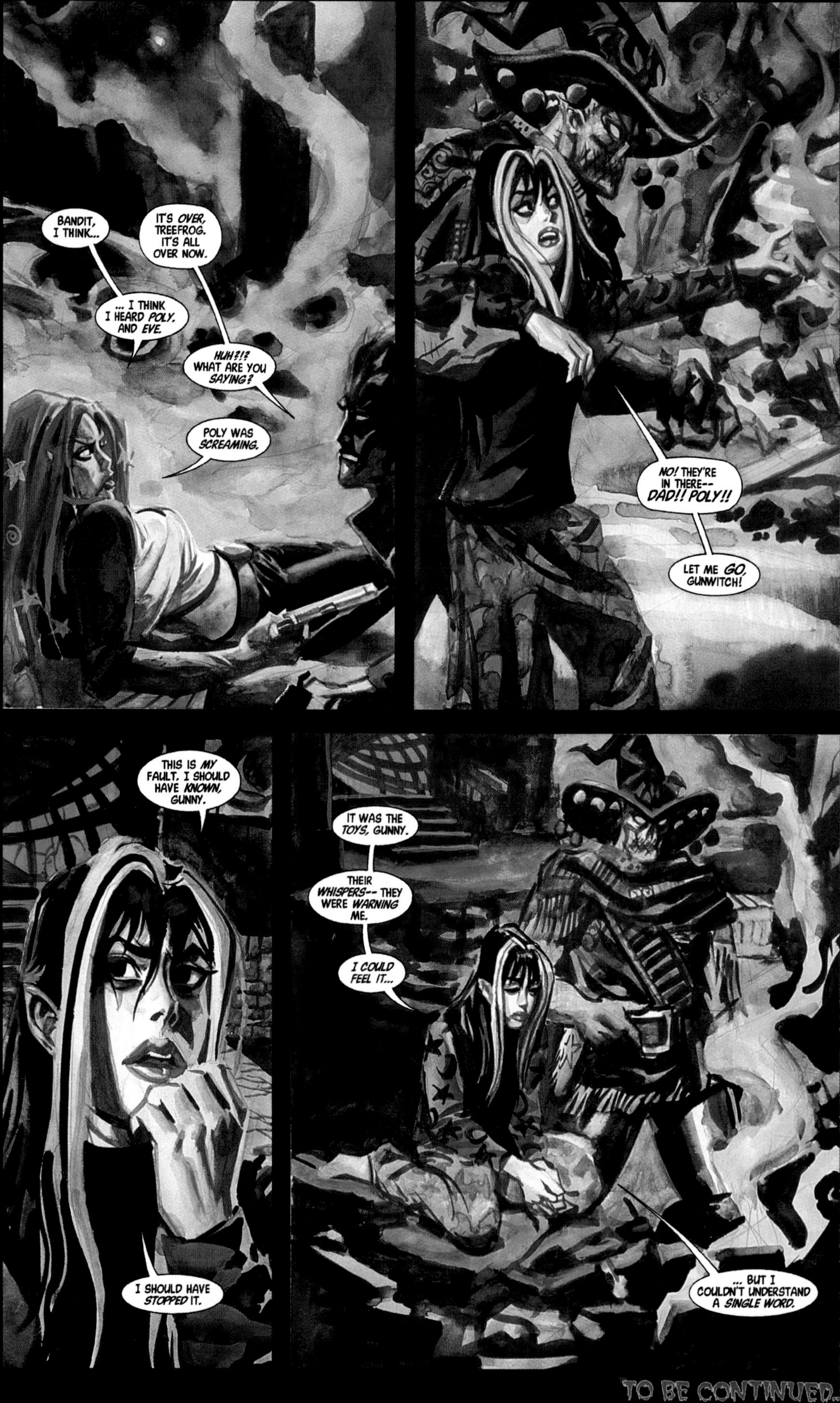

BANDIT, I THINK...
IT'S *OVER*, TREEFROG. IT'S ALL OVER NOW.
... I THINK I HEARD *POLY*. AND *EVE*.
HUH?!? WHAT ARE YOU *SAYING?*
POLY WAS *SCREAMING*.
NO! THEY'RE IN THERE-- *DAD!! POLY!!*
LET ME *GO*, GUNWITCH!
THIS IS *MY* FAULT. I SHOULD HAVE *KNOWN*, GUNNY.
I SHOULD HAVE *STOPPED* IT.
IT WAS THE *TOYS*, GUNNY.
THEIR *WHISPERS*-- THEY WERE *WARNING* ME.
I COULD FEEL IT...
... BUT I COULDN'T UNDERSTAND A *SINGLE WORD*.
TO BE CONTINUED.

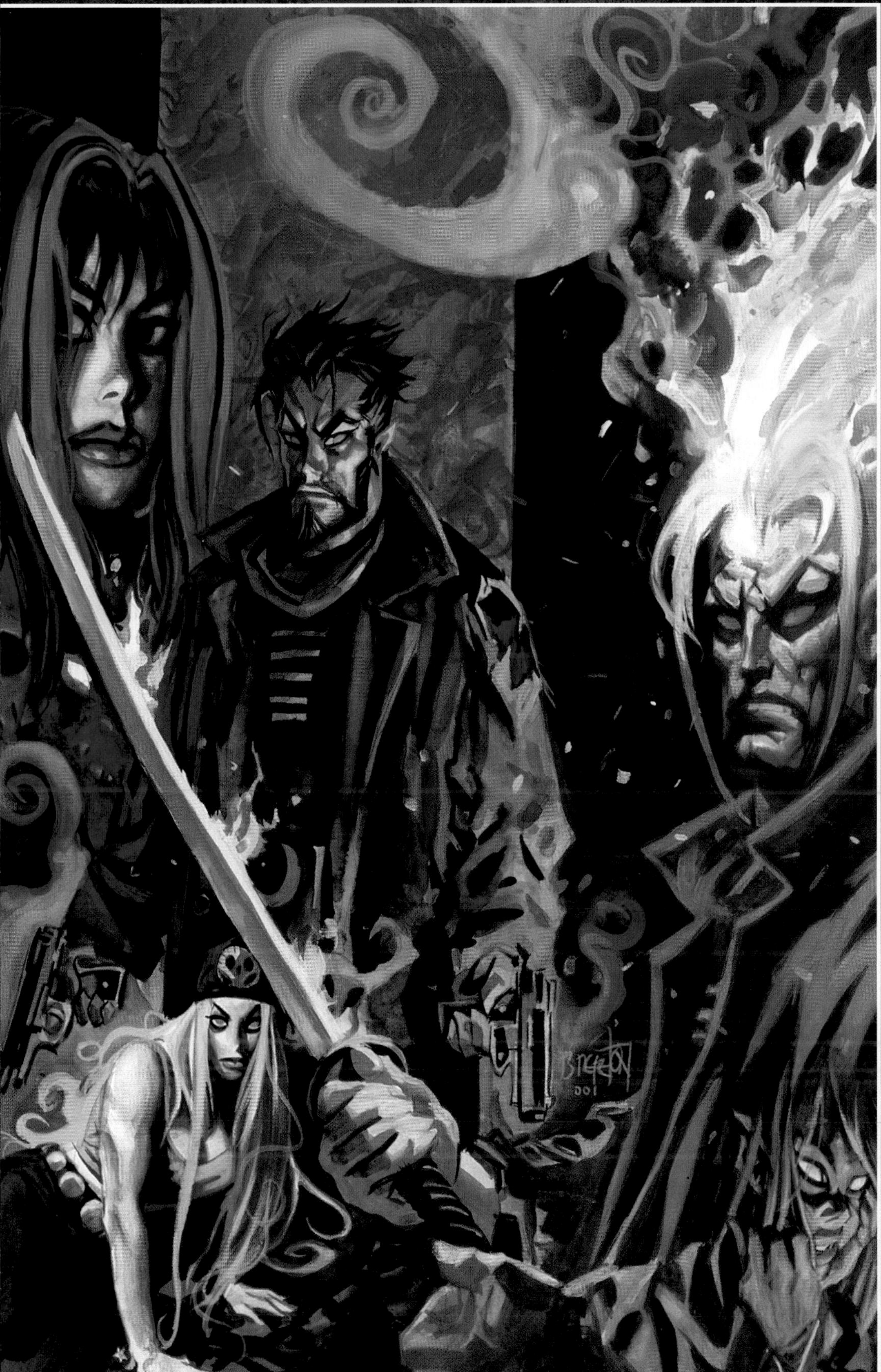

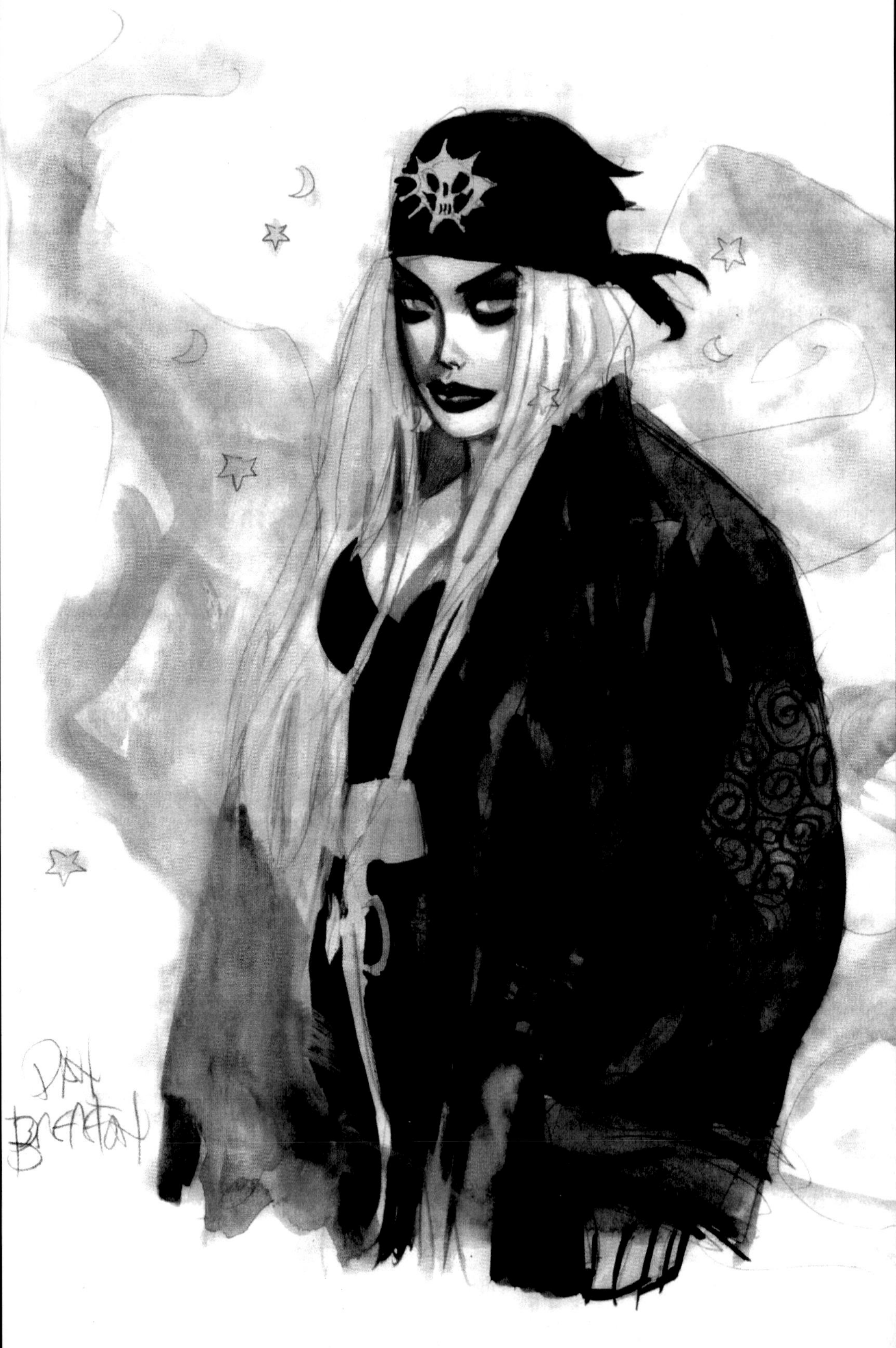
Dan Brereton

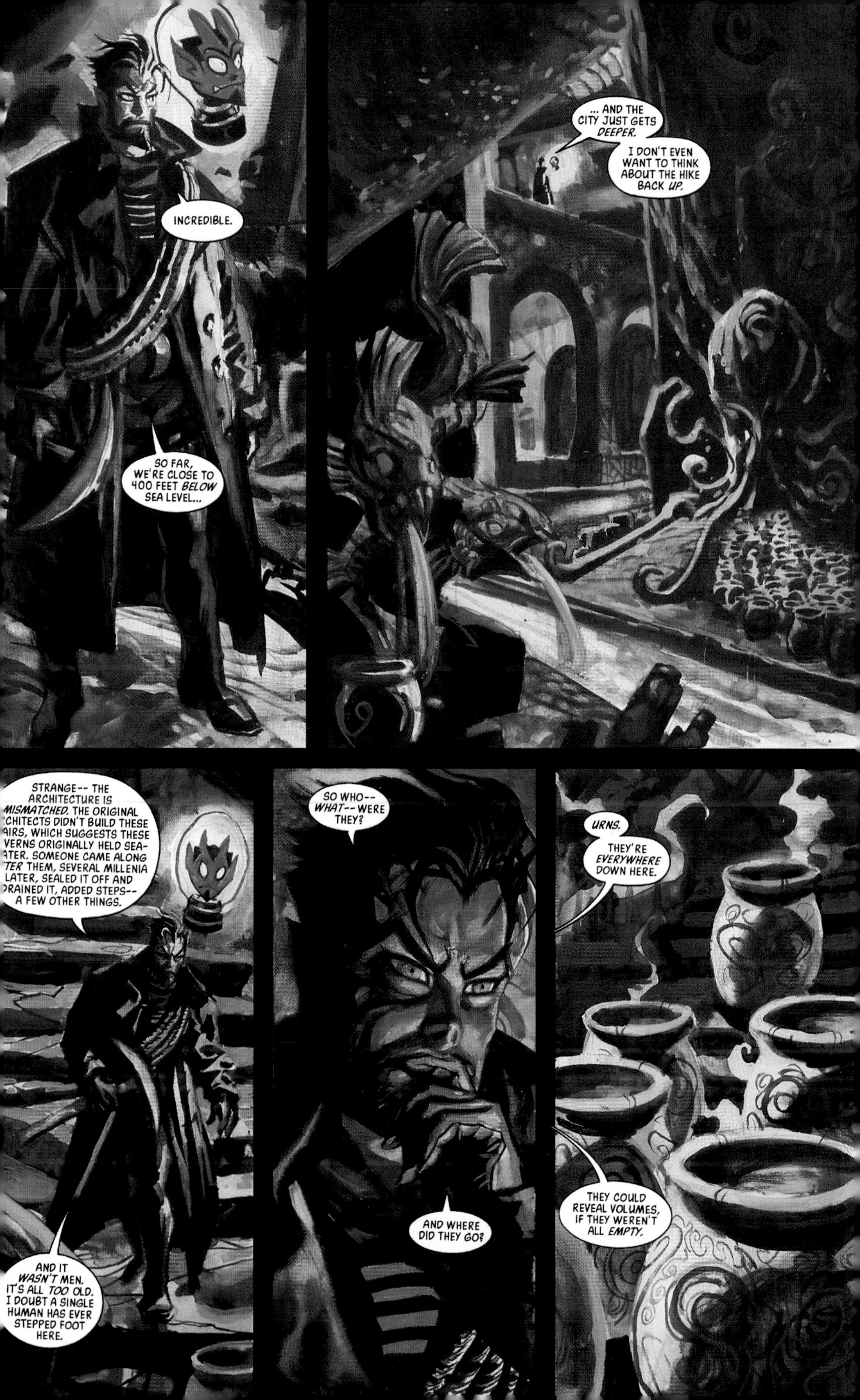
INCREDIBLE.
SO FAR, WE'RE CLOSE TO 400 FEET *BELOW* SEA LEVEL...
... AND THE CITY JUST GETS *DEEPER*.
I DON'T EVEN WANT TO THINK ABOUT THE HIKE BACK *UP*.
STRANGE-- THE ARCHITECTURE IS *MISMATCHED*. THE ORIGINAL CHITECTS DIDN'T BUILD THESE AIRS, WHICH SUGGESTS THESE VERNS ORIGINALLY HELD SEA-ATER. SOMEONE CAME ALONG TER THEM, SEVERAL MILLENIA LATER, SEALED IT OFF AND RAINED IT, ADDED STEPS-- A FEW OTHER THINGS.
AND IT *WASN'T* MEN. IT'S ALL *TOO* OLD. I DOUBT A SINGLE HUMAN HAS EVER STEPPED FOOT HERE.
SO WHO-- *WHAT*-- WERE THEY?
AND WHERE DID THEY GO?
URNS.
THEY'RE *EVERYWHERE* DOWN HERE.
THEY COULD REVEAL VOLUMES, IF THEY WEREN'T ALL *EMPTY*.

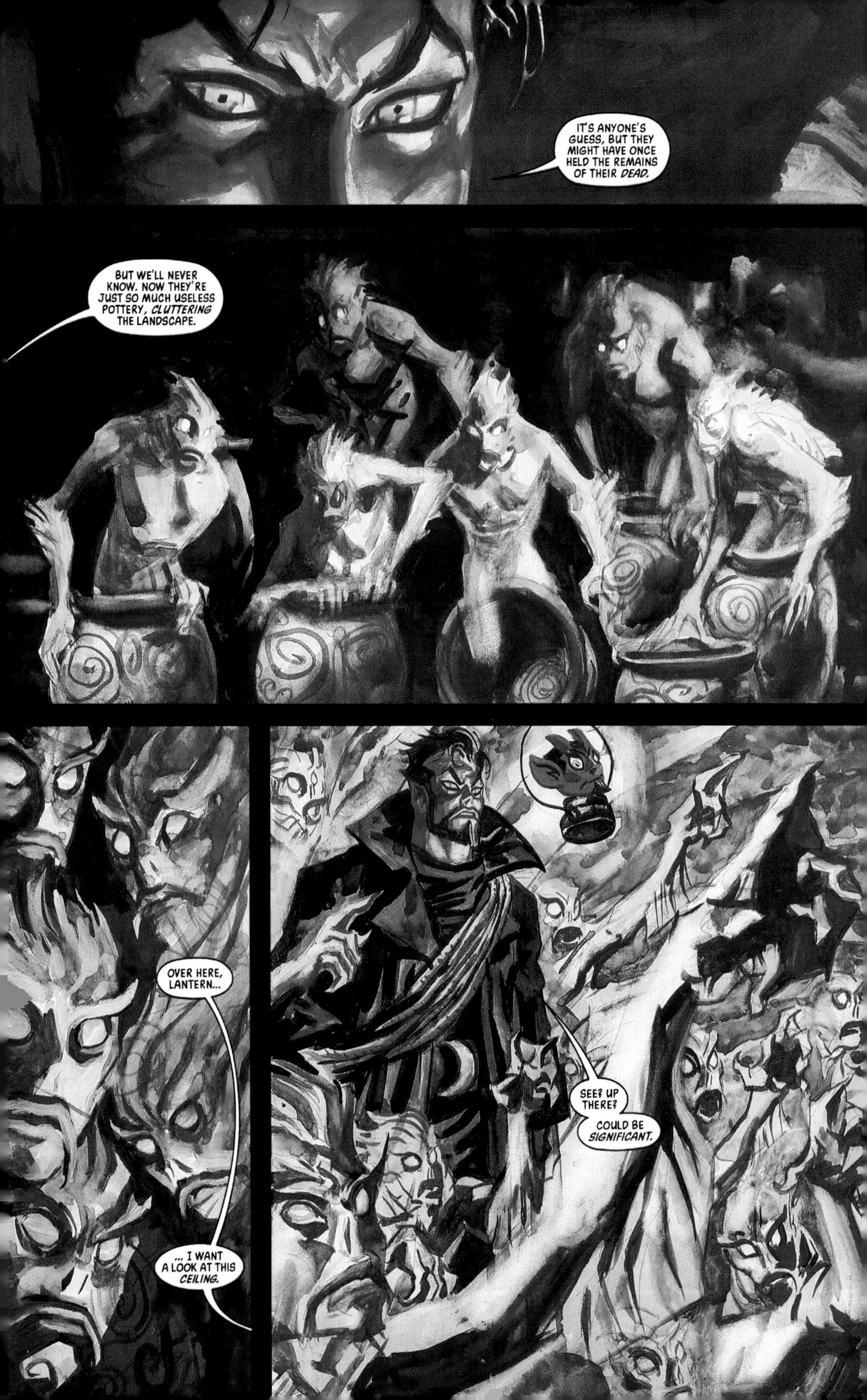
IT'S ANYONE'S GUESS, BUT THEY MIGHT HAVE ONCE HELD THE REMAINS OF THEIR *DEAD.*
BUT WE'LL NEVER KNOW. NOW THEY'RE JUST SO MUCH USELESS POTTERY, *CLUTTERING* THE LANDSCAPE.
OVER HERE, LANTERN...
... I WANT A LOOK AT THIS *CEILING.*
SEE? UP THERE?
COULD BE *SIGNIFICANT.*

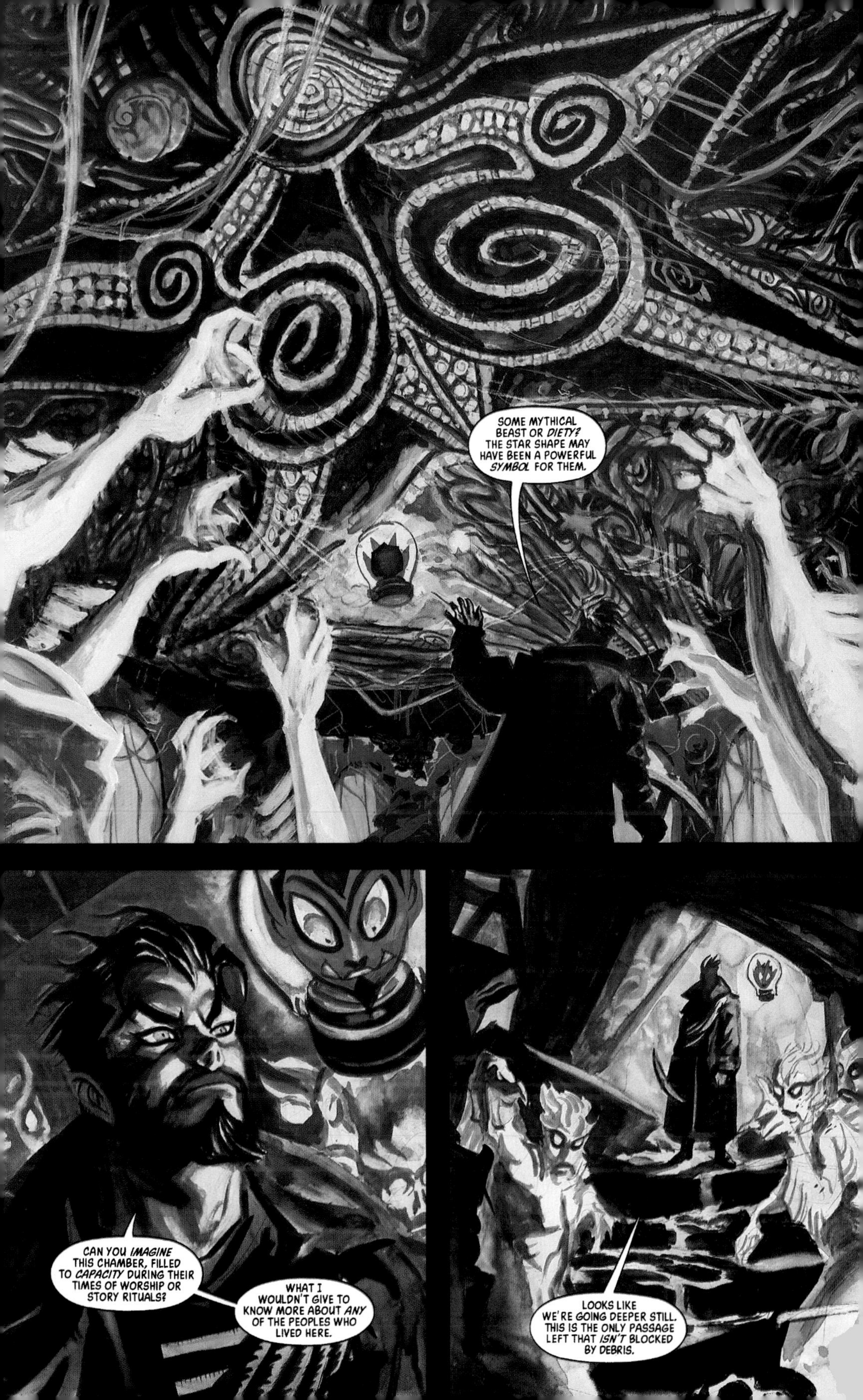
SOME MYTHICAL BEAST OR DIETY? THE STAR SHAPE MAY HAVE BEEN A POWERFUL SYMBOL FOR THEM.
CAN YOU IMAGINE THIS CHAMBER, FILLED TO CAPACITY DURING THEIR TIMES OF WORSHIP OR STORY RITUALS?
WHAT I WOULDN'T GIVE TO KNOW MORE ABOUT ANY OF THE PEOPLES WHO LIVED HERE.
LOOKS LIKE WE'RE GOING DEEPER STILL. THIS IS THE ONLY PASSAGE LEFT THAT ISN'T BLOCKED BY DEBRIS.

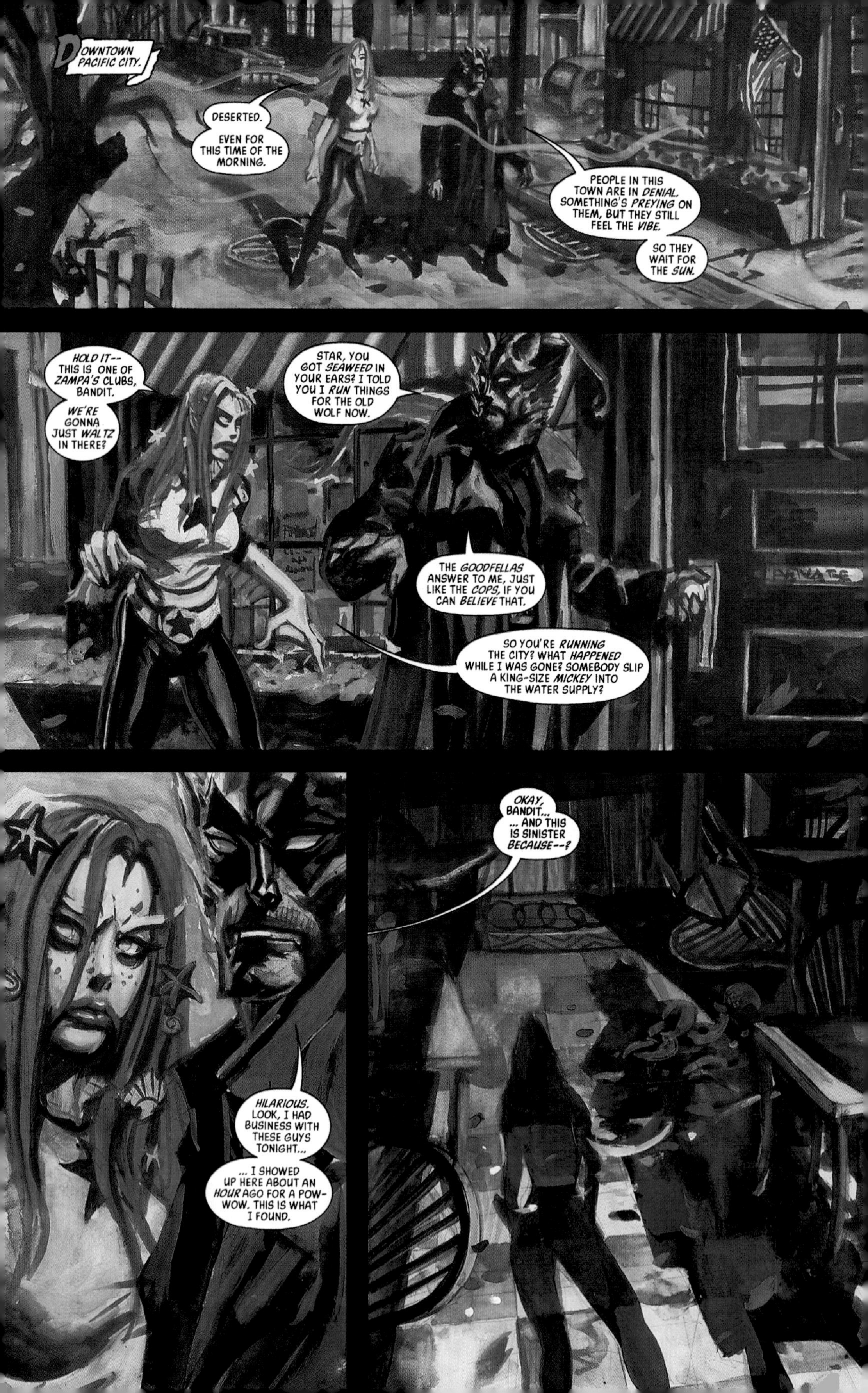
DOWNTOWN PACIFIC CITY.
DESERTED.
EVEN FOR THIS TIME OF THE MORNING.
PEOPLE IN THIS TOWN ARE IN DENIAL. SOMETHING'S PREYING ON THEM, BUT THEY STILL FEEL THE VIBE.
SO THEY WAIT FOR THE SUN.
HOLD IT-- THIS IS ONE OF ZAMPA'S CLUBS, BANDIT.
WE'RE GONNA JUST WALTZ IN THERE?
STAR, YOU GOT SEAWEED IN YOUR EARS? I TOLD YOU I RUN THINGS FOR THE OLD WOLF NOW.
THE GOODFELLAS ANSWER TO ME, JUST LIKE THE COPS, IF YOU CAN BELIEVE THAT.
SO YOU'RE RUNNING THE CITY? WHAT HAPPENED WHILE I WAS GONE? SOMEBODY SLIP A KING-SIZE MICKEY INTO THE WATER SUPPLY?
HILARIOUS. LOOK, I HAD BUSINESS WITH THESE GUYS TONIGHT...
... I SHOWED UP HERE ABOUT AN HOUR AGO FOR A POW-WOW. THIS IS WHAT I FOUND.
OKAY, BANDIT... ... AND THIS IS SINISTER BECAUSE--?

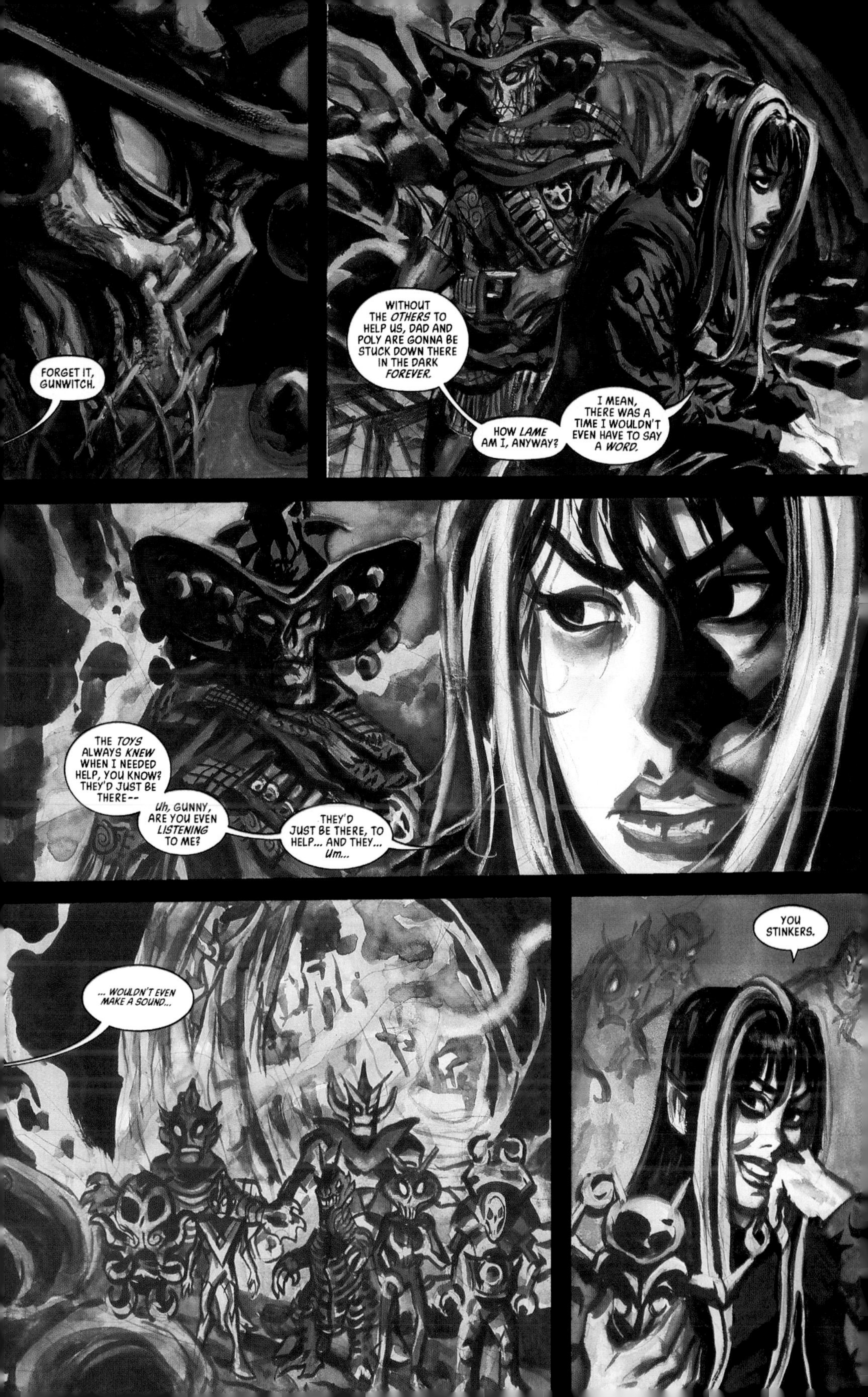
FORGET IT, GUNWITCH.
WITHOUT THE *OTHERS* TO HELP US, DAD AND POLY ARE GONNA BE STUCK DOWN THERE IN THE DARK *FOREVER.*
HOW *LAME* AM I, ANYWAY?
I MEAN, THERE WAS A TIME I WOULDN'T EVEN HAVE TO SAY A *WORD.*
THE *TOYS* ALWAYS *KNEW* WHEN I NEEDED HELP, YOU KNOW? THEY'D JUST BE THERE--
UH, GUNNY, ARE YOU EVEN *LISTENING* TO ME?
THEY'D JUST BE THERE, TO HELP... AND THEY... *UM...*
... WOULDN'T EVEN MAKE A SOUND...
YOU STINKERS.

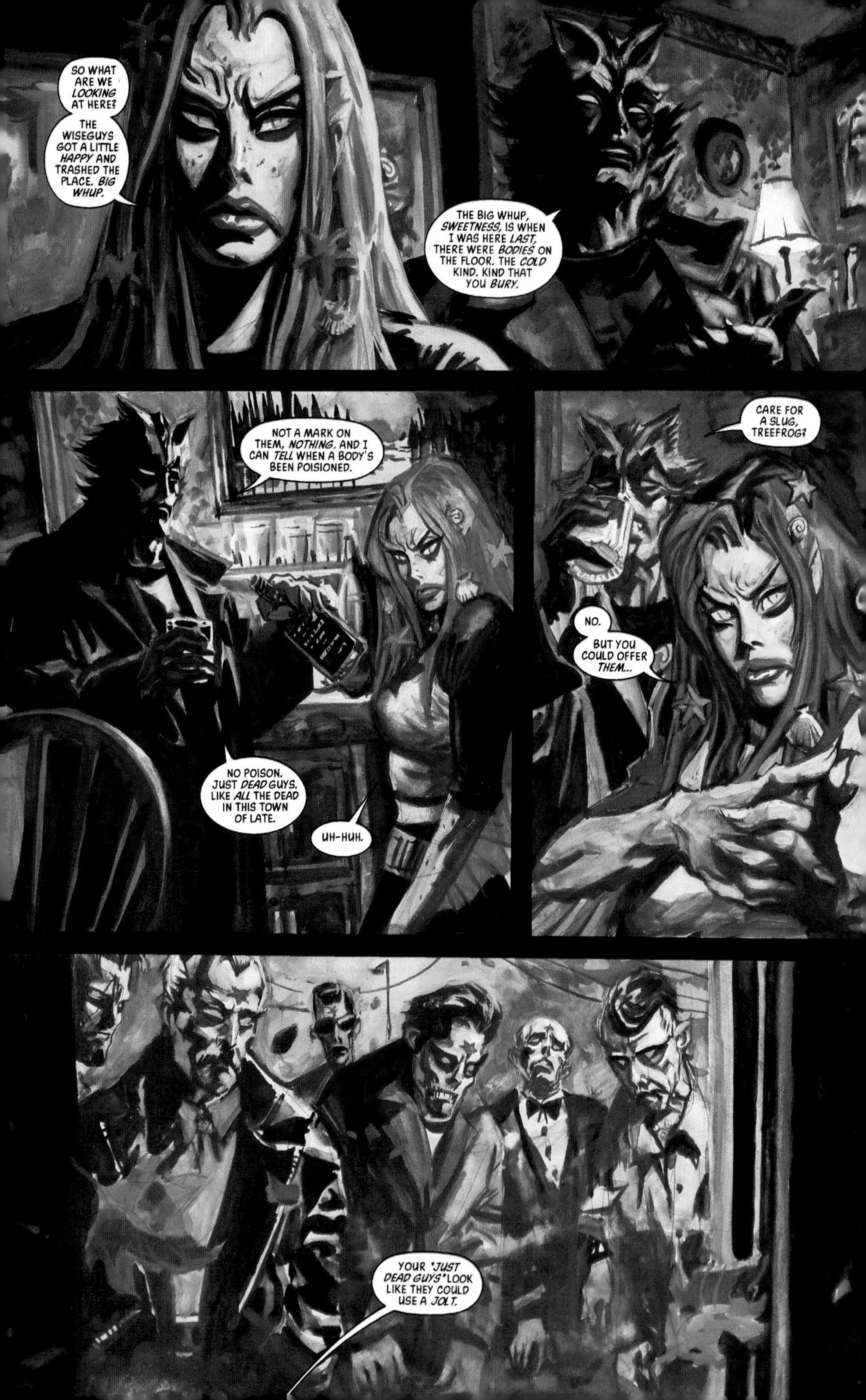
SO WHAT ARE WE LOOKING AT HERE?
THE WISEGUYS GOT A LITTLE HAPPY AND TRASHED THE PLACE. BIG WHUP.
THE BIG WHUP, SWEETNESS, IS WHEN I WAS HERE LAST, THERE WERE BODIES ON THE FLOOR. THE COLD KIND. KIND THAT YOU BURY.
NOT A MARK ON THEM, NOTHING. AND I CAN TELL WHEN A BODY'S BEEN POISONED.
NO POISON. JUST DEAD GUYS. LIKE ALL THE DEAD IN THIS TOWN OF LATE.
UH-HUH.
CARE FOR A SLUG, TREEFROG?
NO.
BUT YOU COULD OFFER THEM...
YOUR "JUST DEAD GUYS" LOOK LIKE THEY COULD USE A JOLT.

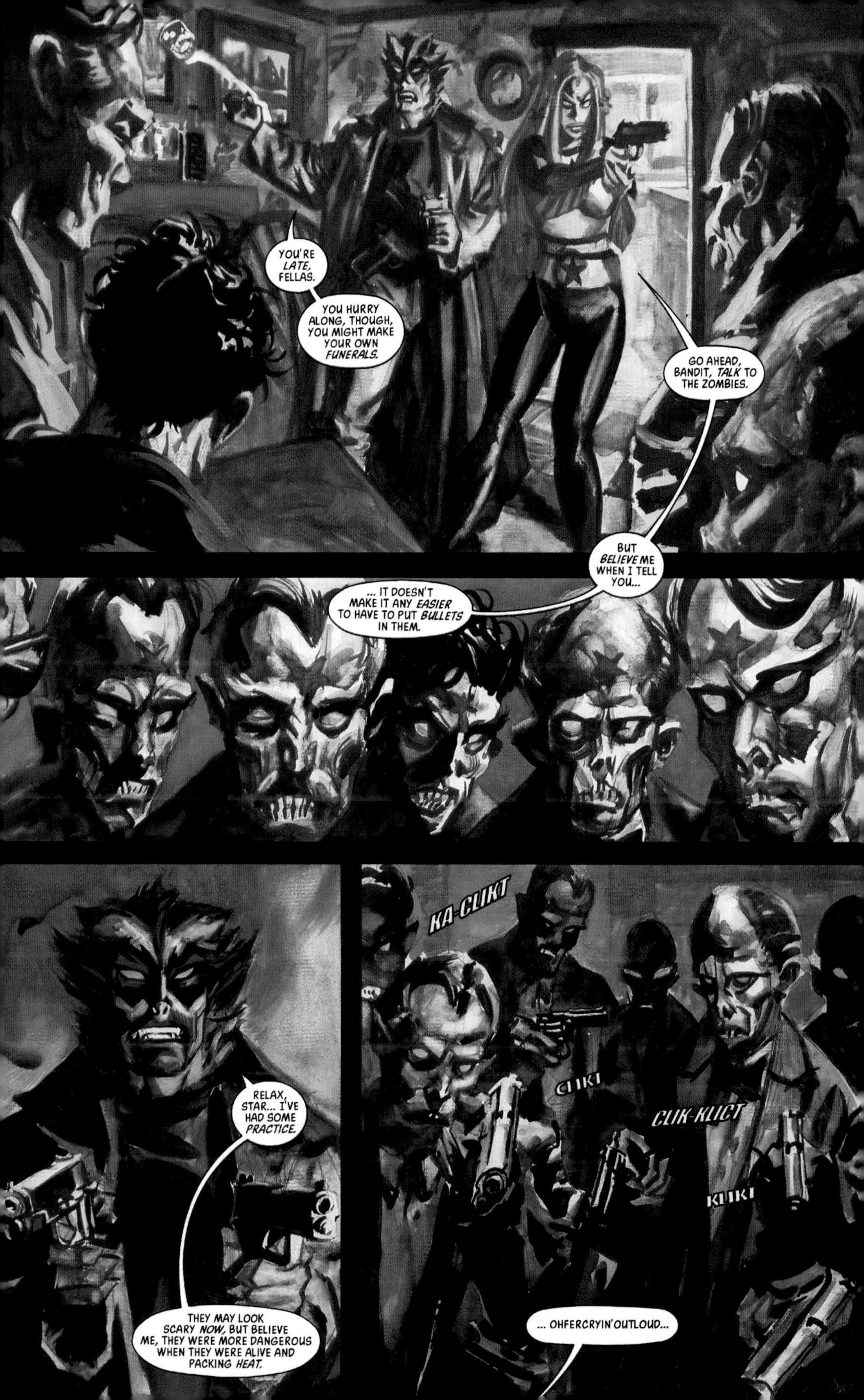
YOU'RE *LATE*, FELLAS.
YOU HURRY ALONG, THOUGH, YOU MIGHT MAKE YOUR OWN *FUNERALS*.
GO AHEAD, BANDIT, *TALK* TO THE ZOMBIES.
BUT *BELIEVE* ME WHEN I TELL YOU...
... IT DOESN'T MAKE IT ANY *EASIER* TO HAVE TO PUT *BULLETS* IN THEM.
RELAX, STAR... I'VE HAD SOME *PRACTICE*.
THEY MAY LOOK SCARY *NOW*, BUT BELIEVE ME, THEY WERE MORE DANGEROUS WHEN THEY WERE ALIVE AND PACKING *HEAT*.
KA-CLIKT
CLIK
CLIK-KLICT
KLIK
... OHFERCRYIN'OUTLOUD...

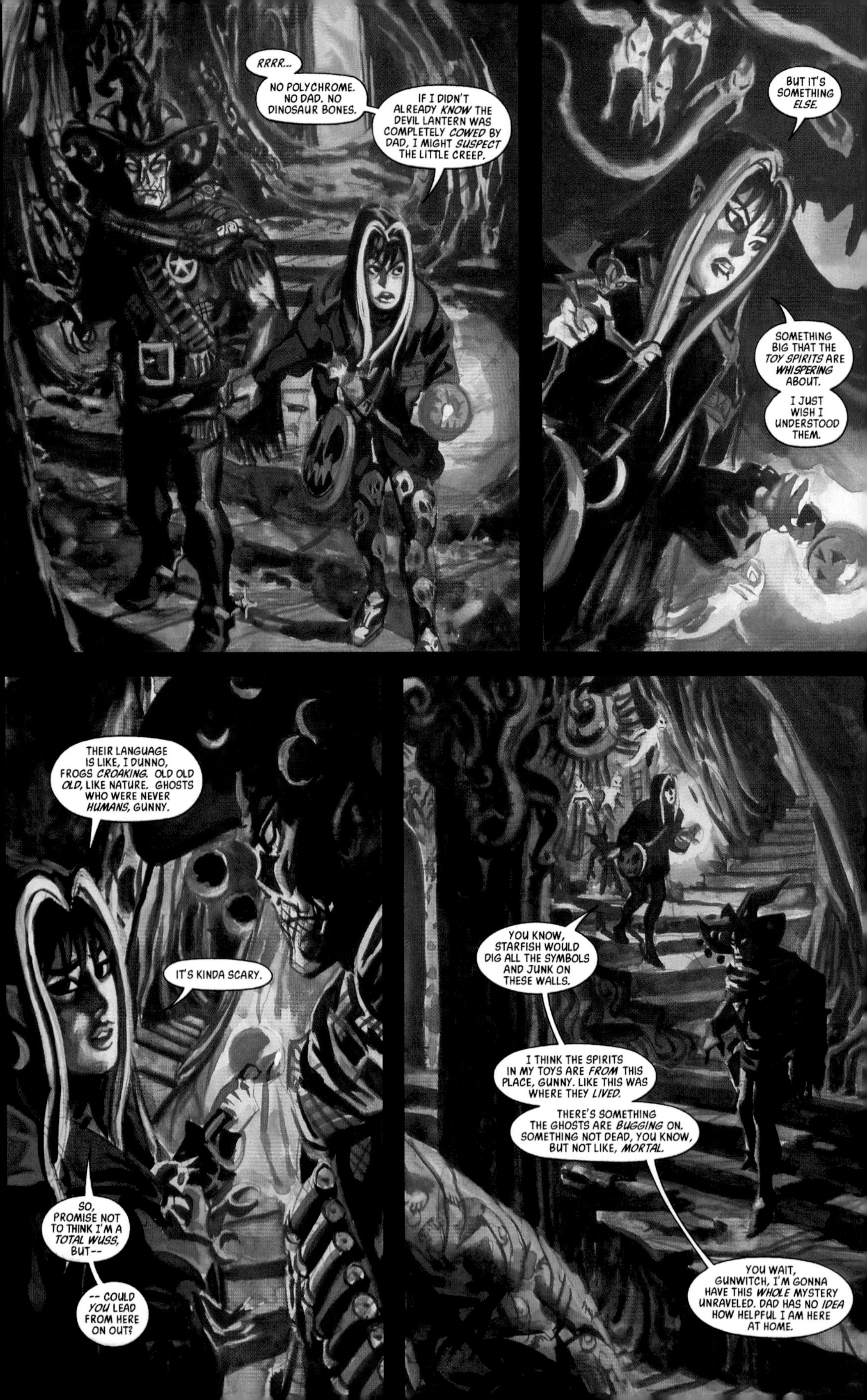

RRRR...
NO POLYCHROME. NO DAD. NO DINOSAUR BONES.
IF I DIDN'T ALREADY *KNOW* THE DEVIL LANTERN WAS COMPLETELY *COWED* BY DAD, I MIGHT *SUSPECT* THE LITTLE CREEP.
BUT IT'S SOMETHING *ELSE.*
SOMETHING BIG THAT THE *TOY SPIRITS* ARE *WHISPERING* ABOUT.
I JUST WISH I UNDERSTOOD THEM.
THEIR LANGUAGE IS LIKE, I DUNNO, FROGS *CROAKING.* OLD OLD *OLD*, LIKE NATURE. GHOSTS WHO WERE NEVER *HUMANS*, GUNNY.
IT'S KINDA SCARY.
SO, PROMISE NOT TO THINK I'M A *TOTAL WUSS*, BUT--
-- COULD *YOU* LEAD FROM HERE ON OUT?
YOU KNOW, STARFISH WOULD DIG ALL THE SYMBOLS AND JUNK ON THESE WALLS.
I THINK THE SPIRITS IN MY TOYS ARE *FROM* THIS PLACE, GUNNY. LIKE THIS WAS WHERE THEY *LIVED.*
THERE'S SOMETHING THE GHOSTS ARE *BUGGING* ON. SOMETHING NOT DEAD, YOU KNOW, BUT NOT LIKE, *MORTAL.*
YOU WAIT, GUNWITCH, I'M GONNA HAVE THIS *WHOLE* MYSTERY UNRAVELED. DAD HAS NO *IDEA* HOW HELPFUL I AM HERE AT HOME.

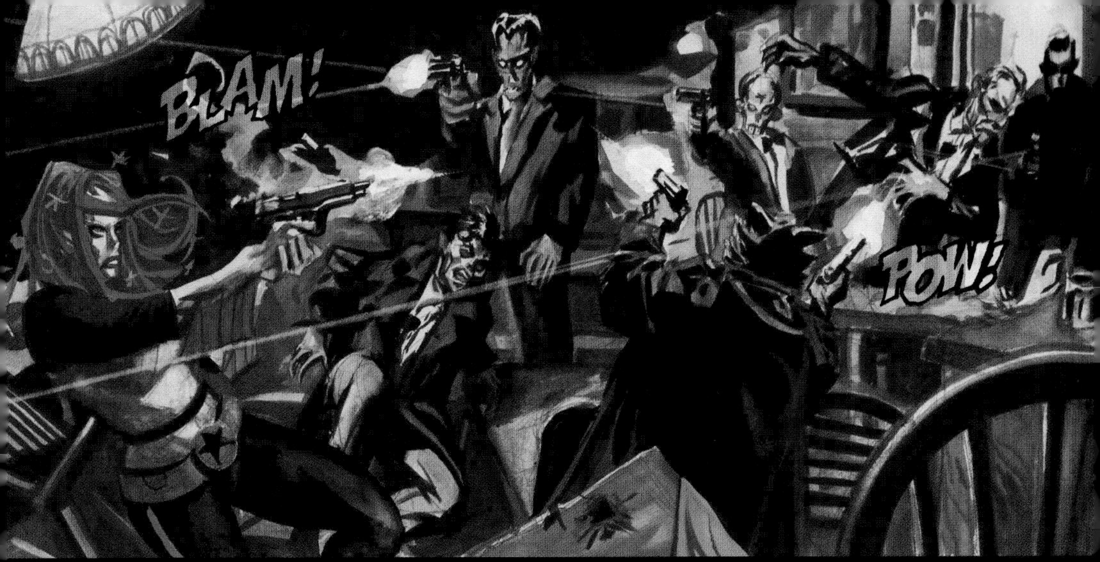
BLAM!
POW!

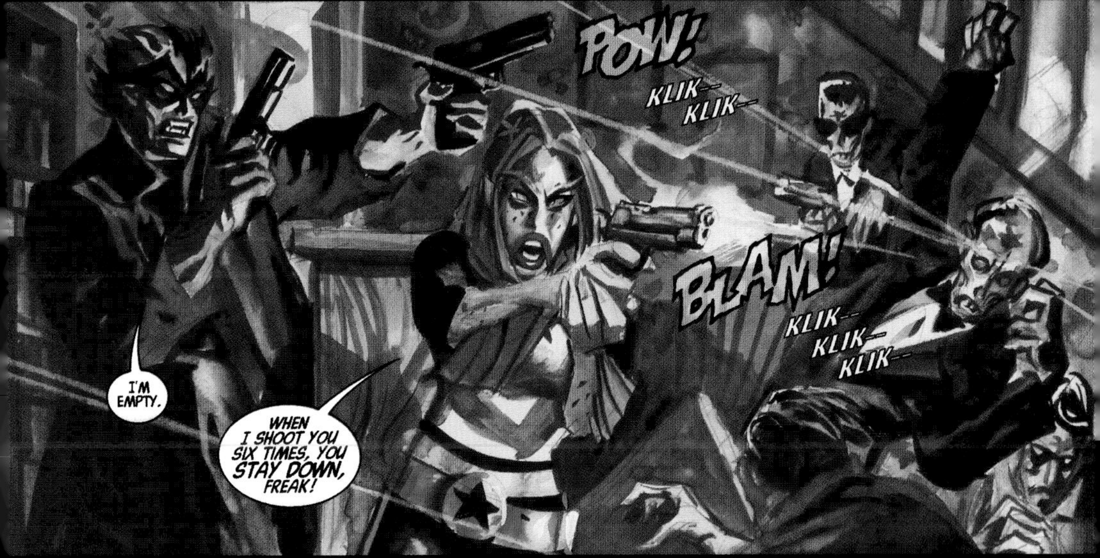
POW!
KLIK-- KLIK--
BLAM!
KLIK-- KLIK-- KLIK--
I'M EMPTY.
WHEN I SHOOT YOU SIX TIMES, YOU STAY DOWN, FREAK!

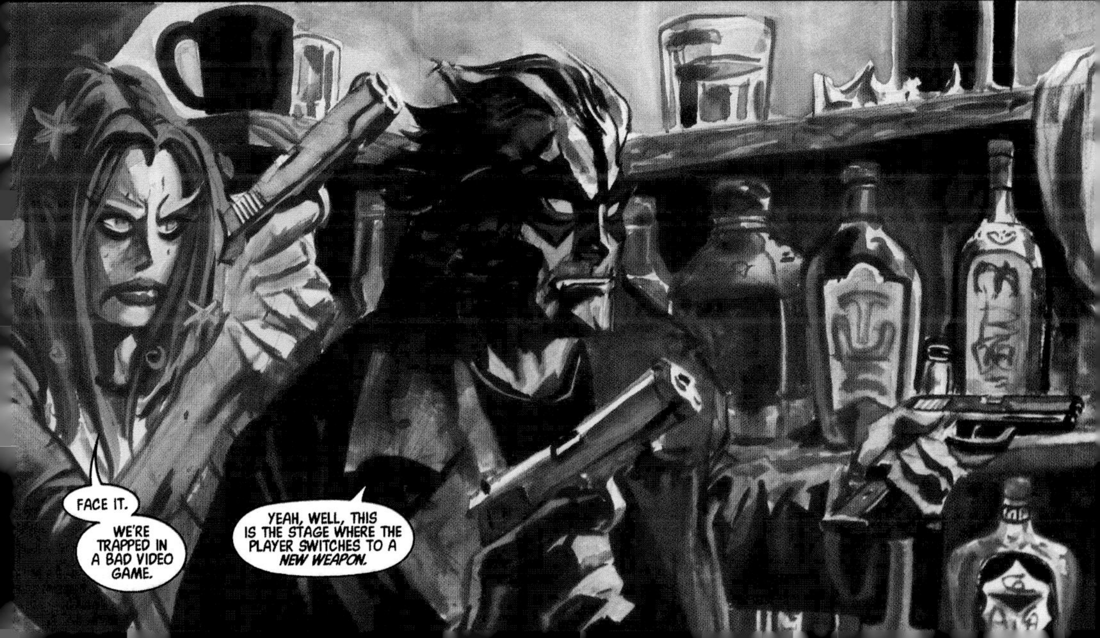
FACE IT.
WE'RE TRAPPED IN A BAD VIDEO GAME.
YEAH, WELL, THIS IS THE STAGE WHERE THE PLAYER SWITCHES TO A NEW WEAPON.

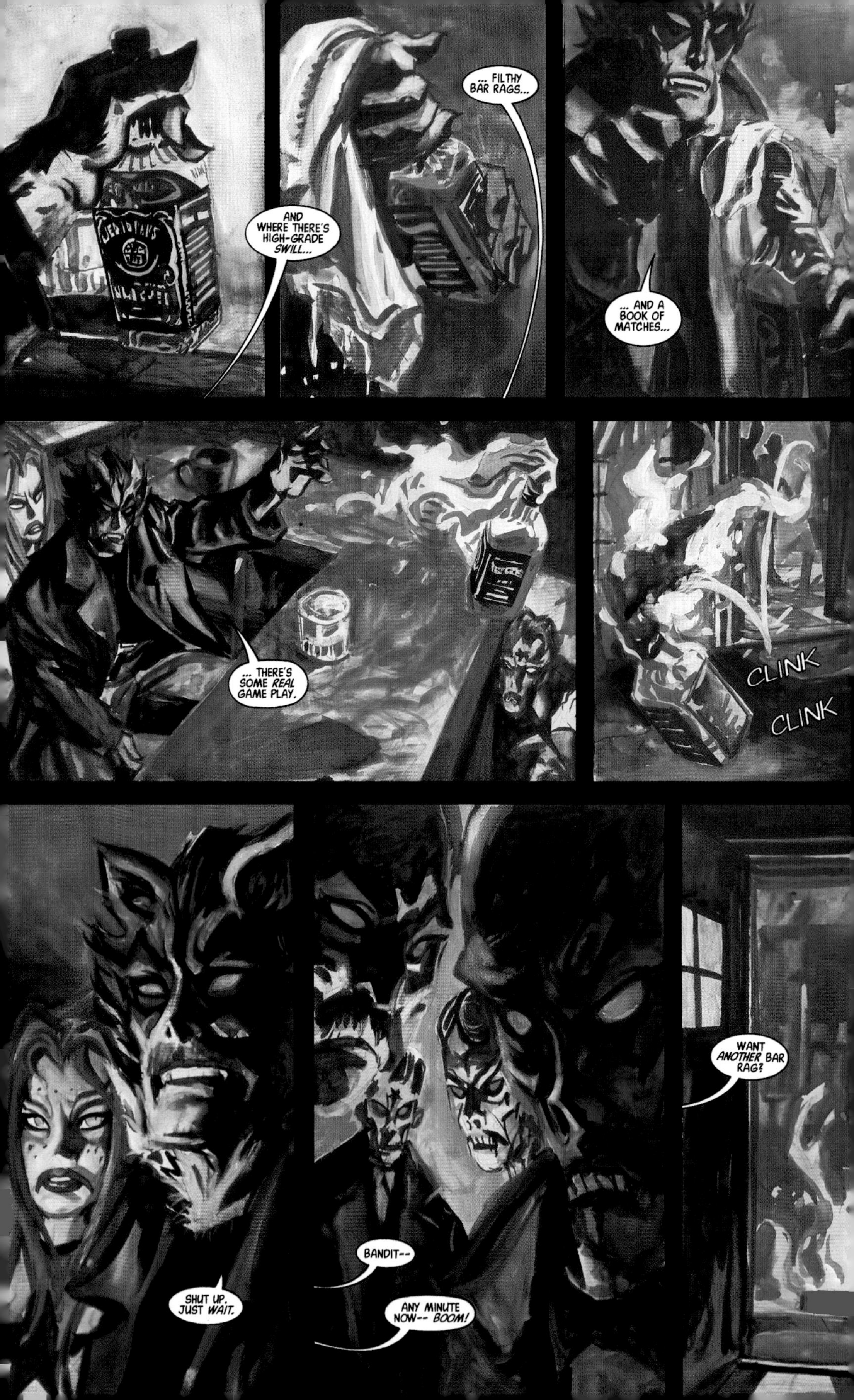
AND WHERE THERE'S HIGH-GRADE SWILL...
... FILTHY BAR RAGS...
... AND A BOOK OF MATCHES...
... THERE'S SOME REAL GAME PLAY.
CLINK
CLINK
SHUT UP. JUST WAIT.
BANDIT--
ANY MINUTE NOW-- BOOM!
WANT ANOTHER BAR RAG?

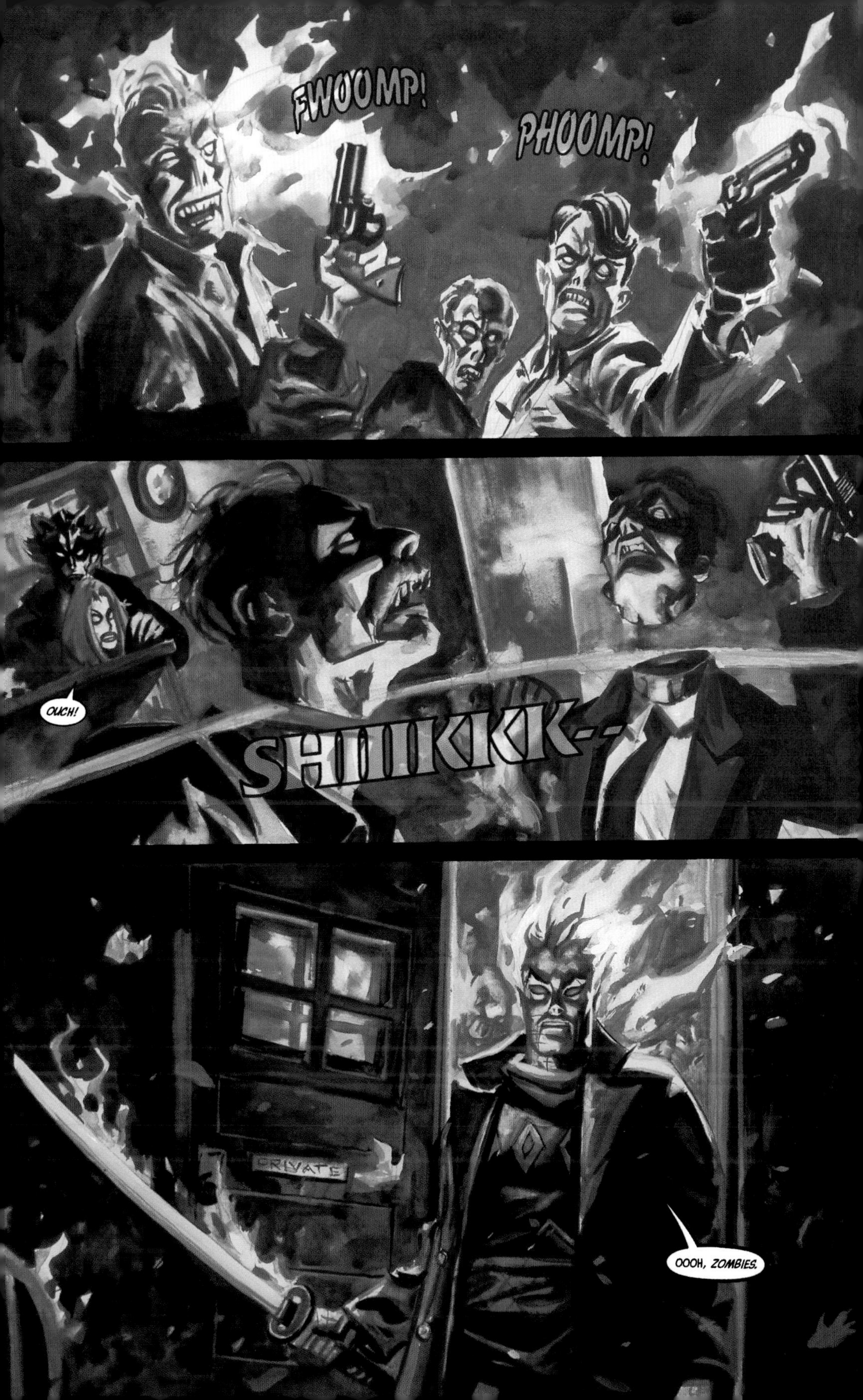
FWOOMP!
PHOOMP!
OUCH!
SHIIIIKKK--
PRIVATE
OOOH, ZOMBIES.

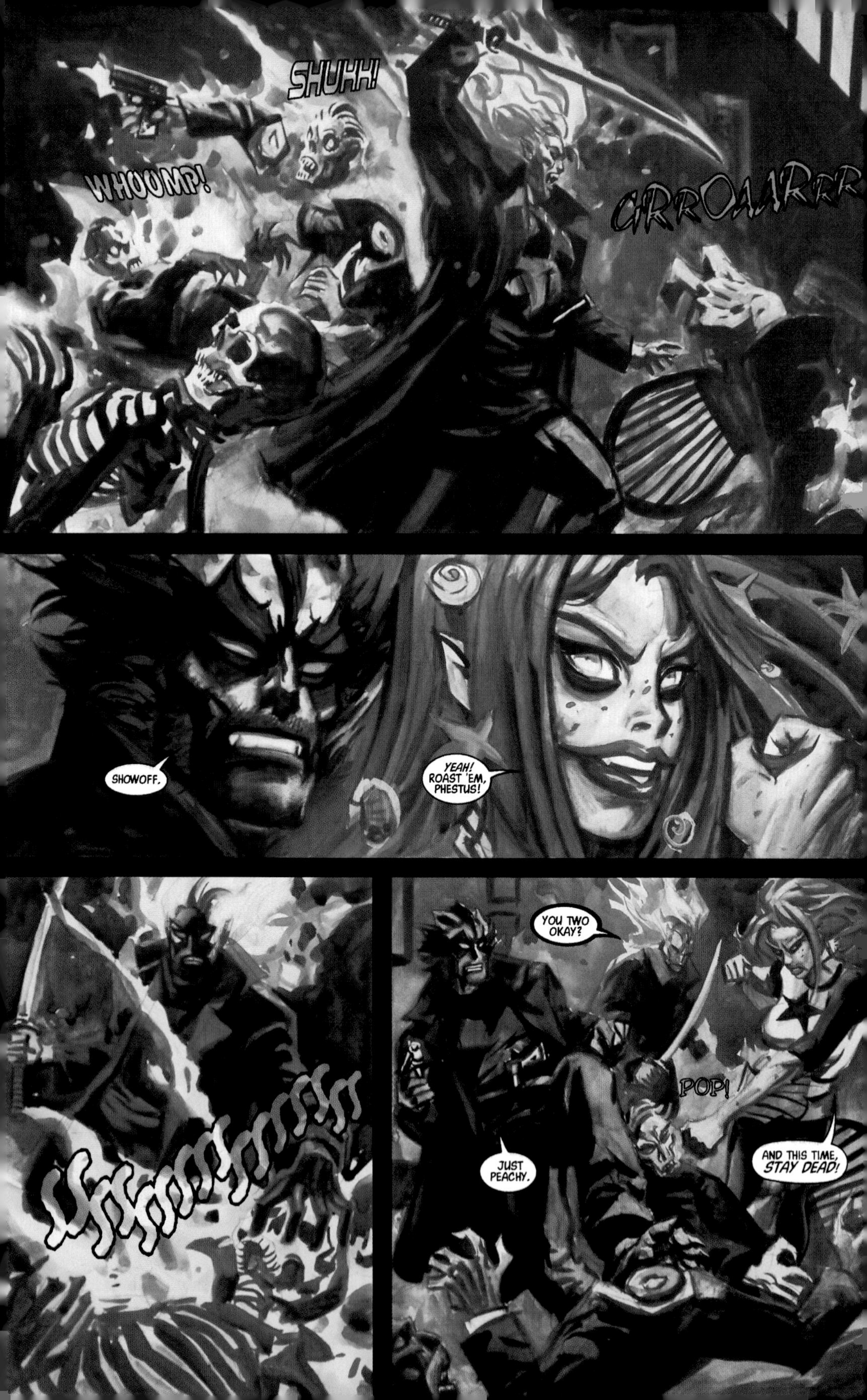
SHUHH!
WHOOMP!
GRROAARRR
SHOWOFF.
YEAH! ROAST 'EM, PHESTUS!
YOU TWO OKAY?
POP!
JUST PEACHY.
AND THIS TIME, STAY DEAD!

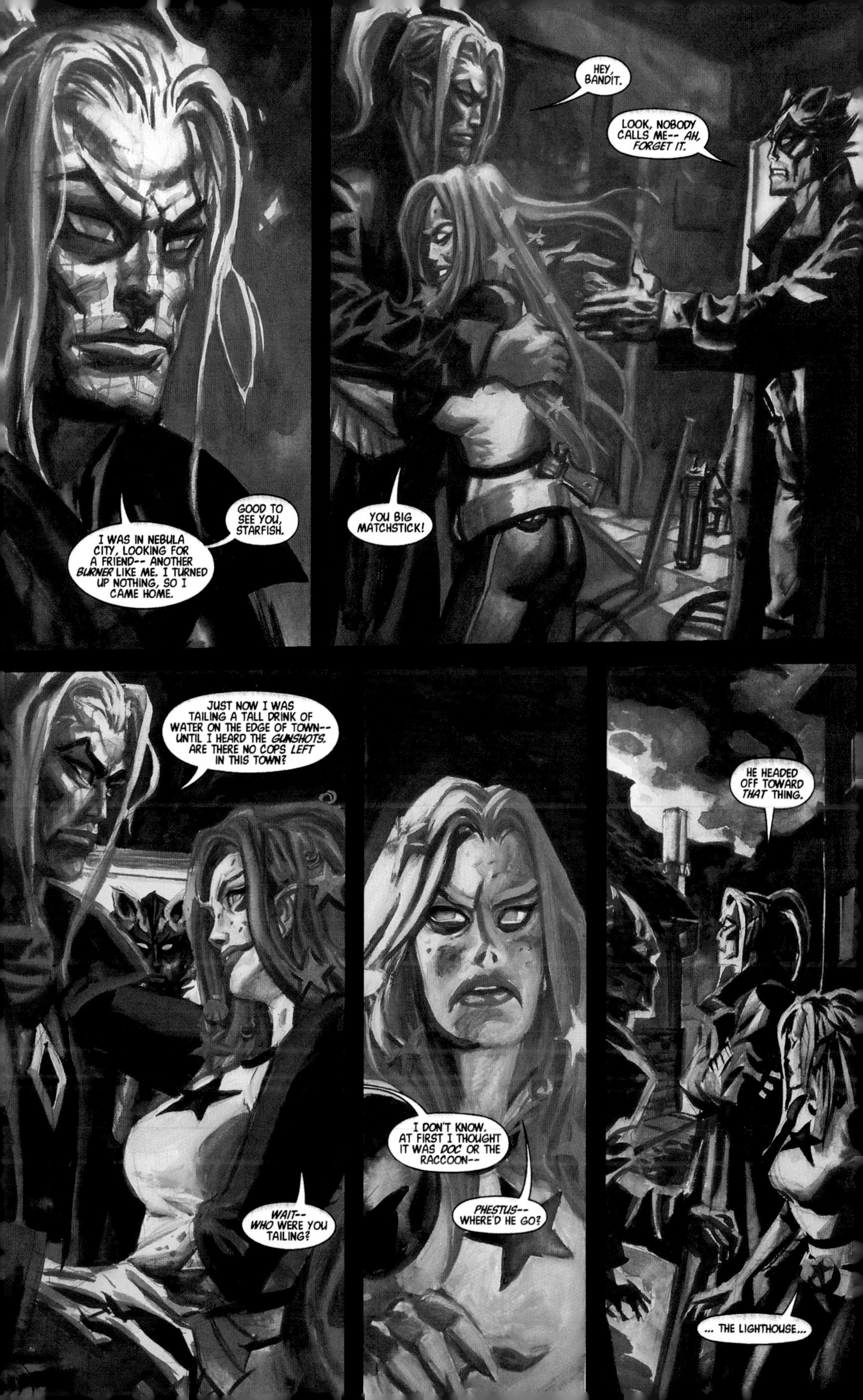
I WAS IN NEBULA CITY, LOOKING FOR A FRIEND-- ANOTHER BURNER LIKE ME. I TURNED UP NOTHING, SO I CAME HOME.
GOOD TO SEE YOU, STARFISH.
HEY, BANDÍT.
LOOK, NOBODY CALLS ME-- AH, FORGET IT.
YOU BIG MATCHSTICK!
JUST NOW I WAS TAILING A TALL DRINK OF WATER ON THE EDGE OF TOWN-- UNTIL I HEARD THE GUNSHOTS. ARE THERE NO COPS LEFT IN THIS TOWN?
WAIT-- WHO WERE YOU TAILING?
I DON'T KNOW. AT FIRST I THOUGHT IT WAS DOC OR THE RACCOON--
PHESTUS-- WHERE'D HE GO?
HE HEADED OFF TOWARD THAT THING.
... THE LIGHTHOUSE...

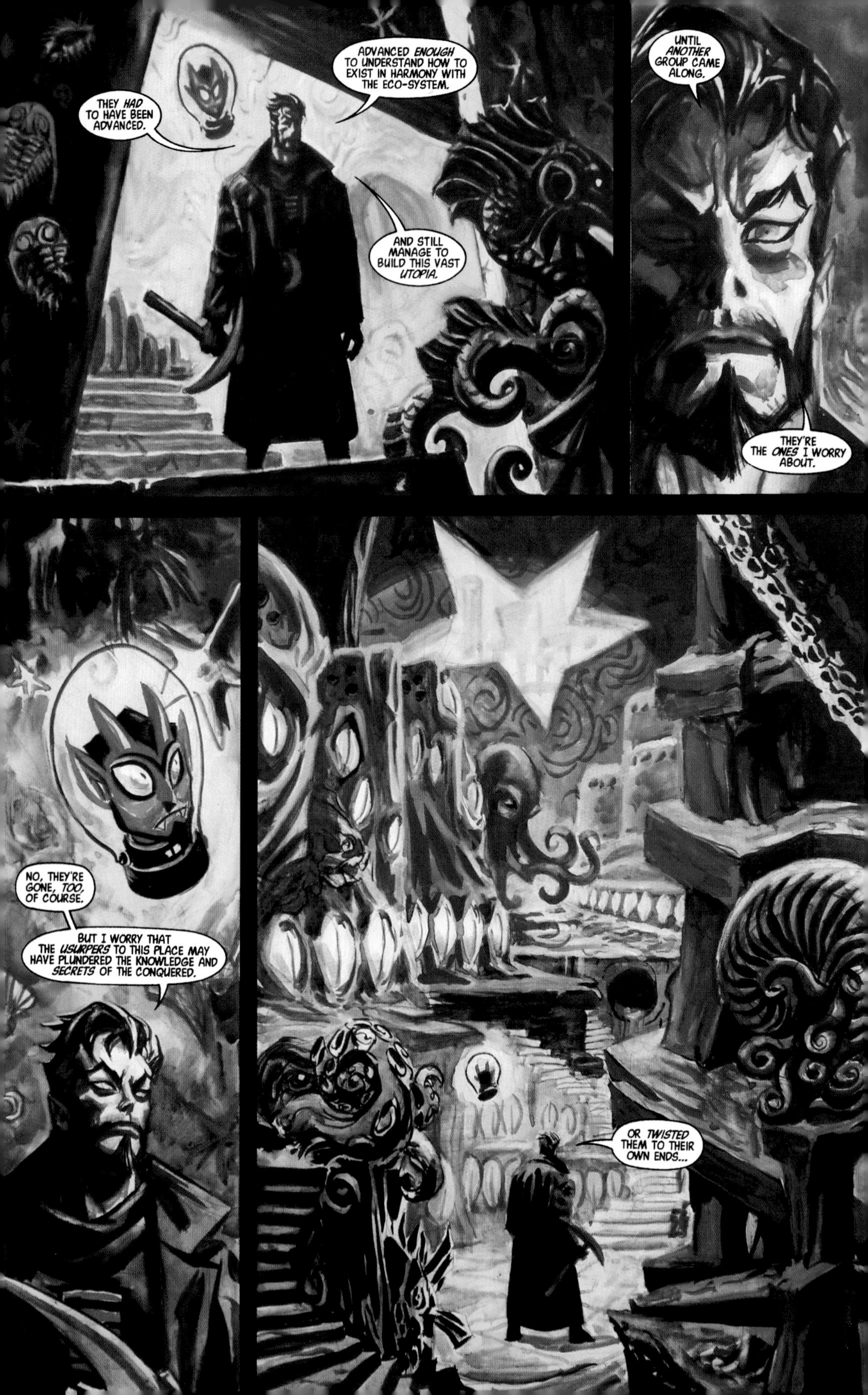
THEY HAD TO HAVE BEEN ADVANCED.
ADVANCED ENOUGH TO UNDERSTAND HOW TO EXIST IN HARMONY WITH THE ECO-SYSTEM.
AND STILL MANAGE TO BUILD THIS VAST UTOPIA.
UNTIL ANOTHER GROUP CAME ALONG.
THEY'RE THE ONES I WORRY ABOUT.
NO, THEY'RE GONE, TOO, OF COURSE.
BUT I WORRY THAT THE USURPERS TO THIS PLACE MAY HAVE PLUNDERED THE KNOWLEDGE AND SECRETS OF THE CONQUERED.
OR TWISTED THEM TO THEIR OWN ENDS...

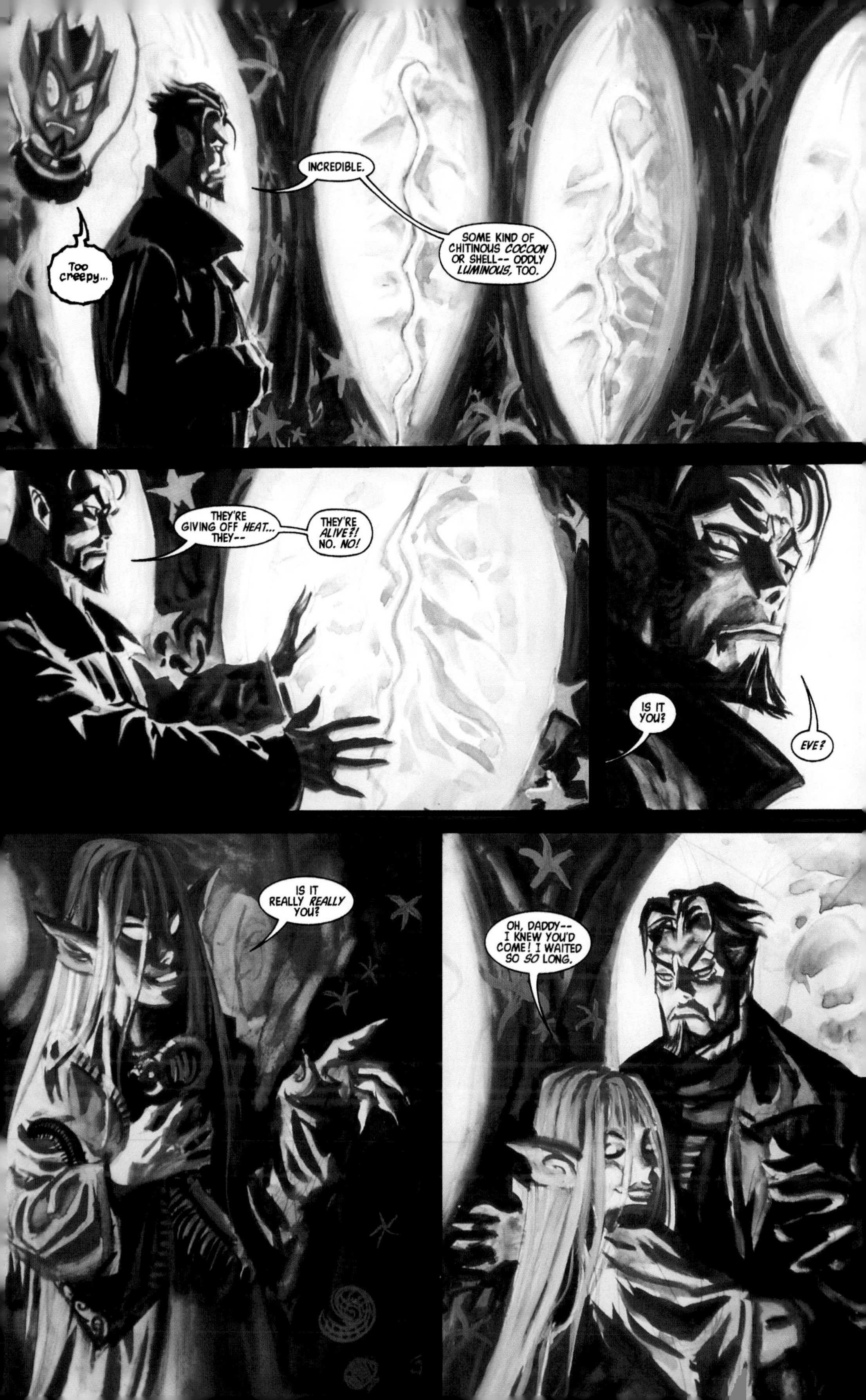
INCREDIBLE.
SOME KIND OF CHITINOUS *COCOON* OR SHELL-- ODDLY *LUMINOUS,* TOO.
Too creepy...
THEY'RE GIVING OFF *HEAT*... THEY--
THEY'RE *ALIVE*?! NO. *NO!*
IS IT YOU?
EVE?
IS IT REALLY *REALLY* YOU?
OH, DADDY-- I KNEW YOU'D COME! I WAITED SO *SO* LONG.

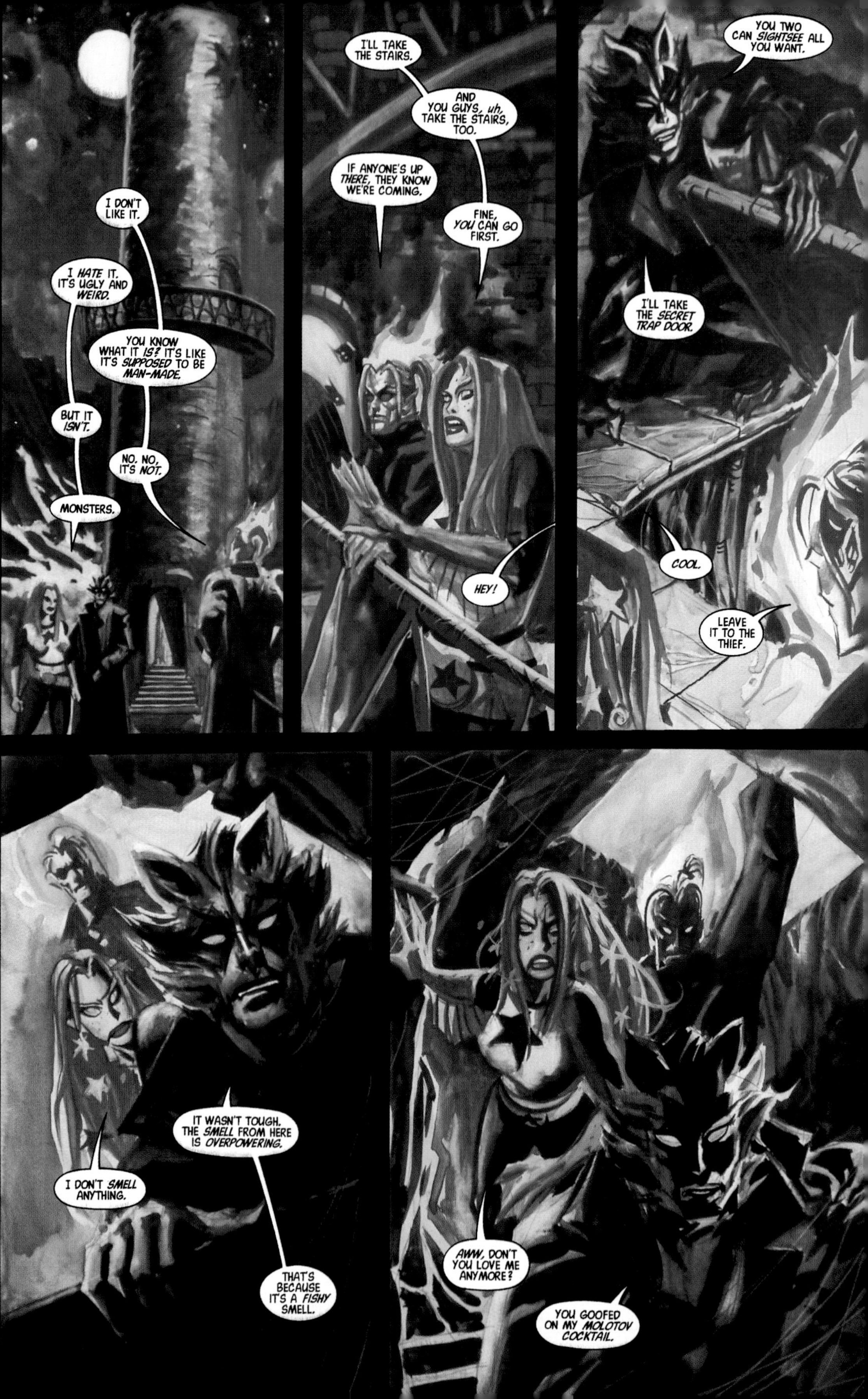

I DON'T LIKE IT.
I *HATE* IT. IT'S UGLY AND *WEIRD*.
YOU KNOW WHAT IT *IS*? IT'S LIKE IT'S *SUPPOSED* TO BE *MAN-MADE*.
BUT IT *ISN'T*.
NO. NO, IT'S *NOT*.
MONSTERS.
I'LL TAKE THE STAIRS.
AND YOU GUYS, *uh*, TAKE THE STAIRS, TOO.
IF ANYONE'S UP *THERE*, THEY KNOW WE'RE COMING.
FINE, *YOU* CAN GO FIRST.
HEY!
YOU TWO CAN *SIGHTSEE* ALL YOU WANT.
I'LL TAKE THE *SECRET TRAP DOOR*.
COOL.
LEAVE IT TO THE THIEF.
IT WASN'T TOUGH. THE *SMELL* FROM HERE IS *OVERPOWERING*.
I DON'T *SMELL* ANYTHING.
THAT'S BECAUSE IT'S A *FISHY* SMELL.
AWW, DON'T YOU LOVE ME ANYMORE?
YOU GOOFED ON MY *MOLOTOV COCKTAIL*.

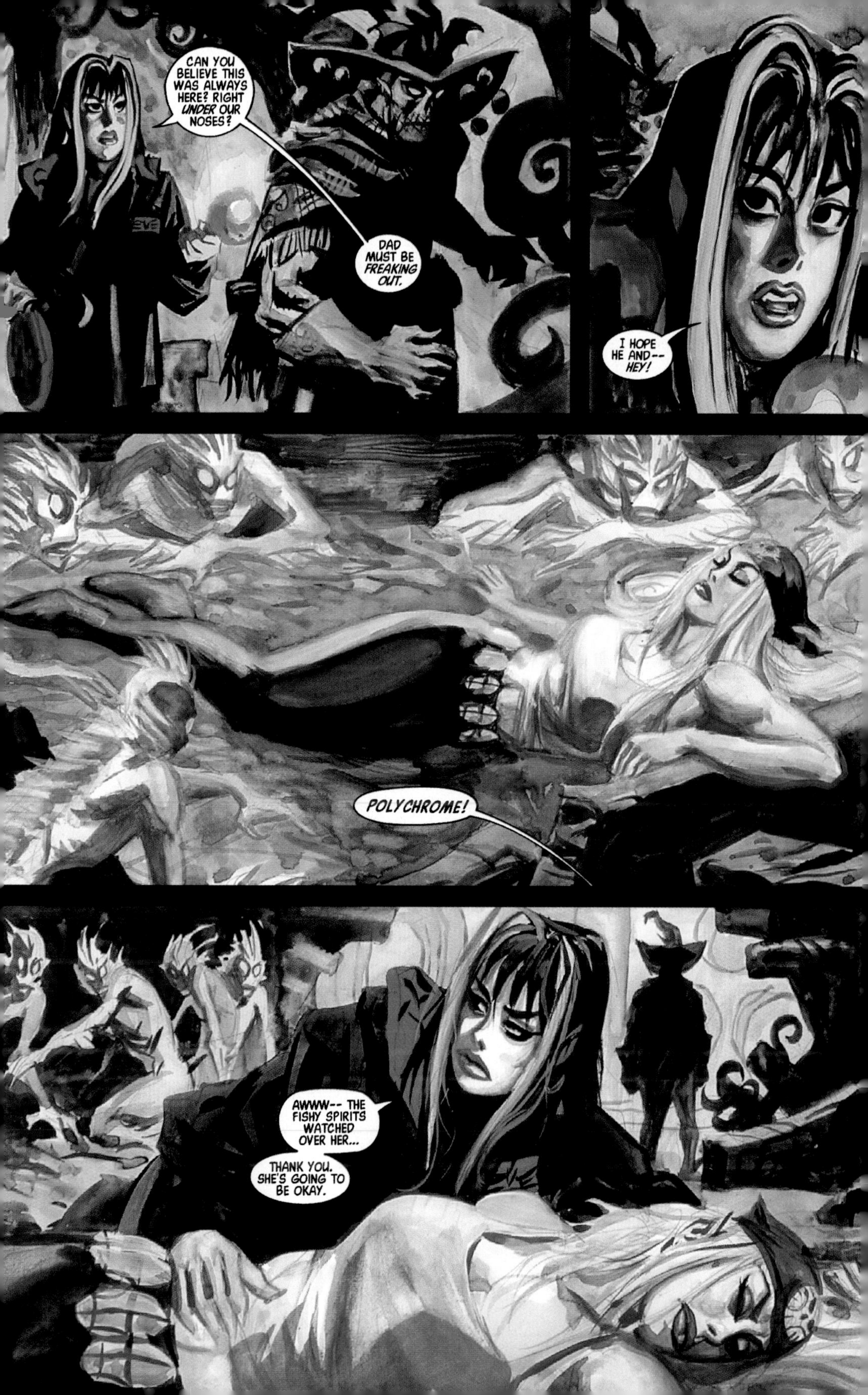
CAN YOU BELIEVE THIS WAS ALWAYS HERE? RIGHT *UNDER* OUR NOSES?
DAD MUST BE *FREAKING* OUT.
I HOPE HE AND-- *HEY!*
POLYCHROME!
AWWW-- THE FISHY SPIRITS WATCHED OVER HER...
THANK YOU. SHE'S GOING TO BE OKAY.

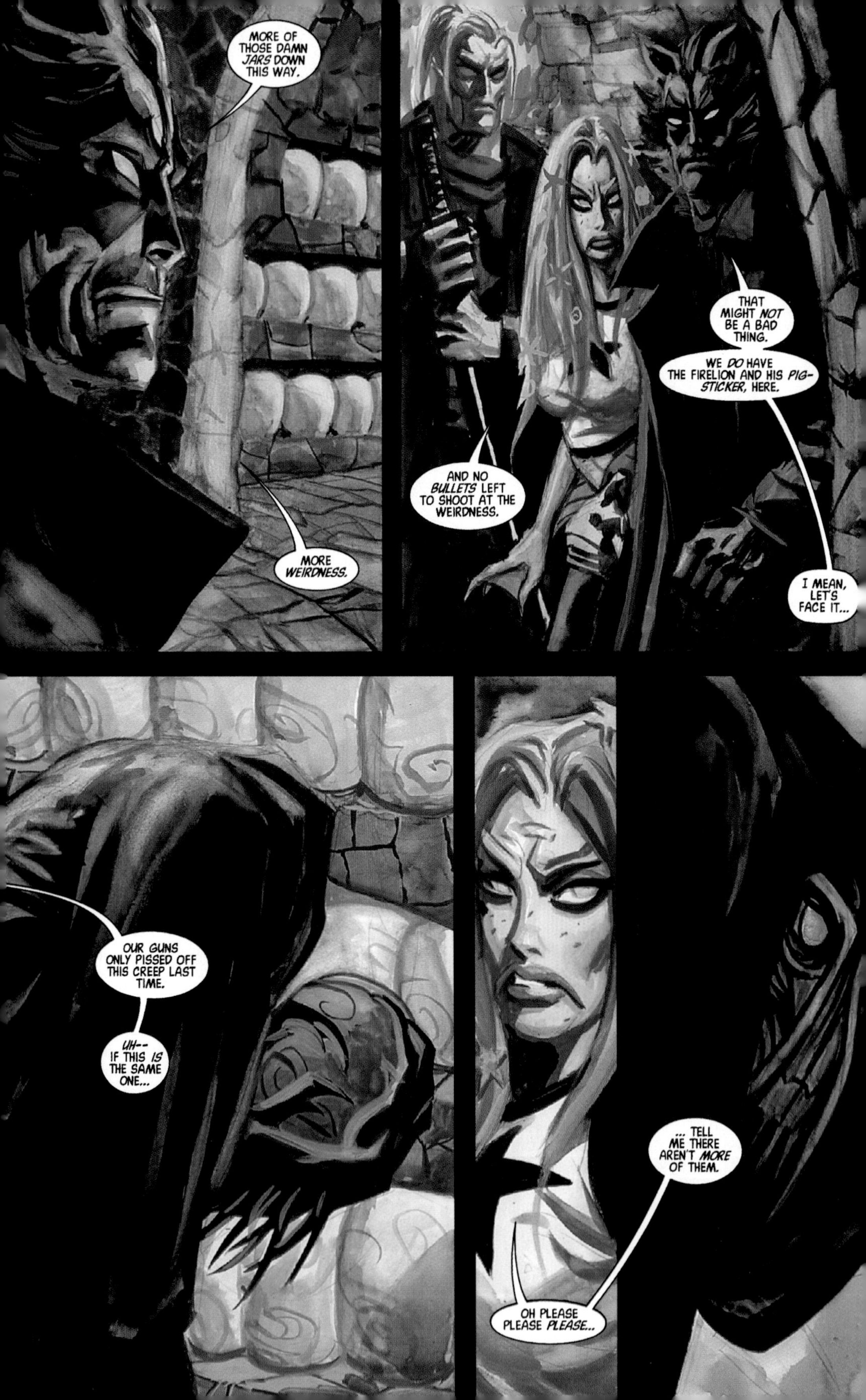
MORE OF THOSE DAMN JARS DOWN THIS WAY.
MORE WEIRDNESS.
AND NO BULLETS LEFT TO SHOOT AT THE WEIRDNESS.
THAT MIGHT NOT BE A BAD THING.
WE DO HAVE THE FIRELION AND HIS PIG-STICKER, HERE.
I MEAN, LET'S FACE IT...
OUR GUNS ONLY PISSED OFF THIS CREEP LAST TIME.
UH-- IF THIS IS THE SAME ONE...
... TELL ME THERE AREN'T MORE OF THEM.
OH PLEASE PLEASE PLEASE...

HSSSSSSSS!

THAT'S... NOT A ZOMBIE.

LEMME GO, BANDIT!

FORGET IT, TREEFROG...

... IT'S TIME WE HIGH-TAILED IT...

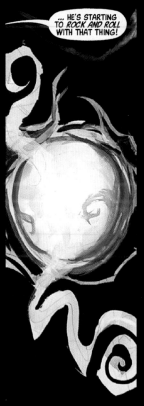

... HE'S STARTING TO ROCK AND ROLL WITH THAT THING!

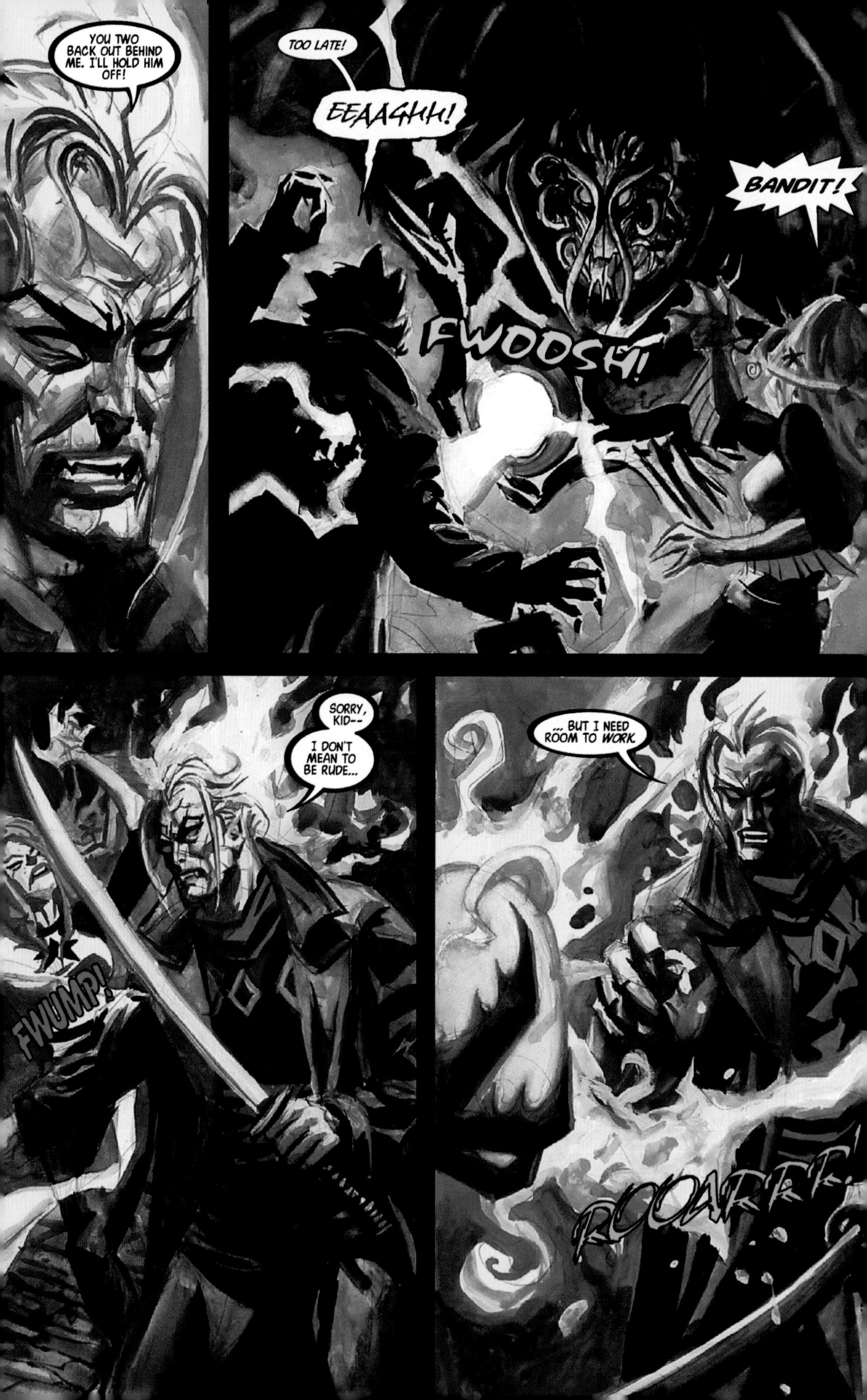
YOU TWO BACK OUT BEHIND ME. I'LL HOLD HIM OFF!
TOO LATE!
EEAAGHH!
BANDIT!
FWOOSH!
SORRY, KID--
I DON'T MEAN TO BE RUDE...
FWUMP!
... BUT I NEED ROOM TO WORK.
ROOARRR!

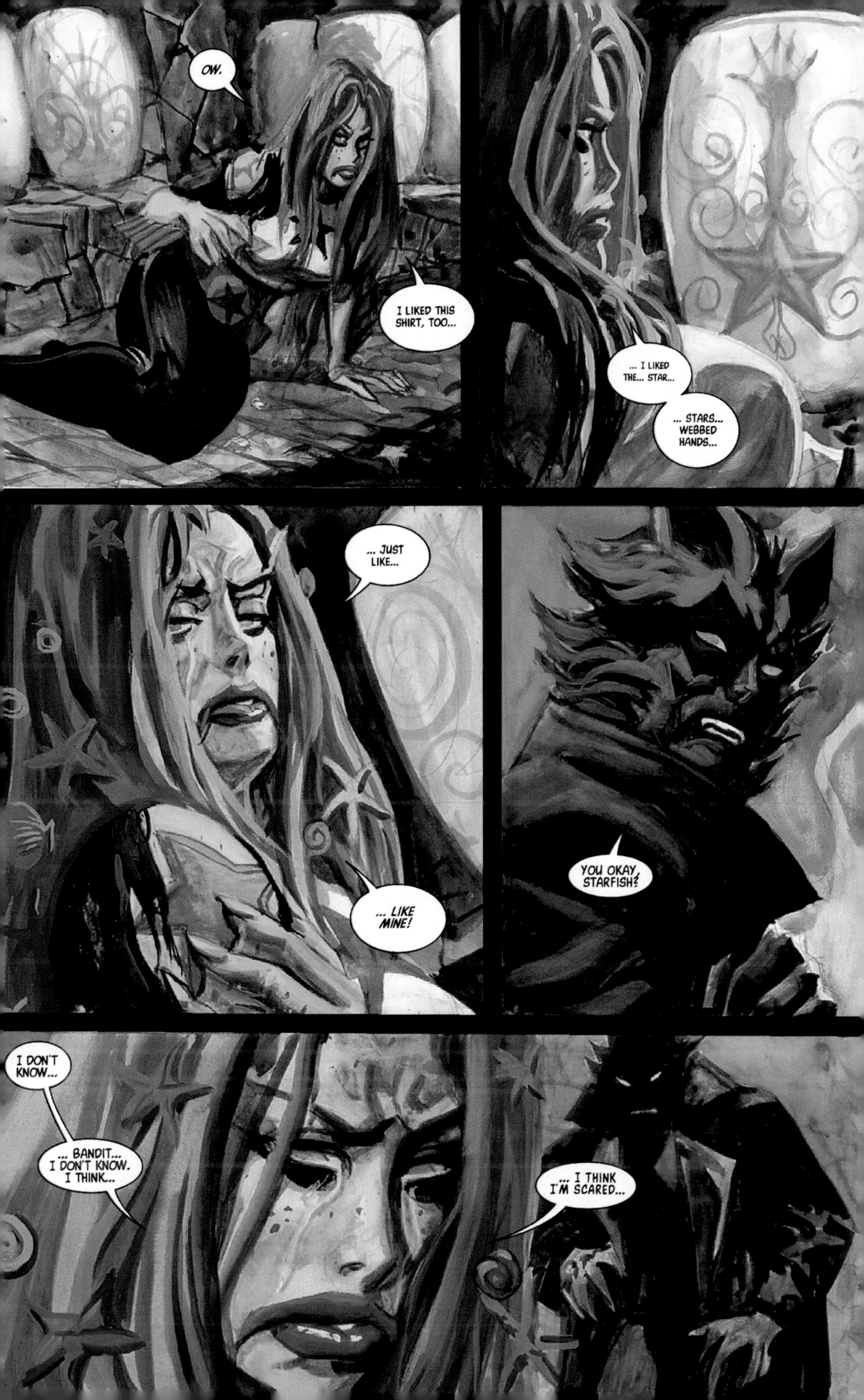
OW.
I LIKED THIS SHIRT, TOO...
... I LIKED THE... STAR...
... STARS... WEBBED HANDS...
... JUST LIKE...
... LIKE MINE!
YOU OKAY, STARFISH?
I DON'T KNOW...
... BANDIT... I DON'T KNOW. I THINK...
... I THINK I'M SCARED...

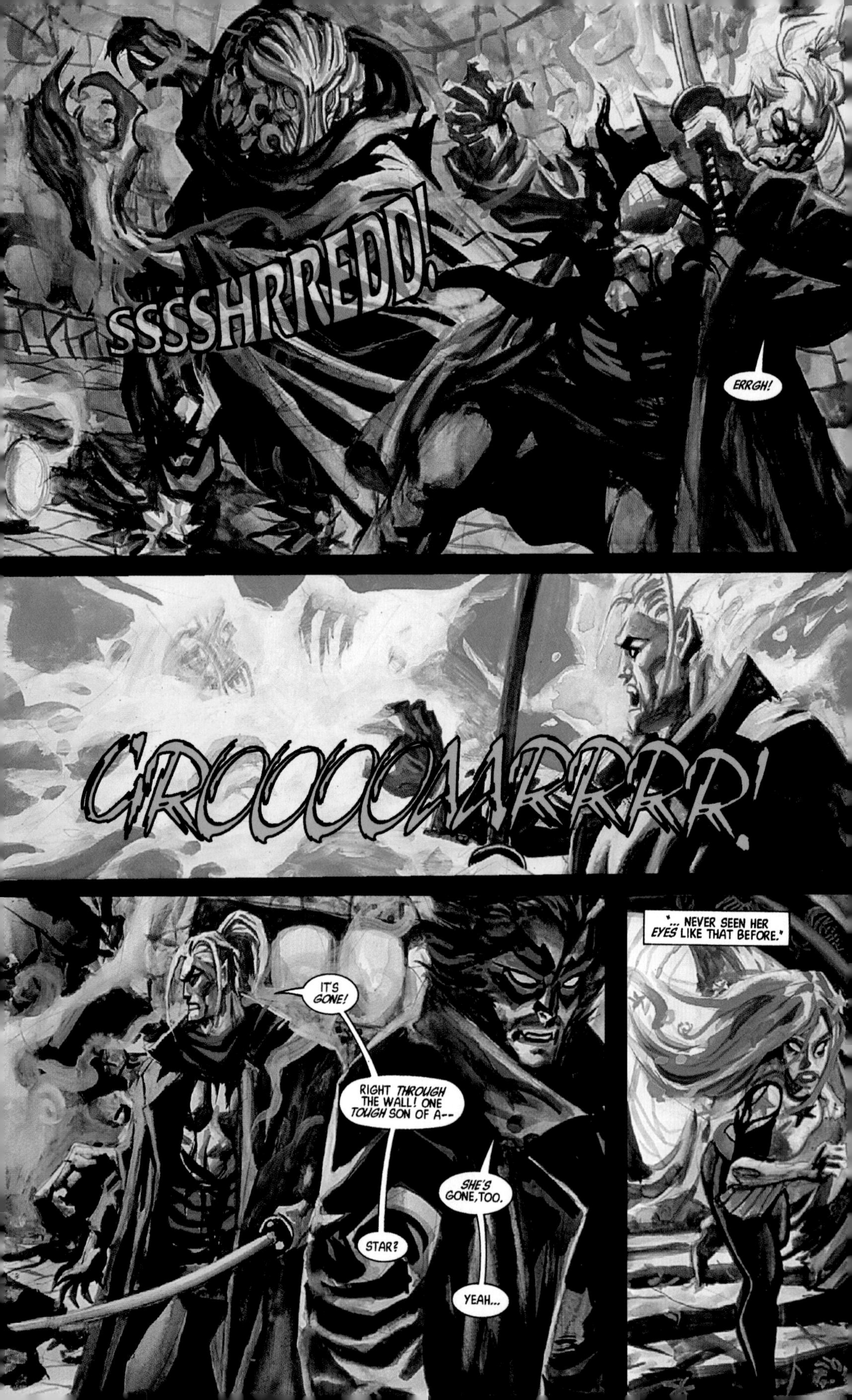
SSSSHRREDD!
ERRGH!
GROOOOOAARRRR!
IT'S GONE!
RIGHT THROUGH THE WALL! ONE TOUGH SON OF A--
STAR?
SHE'S GONE, TOO.
YEAH...
"... NEVER SEEN HER EYES LIKE THAT BEFORE."

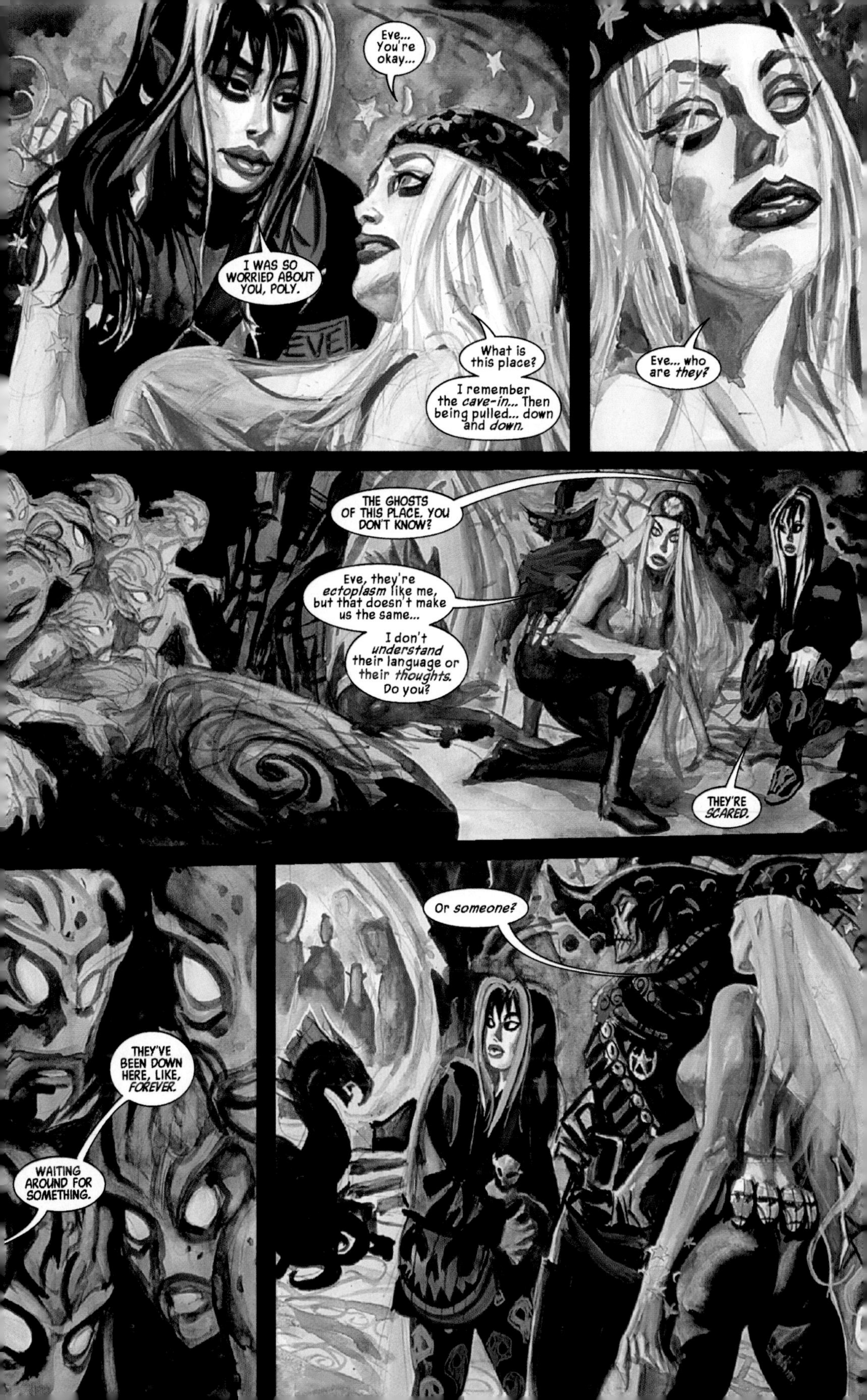

Eve... You're okay...
I WAS SO WORRIED ABOUT YOU, POLY.
EVE
What is this place?
I remember the *cave-in...* Then being pulled... down and *down.*
Eve... who are *they?*
THE GHOSTS OF THIS PLACE. YOU DON'T KNOW?
Eve, they're *ectoplasm* like me, but that doesn't make us the same...
I don't *understand* their language or their *thoughts.* Do you?
THEY'RE *SCARED.*
THEY'VE BEEN DOWN HERE, LIKE, *FOREVER.*
WAITING AROUND FOR SOMETHING.
Or *someone?*

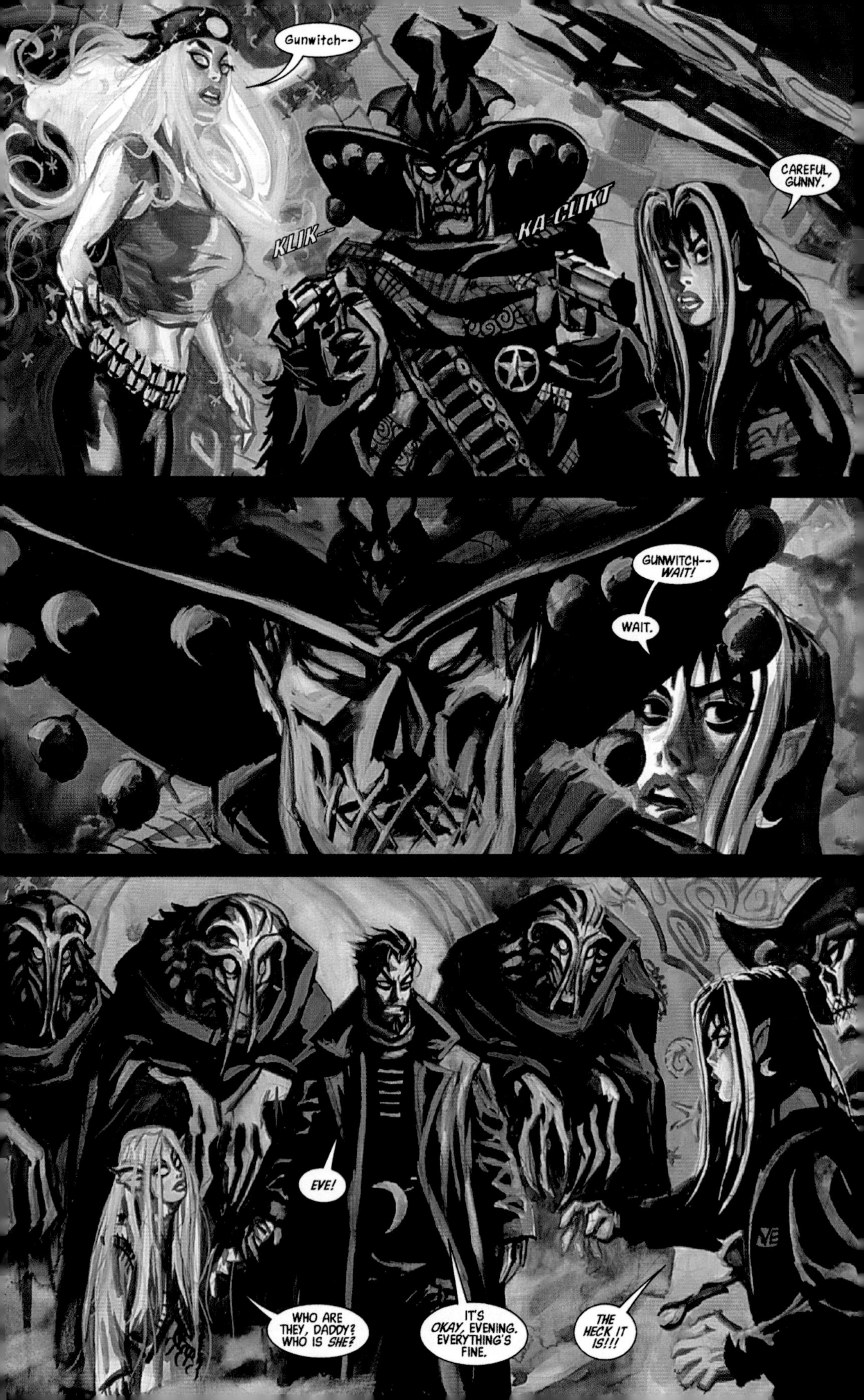

Gunwitch--
KLIK--
KA-CLIKT
CAREFUL, GUNNY.
GUNWITCH-- WAIT!
WAIT.
EVE!
WHO ARE THEY, DADDY? WHO IS SHE?
IT'S OKAY, EVENING. EVERYTHING'S FINE.
THE HECK IT IS!!!

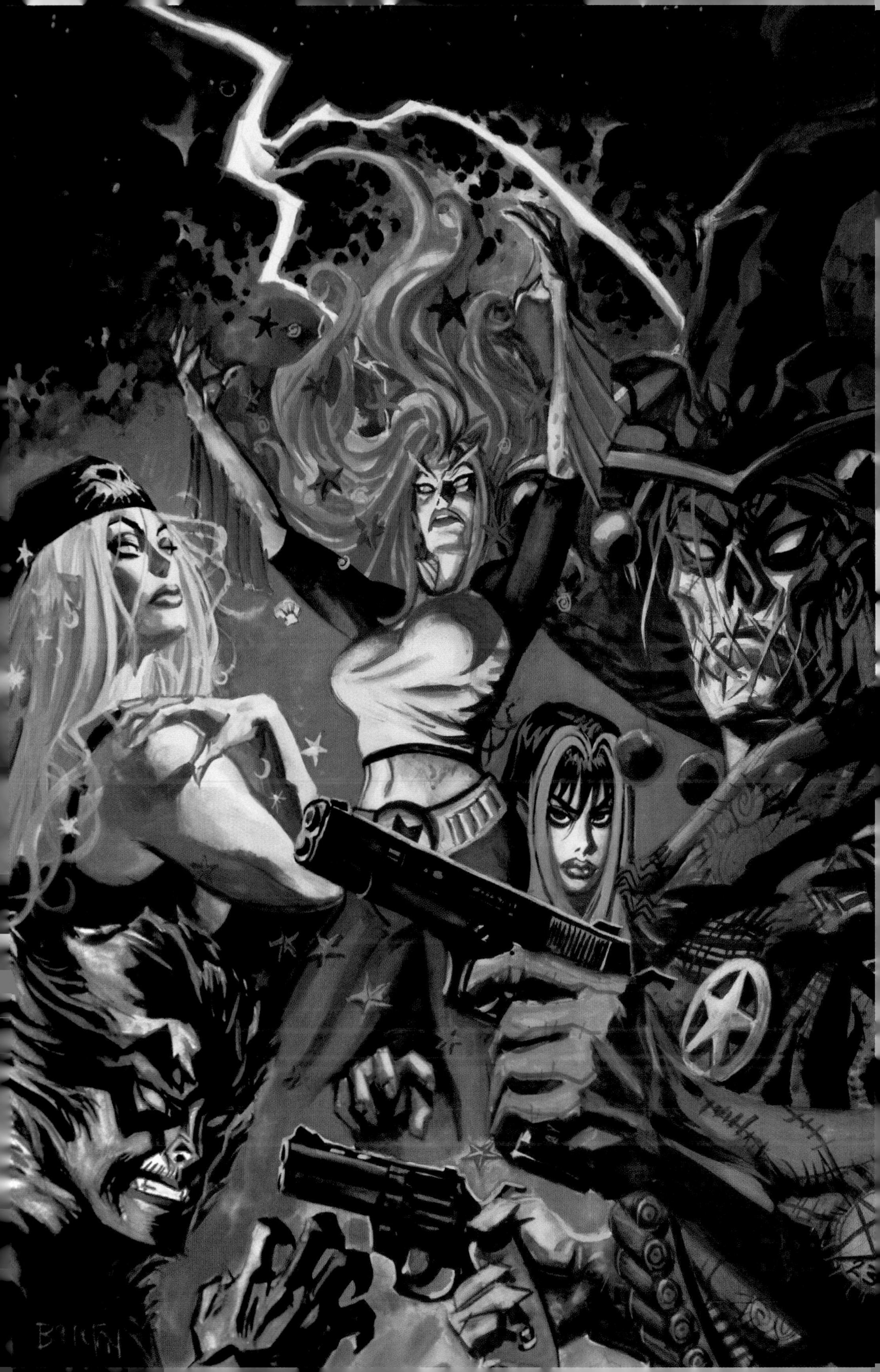

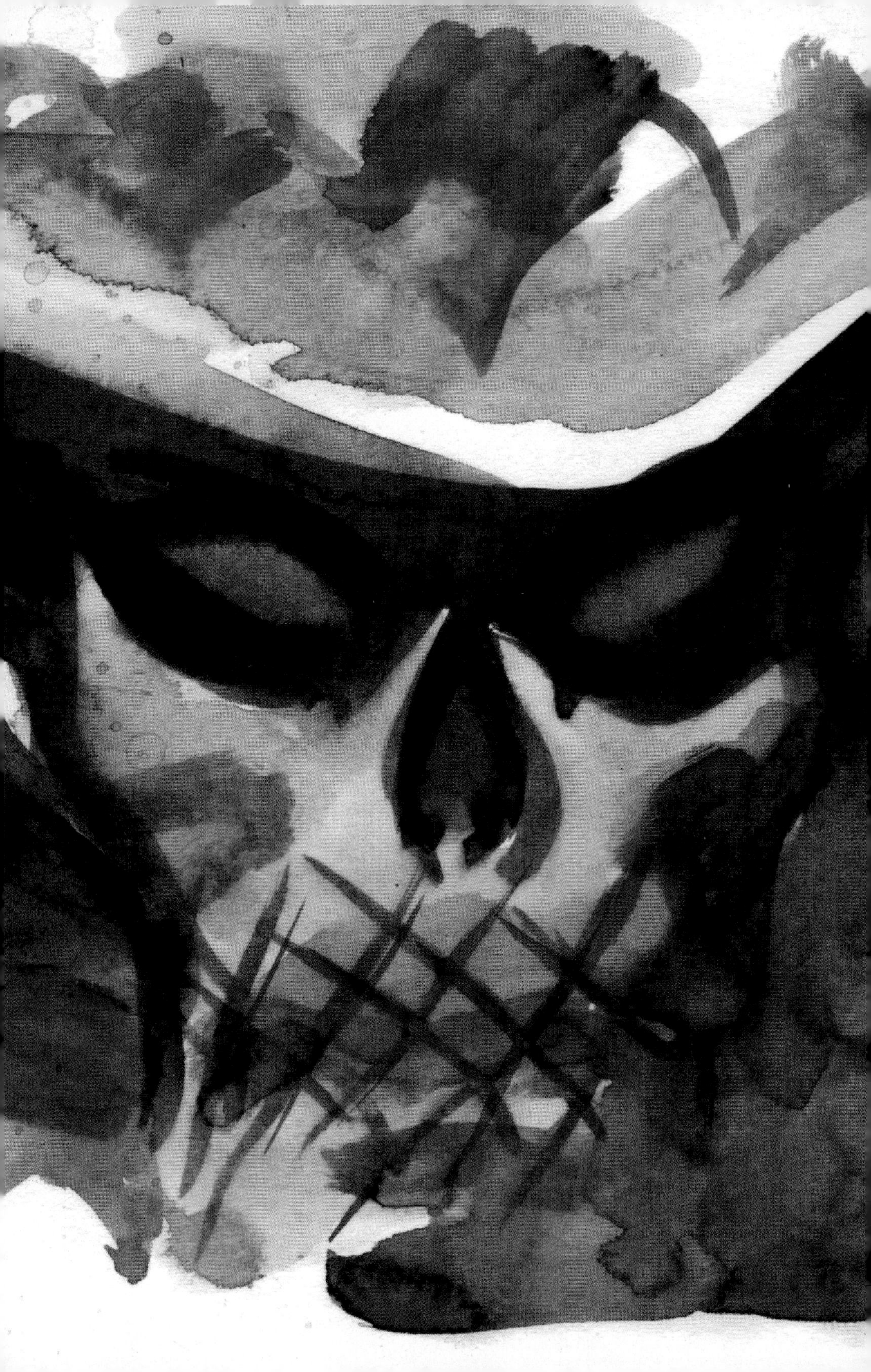

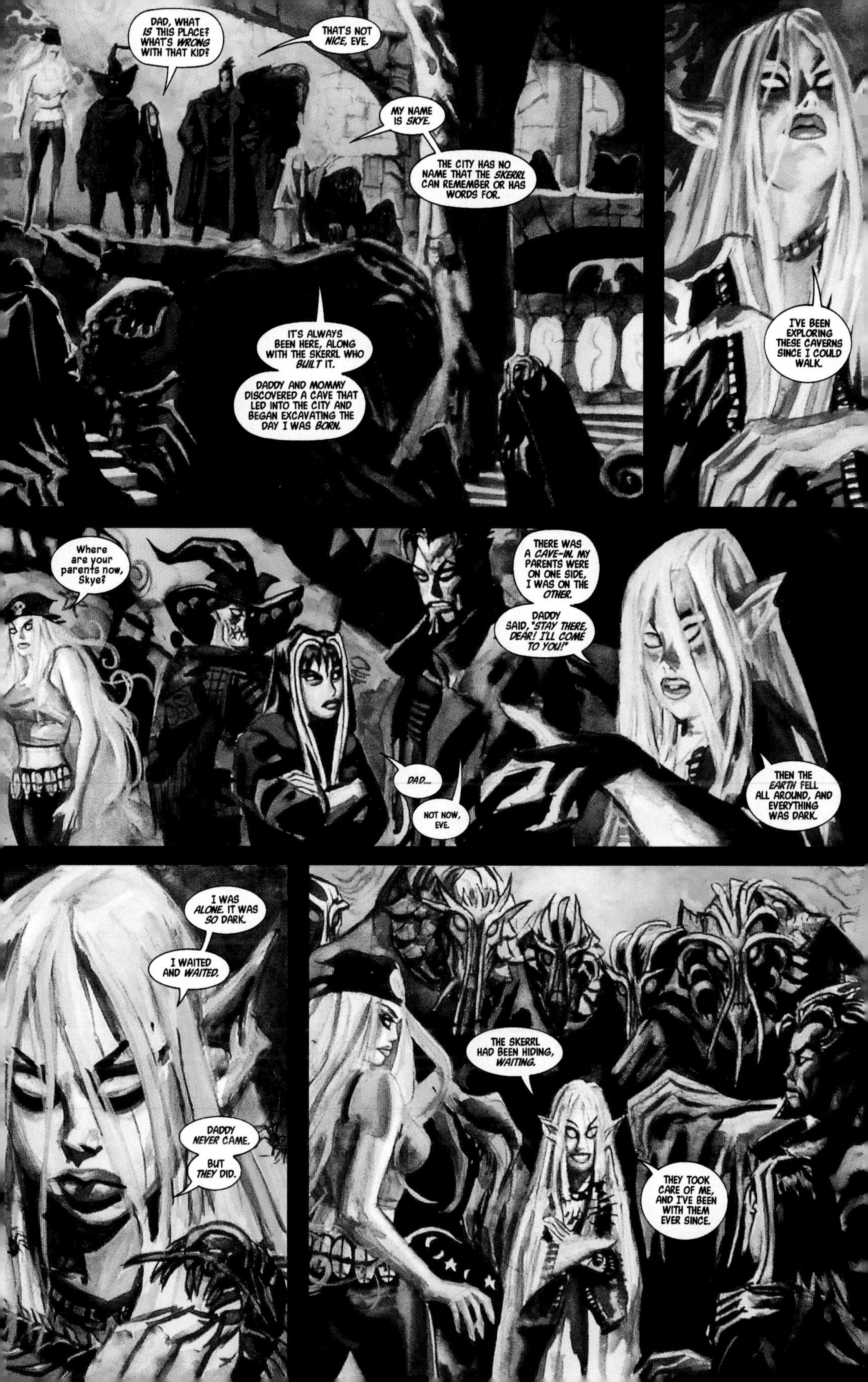
DAD, WHAT IS THIS PLACE? WHAT'S WRONG WITH THAT KID?
THAT'S NOT NICE, EVE.
MY NAME IS SKYE.
THE CITY HAS NO NAME THAT THE SKERRL CAN REMEMBER OR HAS WORDS FOR.
IT'S ALWAYS BEEN HERE, ALONG WITH THE SKERRL WHO BUILT IT.
DADDY AND MOMMY DISCOVERED A CAVE THAT LED INTO THE CITY AND BEGAN EXCAVATING THE DAY I WAS BORN.
I'VE BEEN EXPLORING THESE CAVERNS SINCE I COULD WALK.
Where are your parents now, Skye?
THERE WAS A CAVE-IN. MY PARENTS WERE ON ONE SIDE, I WAS ON THE OTHER.
DADDY SAID, "STAY THERE, DEAR! I'LL COME TO YOU!"
DAD...
NOT NOW, EVE.
THEN THE EARTH FELL ALL AROUND, AND EVERYTHING WAS DARK.
I WAS ALONE. IT WAS SO DARK.
I WAITED AND WAITED.
DADDY NEVER CAME.
BUT THEY DID.
THE SKERRL HAD BEEN HIDING, WAITING.
THEY TOOK CARE OF ME, AND I'VE BEEN WITH THEM EVER SINCE.

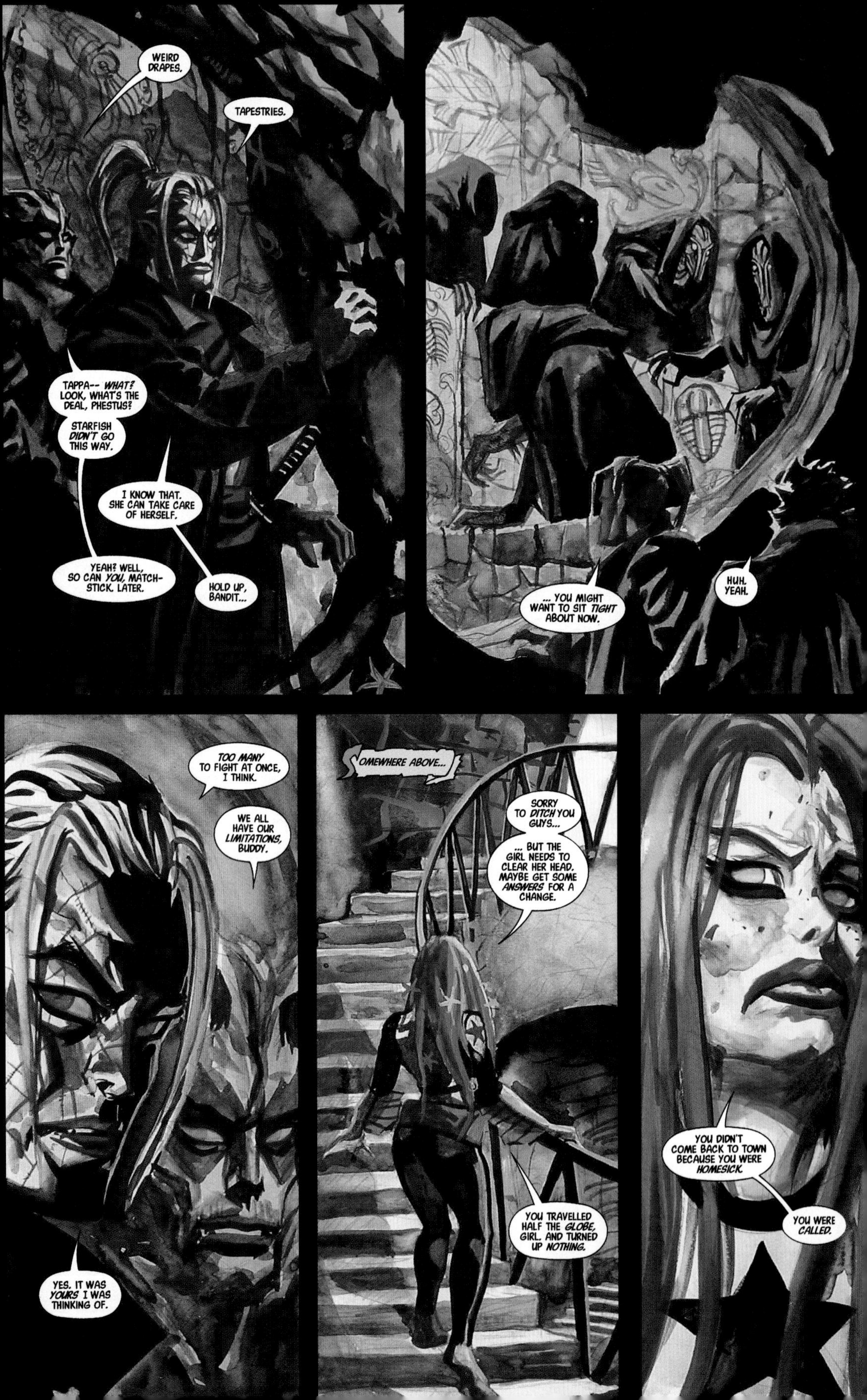
WEIRD DRAPES.
TAPESTRIES.
TAPPA-- WHAT? LOOK, WHAT'S THE DEAL, PHESTUS?
STARFISH DIDN'T GO THIS WAY.
I KNOW THAT. SHE CAN TAKE CARE OF HERSELF.
YEAH? WELL, SO CAN YOU, MATCH-STICK. LATER.
HOLD UP, BANDIT...
... YOU MIGHT WANT TO SIT TIGHT ABOUT NOW.
HUH. YEAH.
TOO MANY TO FIGHT AT ONCE, I THINK.
WE ALL HAVE OUR LIMITATIONS, BUDDY.
YES. IT WAS YOURS I WAS THINKING OF.
SOMEWHERE ABOVE...
SORRY TO DITCH YOU GUYS...
... BUT THE GIRL NEEDS TO CLEAR HER HEAD. MAYBE GET SOME ANSWERS FOR A CHANGE.
YOU TRAVELLED HALF THE GLOBE, GIRL. AND TURNED UP NOTHING.
YOU DIDN'T COME BACK TO TOWN BECAUSE YOU WERE HOMESICK.
YOU WERE CALLED.

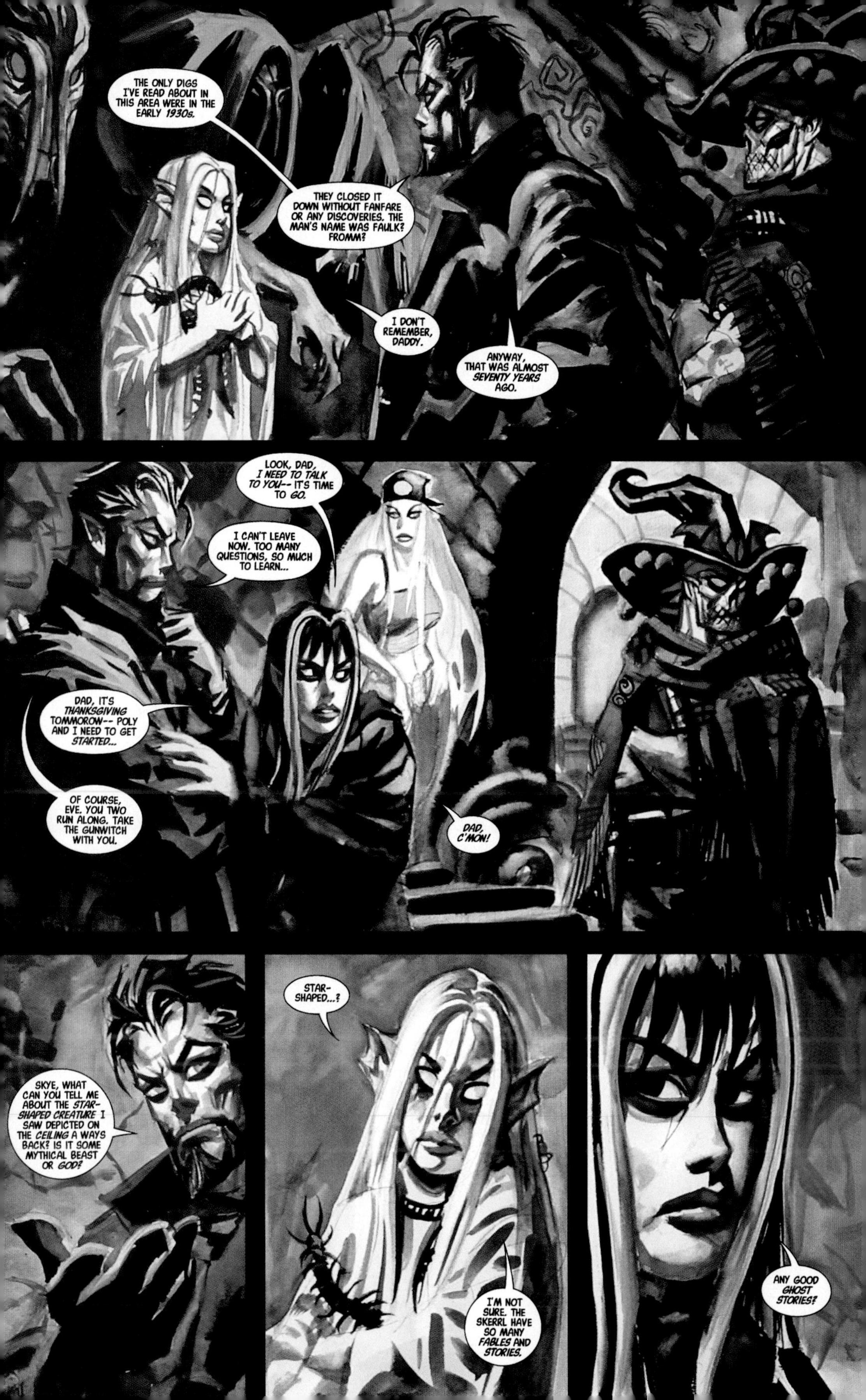

THE ONLY DIGS I'VE READ ABOUT IN THIS AREA WERE IN THE EARLY 1930s.
THEY CLOSED IT DOWN WITHOUT FANFARE OR ANY DISCOVERIES. THE MAN'S NAME WAS FAULK? FROMM?
I DON'T REMEMBER, DADDY.
ANYWAY, THAT WAS ALMOST SEVENTY YEARS AGO.
LOOK, DAD, I NEED TO TALK TO YOU-- IT'S TIME TO GO.
I CAN'T LEAVE NOW. TOO MANY QUESTIONS, SO MUCH TO LEARN...
DAD, IT'S THANKSGIVING TOMMOROW-- POLY AND I NEED TO GET STARTED...
OF COURSE, EVE. YOU TWO RUN ALONG. TAKE THE GUNWITCH WITH YOU.
DAD, C'MON!
SKYE, WHAT CAN YOU TELL ME ABOUT THE STAR-SHAPED CREATURE I SAW DEPICTED ON THE CEILING A WAYS BACK? IS IT SOME MYTHICAL BEAST OR GOD?
STAR-SHAPED...?
I'M NOT SURE. THE SKERRL HAVE SO MANY FABLES AND STORIES.
ANY GOOD GHOST STORIES?

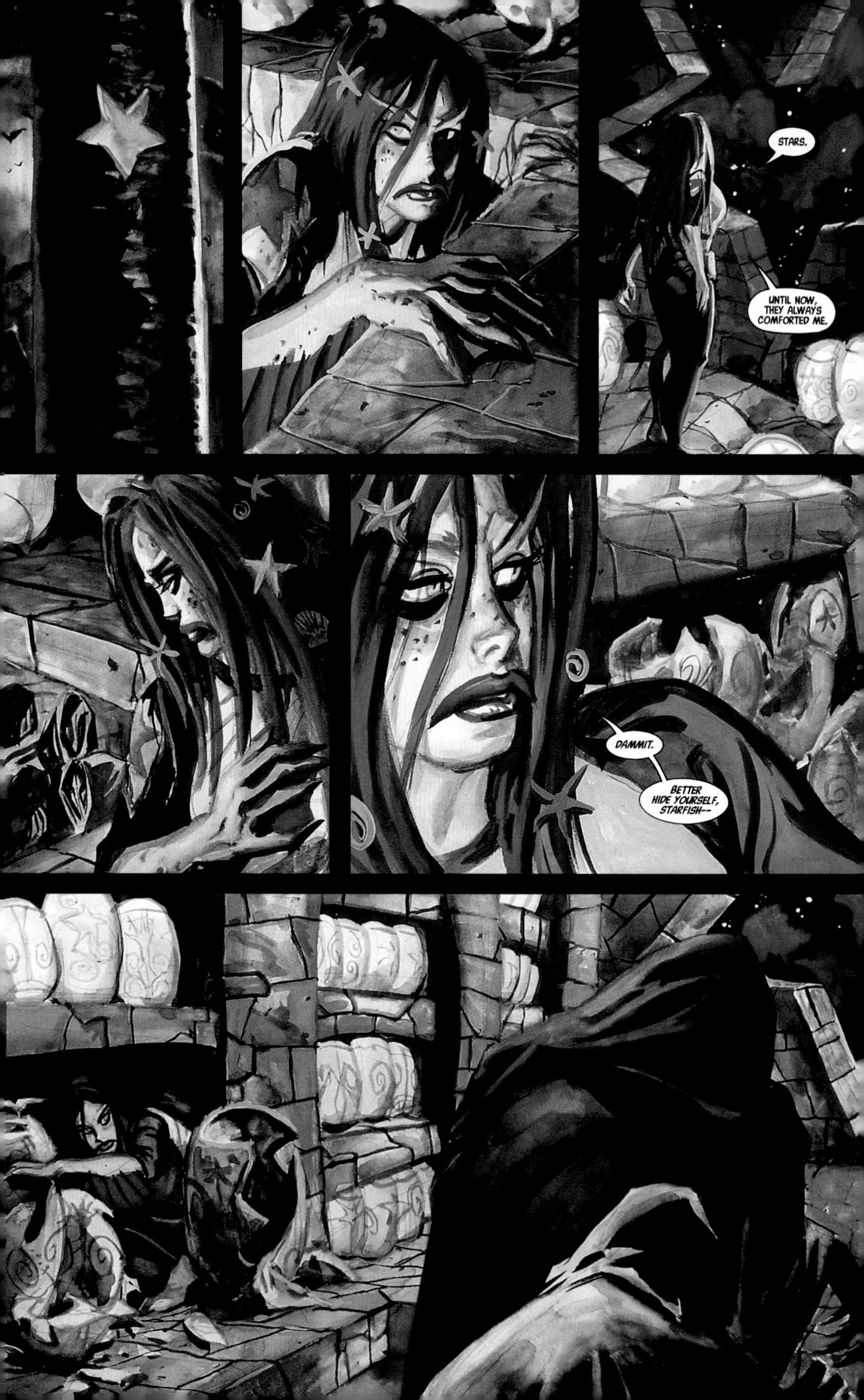
STARS.
UNTIL NOW, THEY ALWAYS COMFORTED ME.
DAMMIT.
BETTER HIDE YOURSELF, STARFISH--

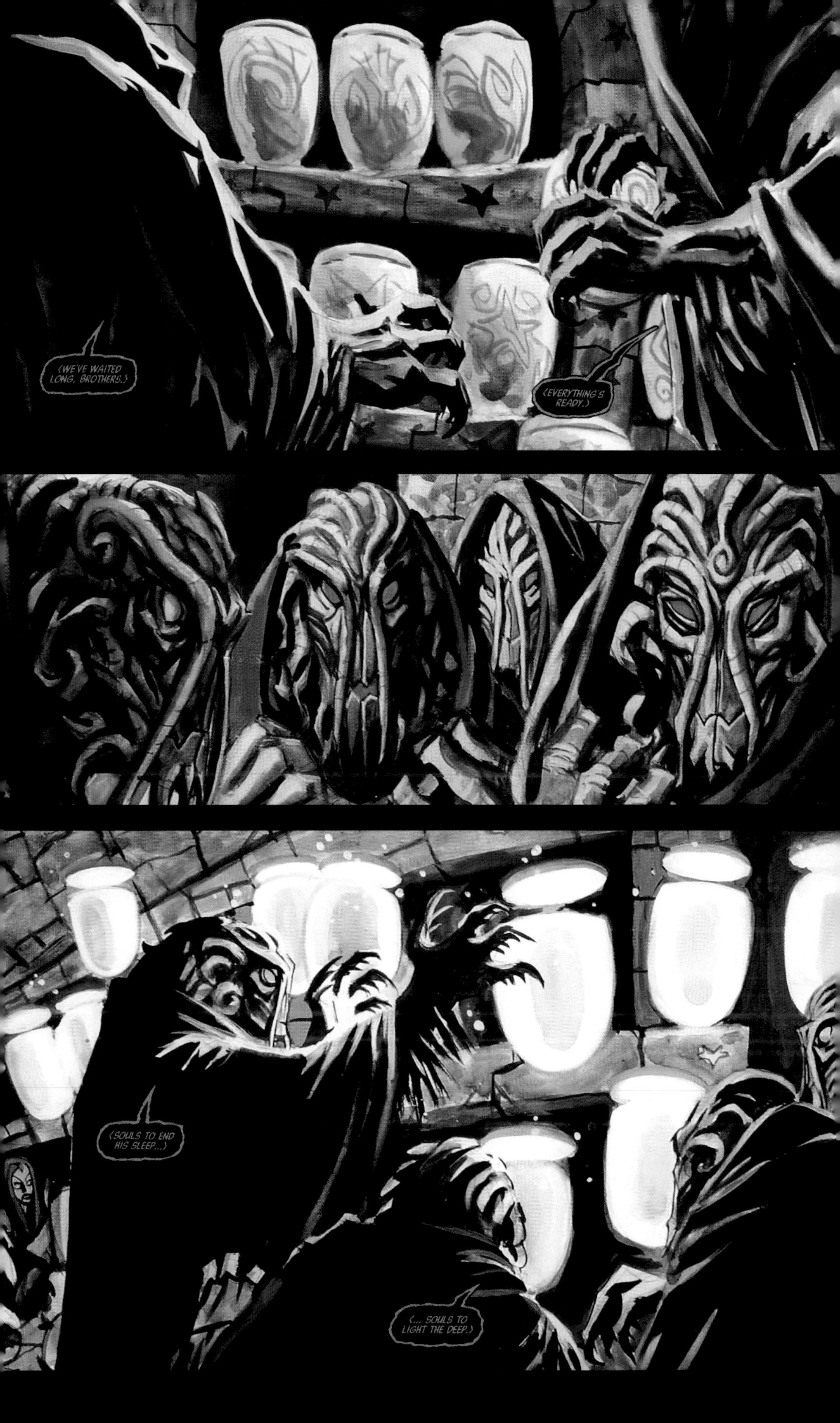
‹WE'VE WAITED LONG, BROTHERS.›
‹EVERYTHING'S READY.›
‹SOULS TO END HIS SLEEP...›
‹... SOULS TO LIGHT THE DEEP.›

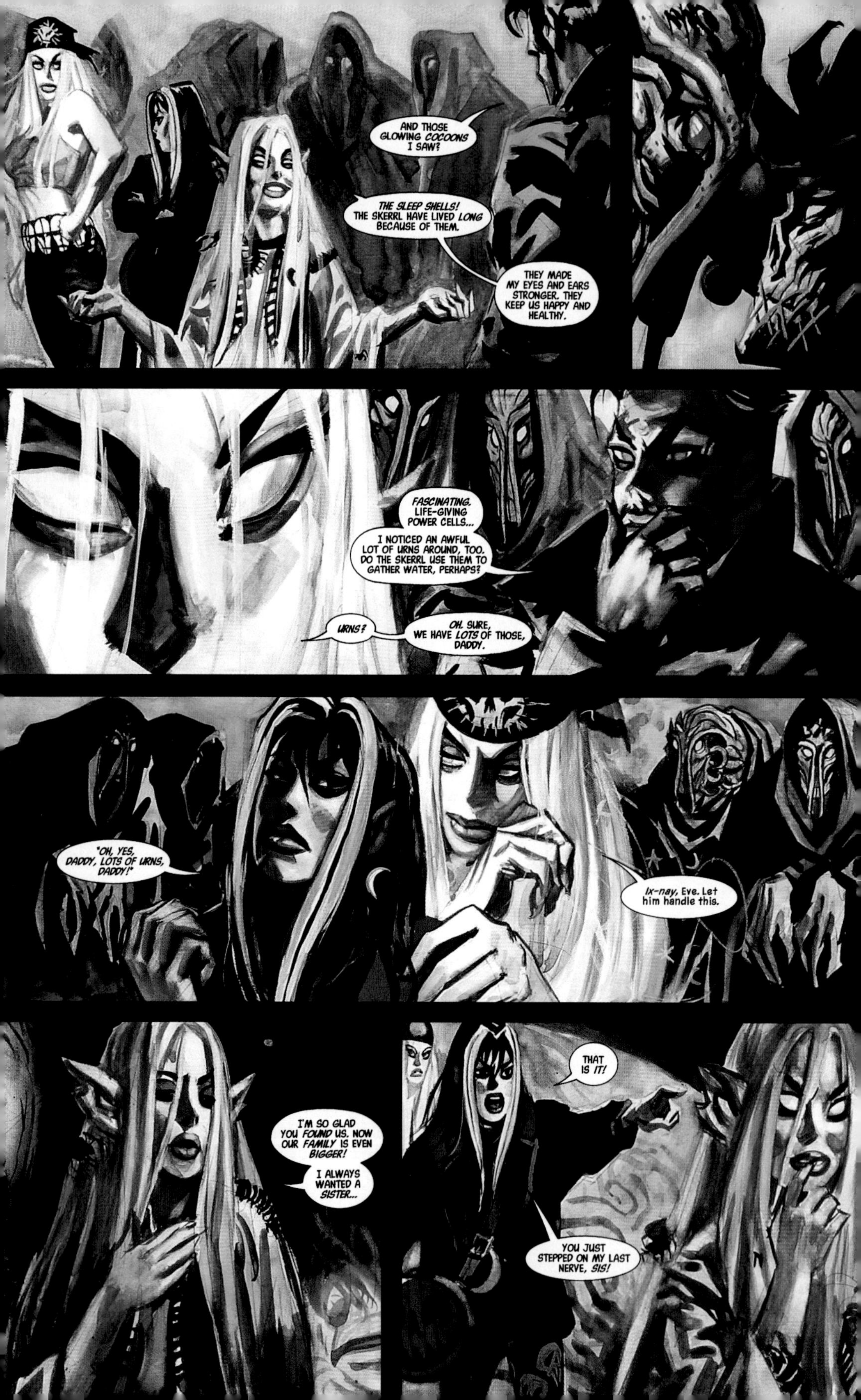
AND THOSE GLOWING *COCOONS* I SAW?
THE SLEEP SHELLS! THE SKERRL HAVE LIVED *LONG* BECAUSE OF THEM.
THEY MADE MY EYES AND EARS STRONGER. THEY KEEP US HAPPY AND HEALTHY.
FASCINATING. LIFE-GIVING POWER CELLS...
I NOTICED AN AWFUL LOT OF URNS AROUND, TOO. DO THE SKERRL USE THEM TO GATHER WATER, PERHAPS?
URNS?
OH. SURE, WE HAVE *LOTS* OF THOSE, DADDY.
"OH, YES, DADDY, LOTS OF URNS, DADDY!"
Ix-nay, Eve. Let him handle this.
I'M SO GLAD YOU *FOUND* US. NOW OUR *FAMILY* IS EVEN *BIGGER!*
I ALWAYS WANTED A *SISTER...*
THAT IS *IT!*
YOU JUST STEPPED ON MY LAST NERVE, *SIS!*

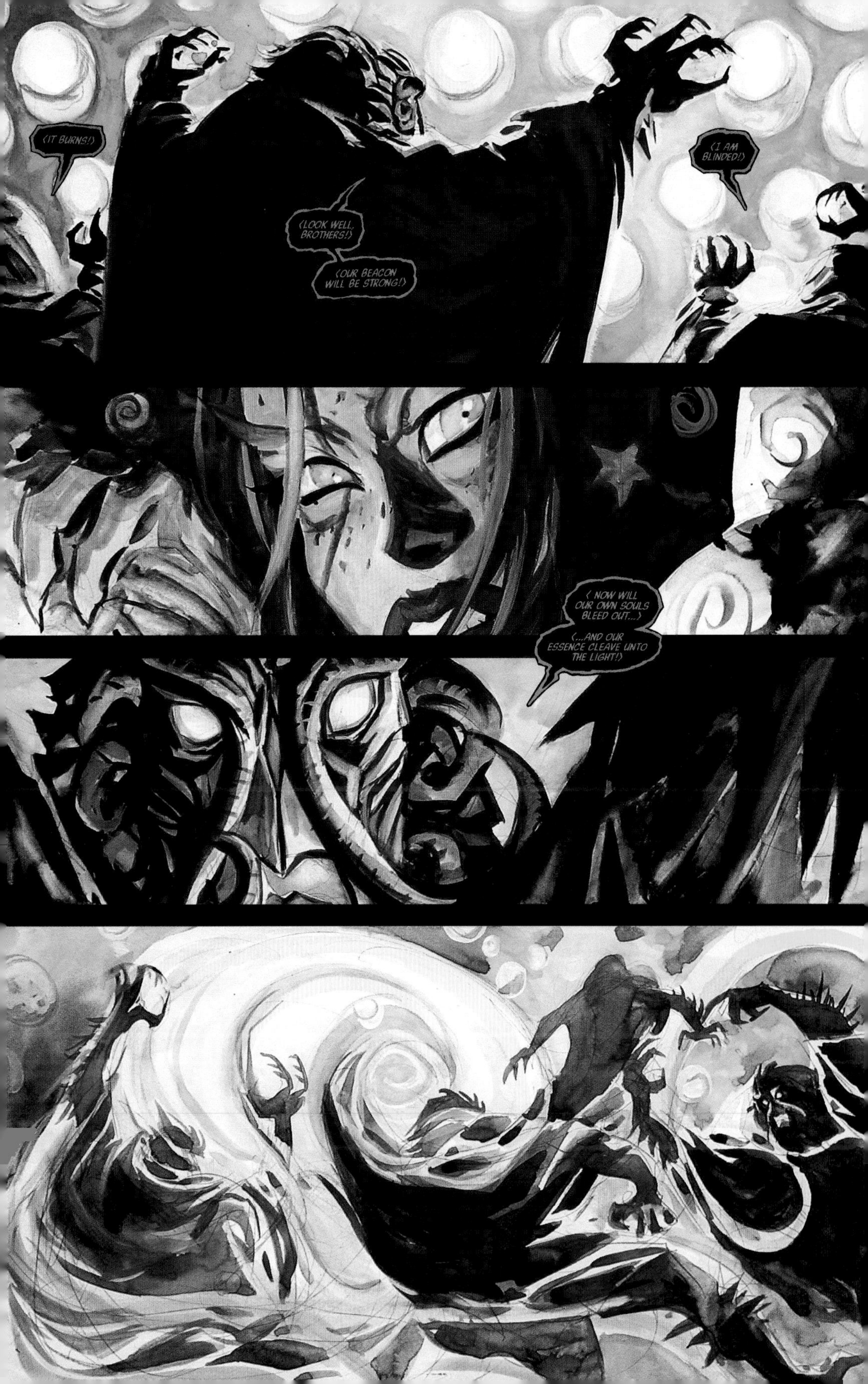
(IT BURNS!)
(LOOK WELL, BROTHERS!)
(OUR BEACON WILL BE STRONG!)
(I AM BLINDED!)
(NOW WILL OUR OWN SOULS BLEED OUT...)
(...AND OUR ESSENCE CLEAVE UNTO THE LIGHT!)

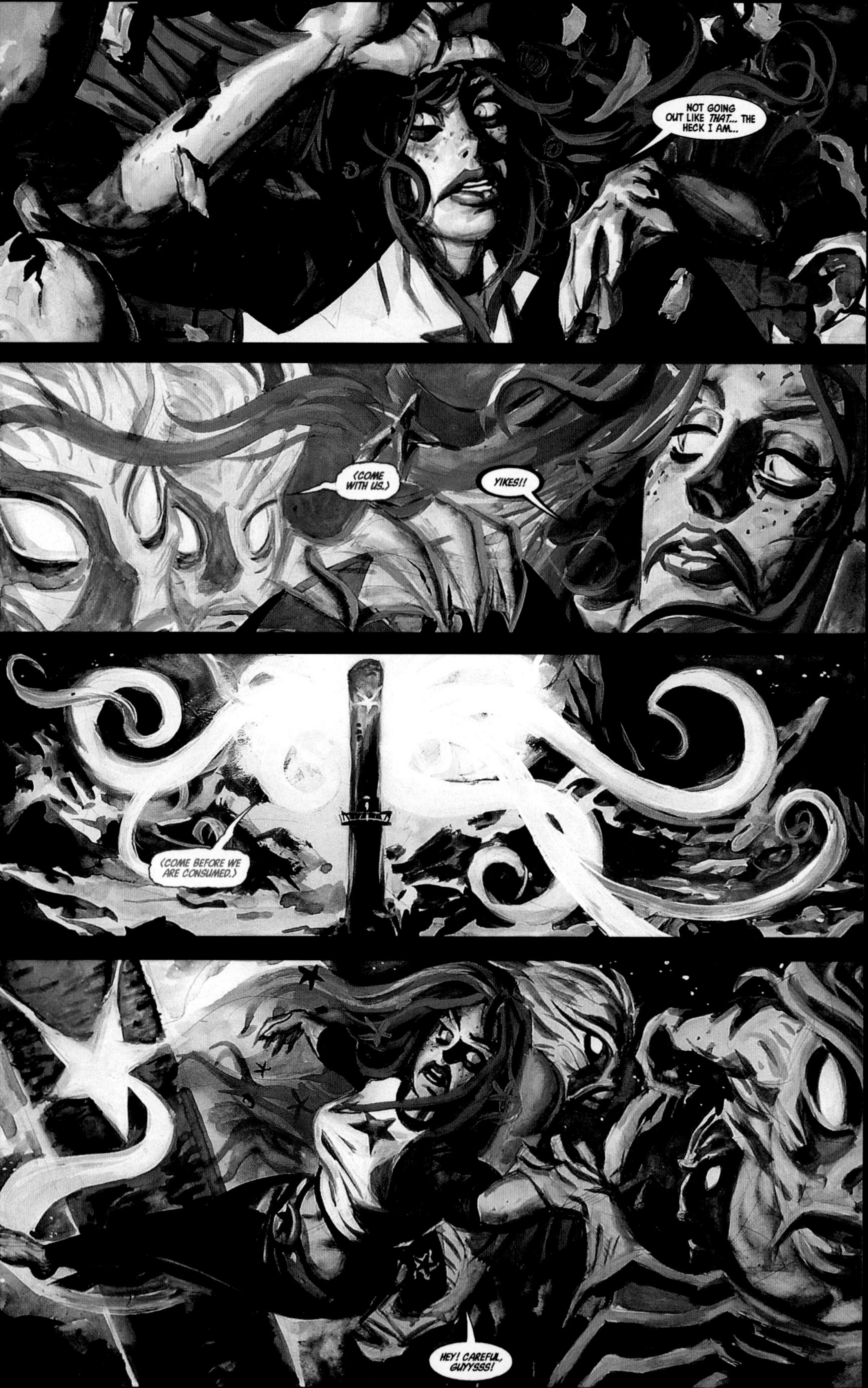
NOT GOING OUT LIKE *THAT*... THE HECK I AM...
(COME WITH US.)
YIKES!!
(COME BEFORE WE ARE CONSUMED.)
HEY! CAREFUL, GUYYSSS!

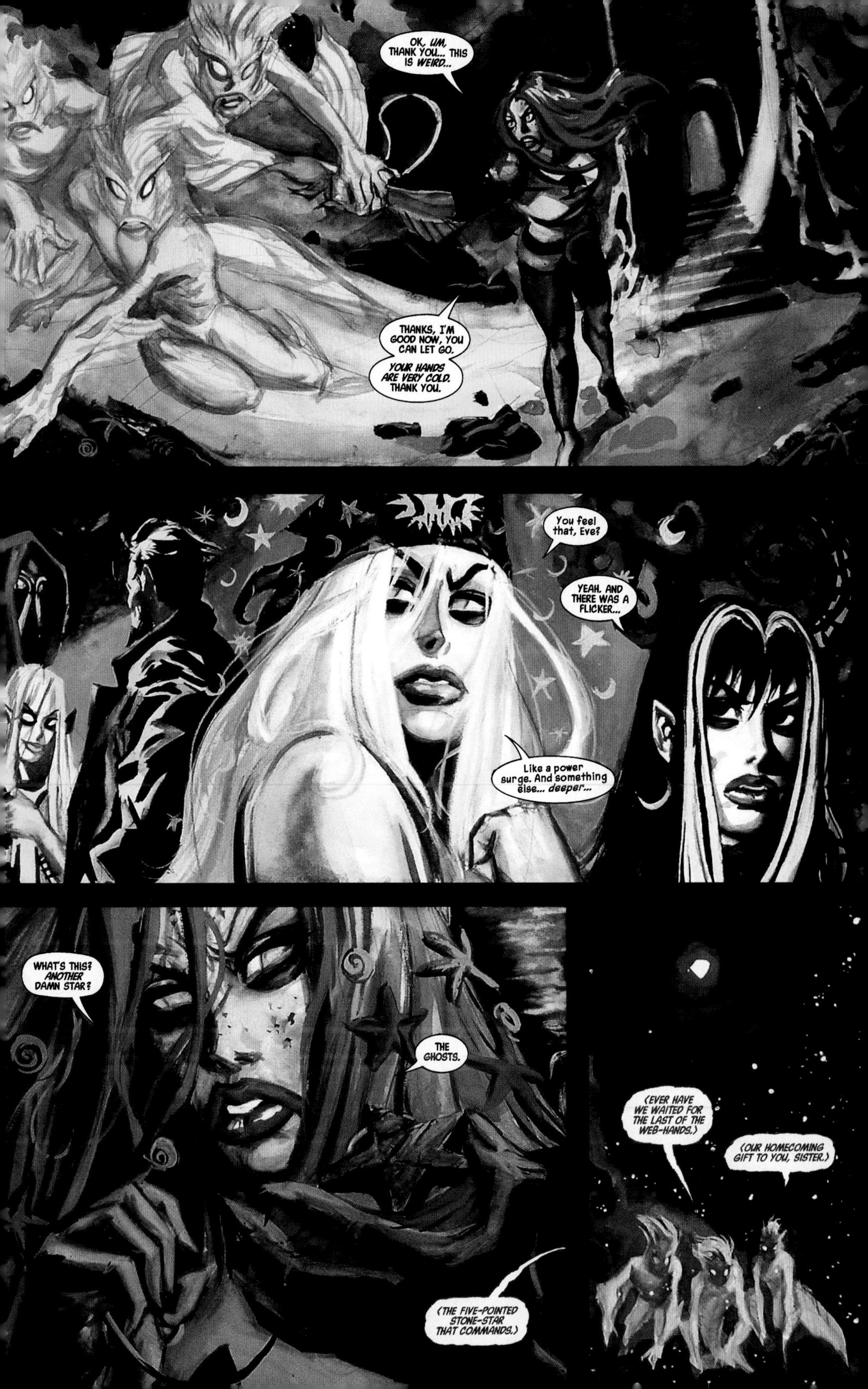

OK, UM, THANK YOU... THIS IS WEIRD...
THANKS, I'M GOOD NOW, YOU CAN LET GO.
YOUR HANDS ARE VERY COLD. THANK YOU.
You feel that, Eve?
YEAH. AND THERE WAS A FLICKER...
Like a power surge. And something else... deeper...
WHAT'S THIS? ANOTHER DAMN STAR?
THE GHOSTS.
(THE FIVE-POINTED STONE-STAR THAT COMMANDS.)
(EVER HAVE WE WAITED FOR THE LAST OF THE WEB-HANDS.)
(OUR HOMECOMING GIFT TO YOU, SISTER.)

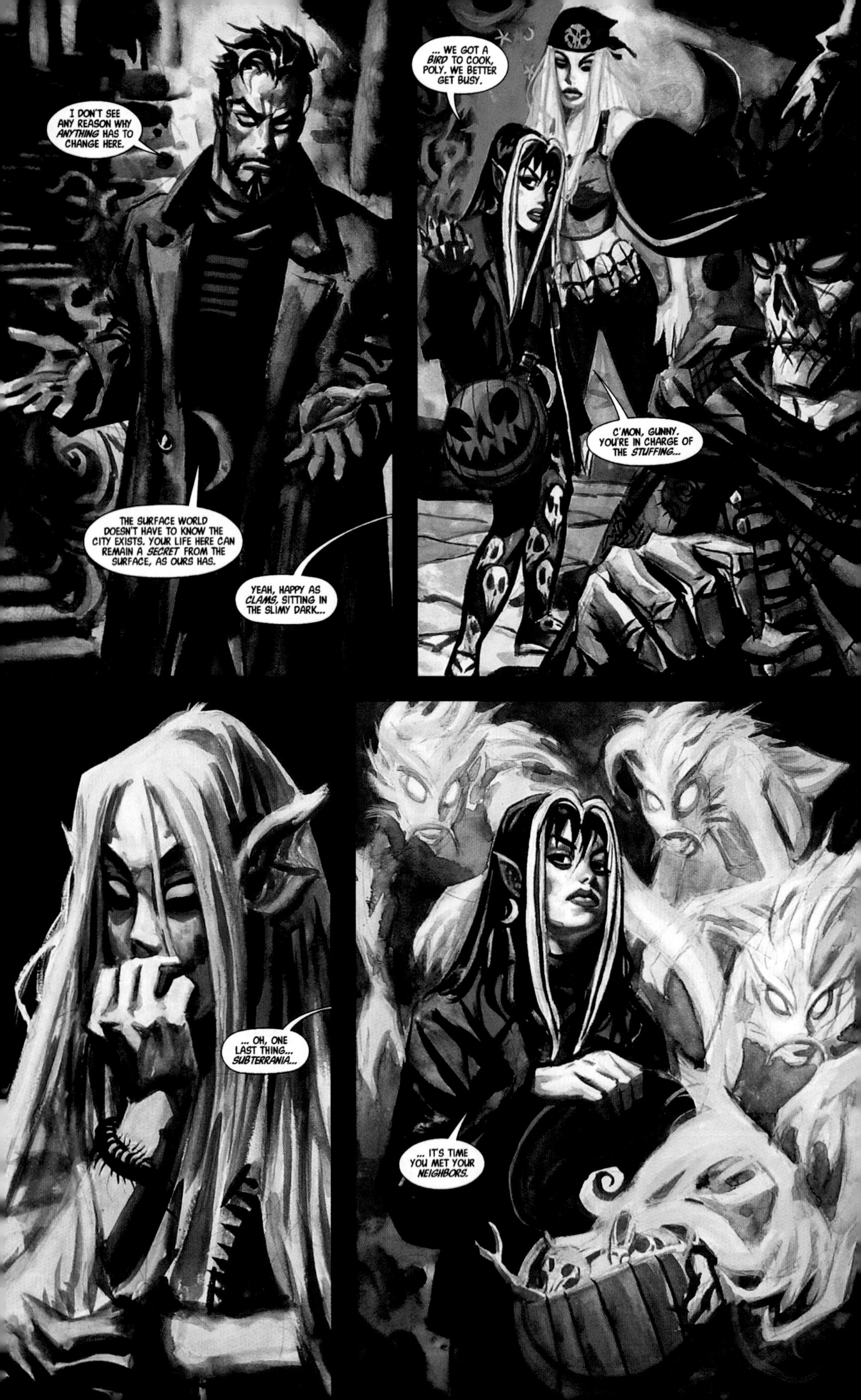
I DON'T SEE ANY REASON WHY ANYTHING HAS TO CHANGE HERE.
THE SURFACE WORLD DOESN'T HAVE TO KNOW THE CITY EXISTS. YOUR LIFE HERE CAN REMAIN A SECRET FROM THE SURFACE, AS OURS HAS.
YEAH, HAPPY AS CLAMS, SITTING IN THE SLIMY DARK...
... WE GOT A BIRD TO COOK, POLY. WE BETTER GET BUSY.
C'MON, GUNNY. YOU'RE IN CHARGE OF THE STUFFING...
... OH, ONE LAST THING... SUBTERRANIA...
... IT'S TIME YOU MET YOUR NEIGHBORS.

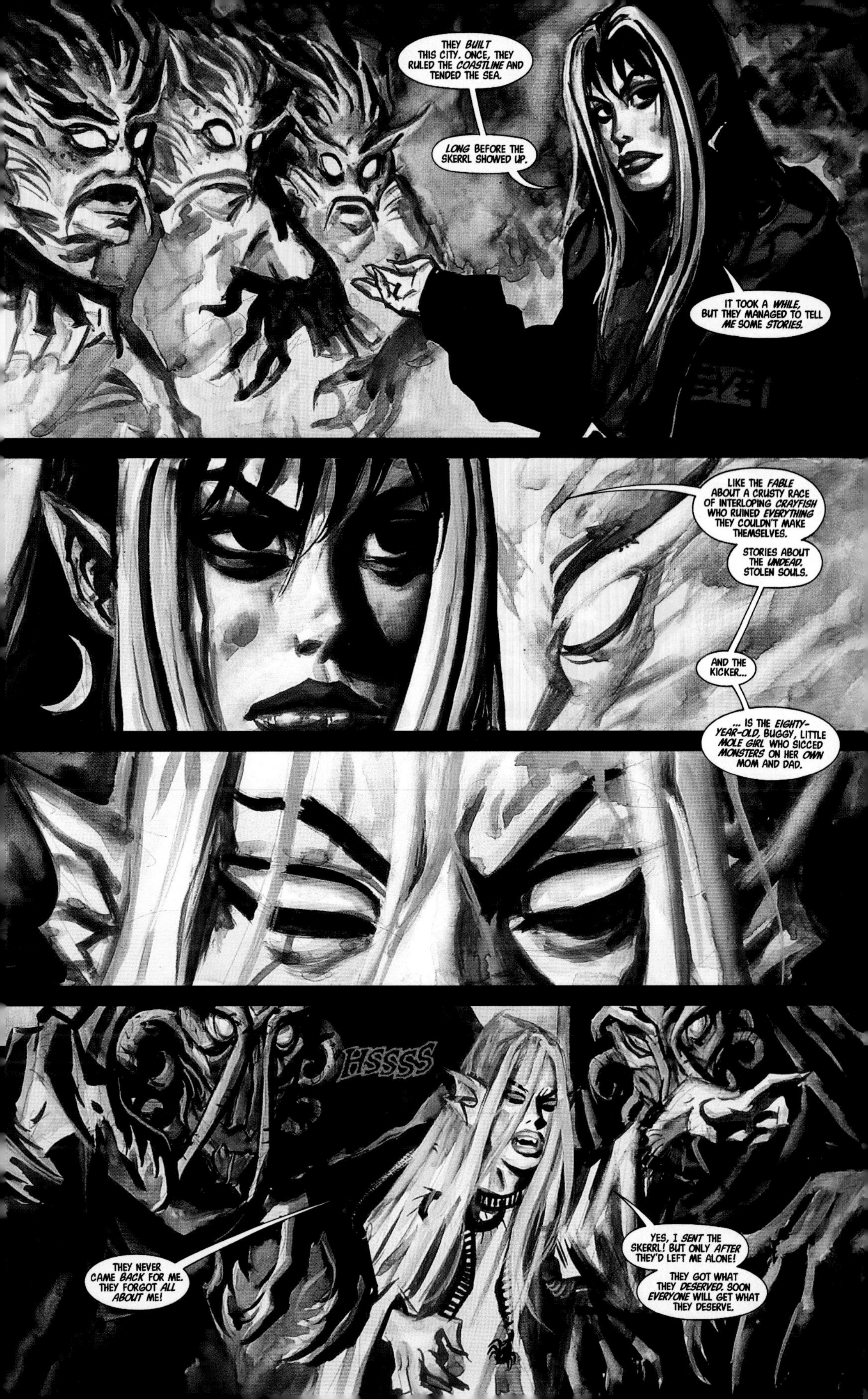
THEY BUILT THIS CITY. ONCE, THEY RULED THE COASTLINE AND TENDED THE SEA.
LONG BEFORE THE SKERRL SHOWED UP.
IT TOOK A WHILE, BUT THEY MANAGED TO TELL ME SOME STORIES.
LIKE THE FABLE ABOUT A CRUSTY RACE OF INTERLOPING CRAYFISH WHO RUINED EVERYTHING THEY COULDN'T MAKE THEMSELVES.
STORIES ABOUT THE UNDEAD. STOLEN SOULS.
AND THE KICKER...
... IS THE EIGHTY-YEAR-OLD, BUGGY, LITTLE MOLE GIRL WHO SICCED MONSTERS ON HER OWN MOM AND DAD.
HSSSS
THEY NEVER CAME BACK FOR ME. THEY FORGOT ALL ABOUT ME!
YES, I SENT THE SKERRL! BUT ONLY AFTER THEY'D LEFT ME ALONE!
THEY GOT WHAT THEY DESERVED. SOON EVERYONE WILL GET WHAT THEY DESERVE.

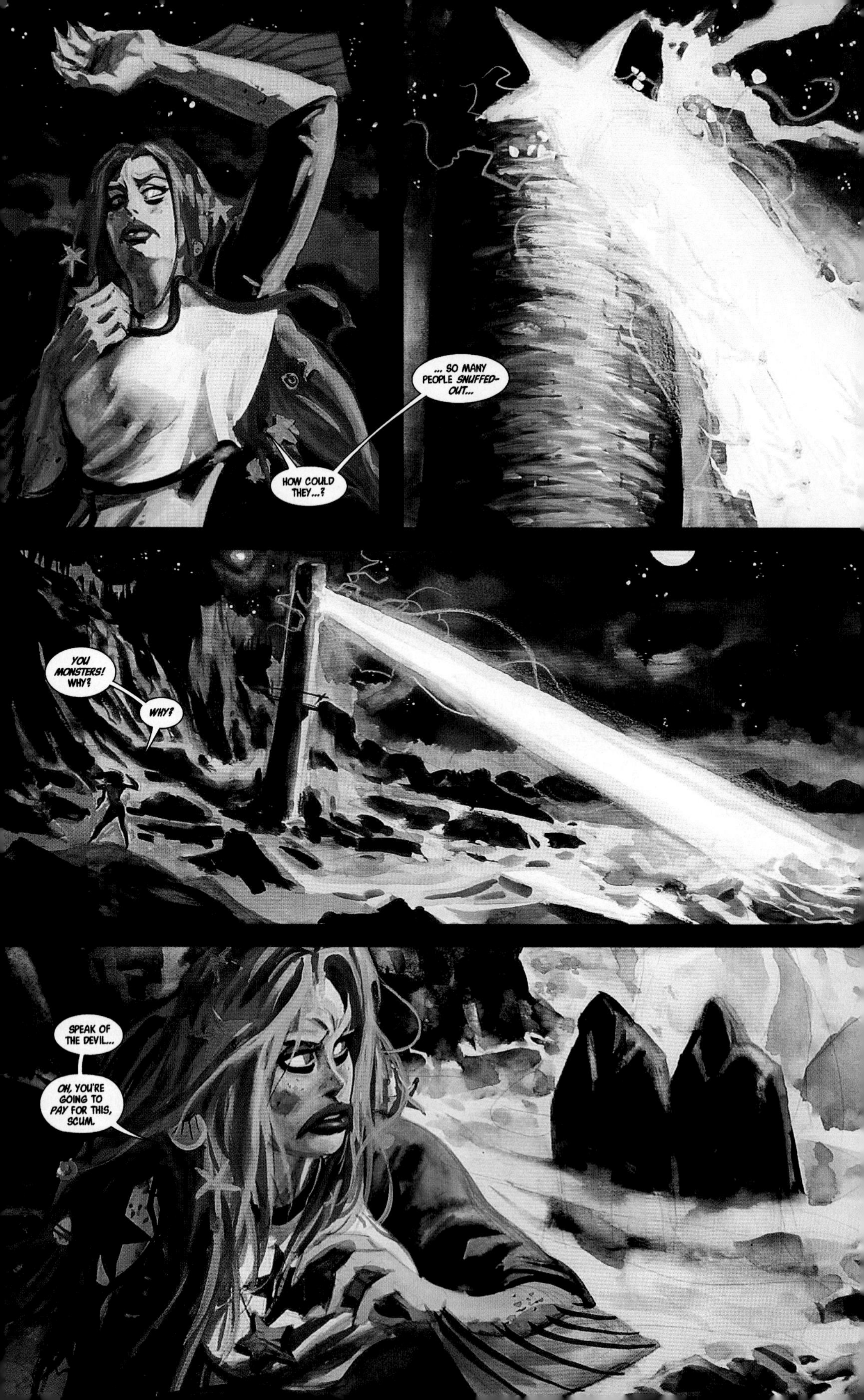

HOW COULD THEY...?
... SO MANY PEOPLE SNUFFED-OUT...
YOU MONSTERS! WHY?
WHY?
SPEAK OF THE DEVIL...
OH, YOU'RE GOING TO PAY FOR THIS, SCUM.

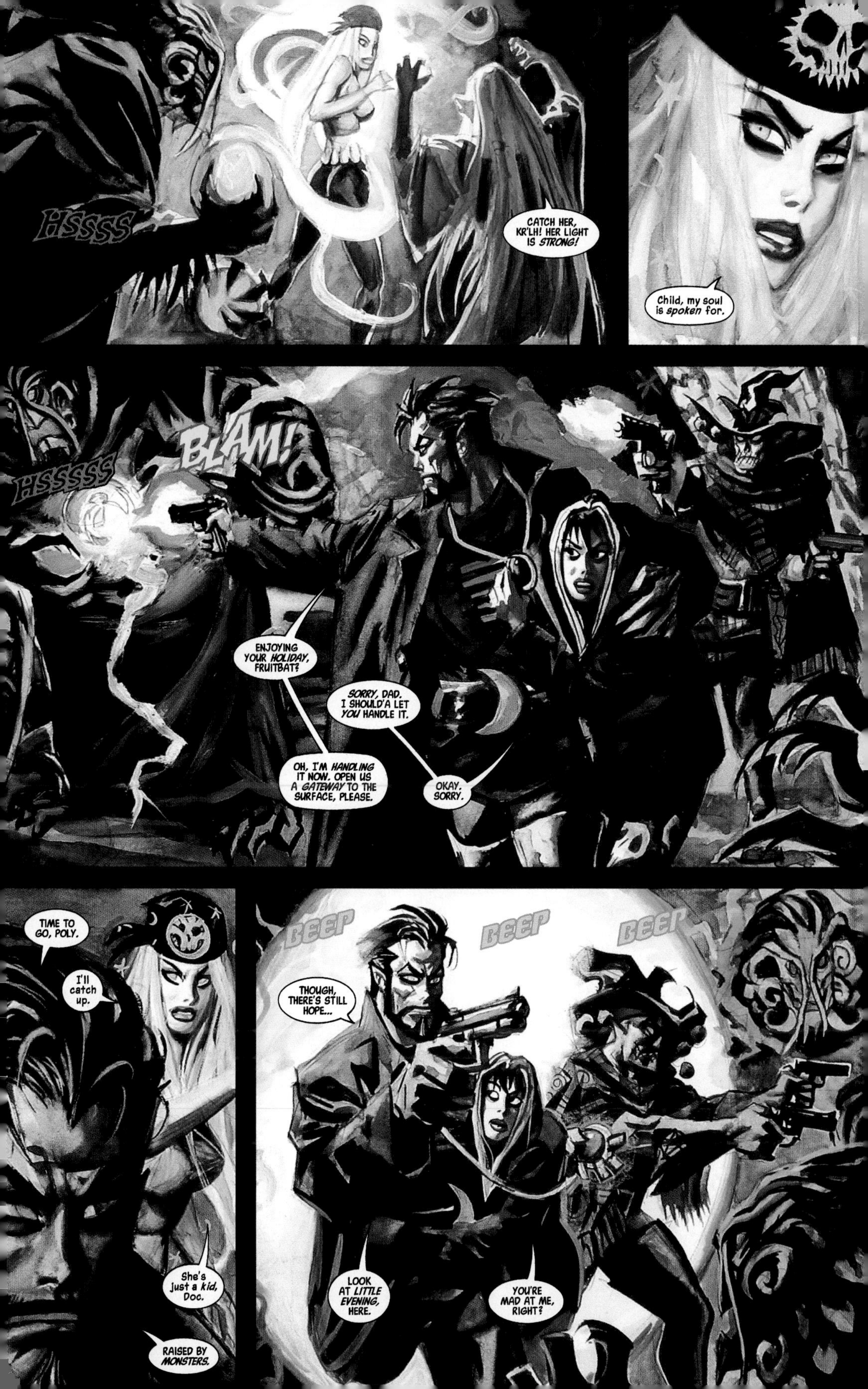
HSSSS
CATCH HER, KR'LH! HER LIGHT IS STRONG!
Child, my soul is spoken for.
HSSSSS
BLAM!
ENJOYING YOUR HOLIDAY, FRUITBAT?
SORRY, DAD. I SHOULD'A LET YOU HANDLE IT.
OH, I'M HANDLING IT NOW. OPEN US A GATEWAY TO THE SURFACE, PLEASE.
OKAY. SORRY.
TIME TO GO, POLY.
I'll catch up.
She's just a kid, Doc.
RAISED BY MONSTERS.
BEEP
BEEP
BEEP
THOUGH, THERE'S STILL HOPE...
LOOK AT LITTLE EVENING, HERE.
YOU'RE MAD AT ME, RIGHT?

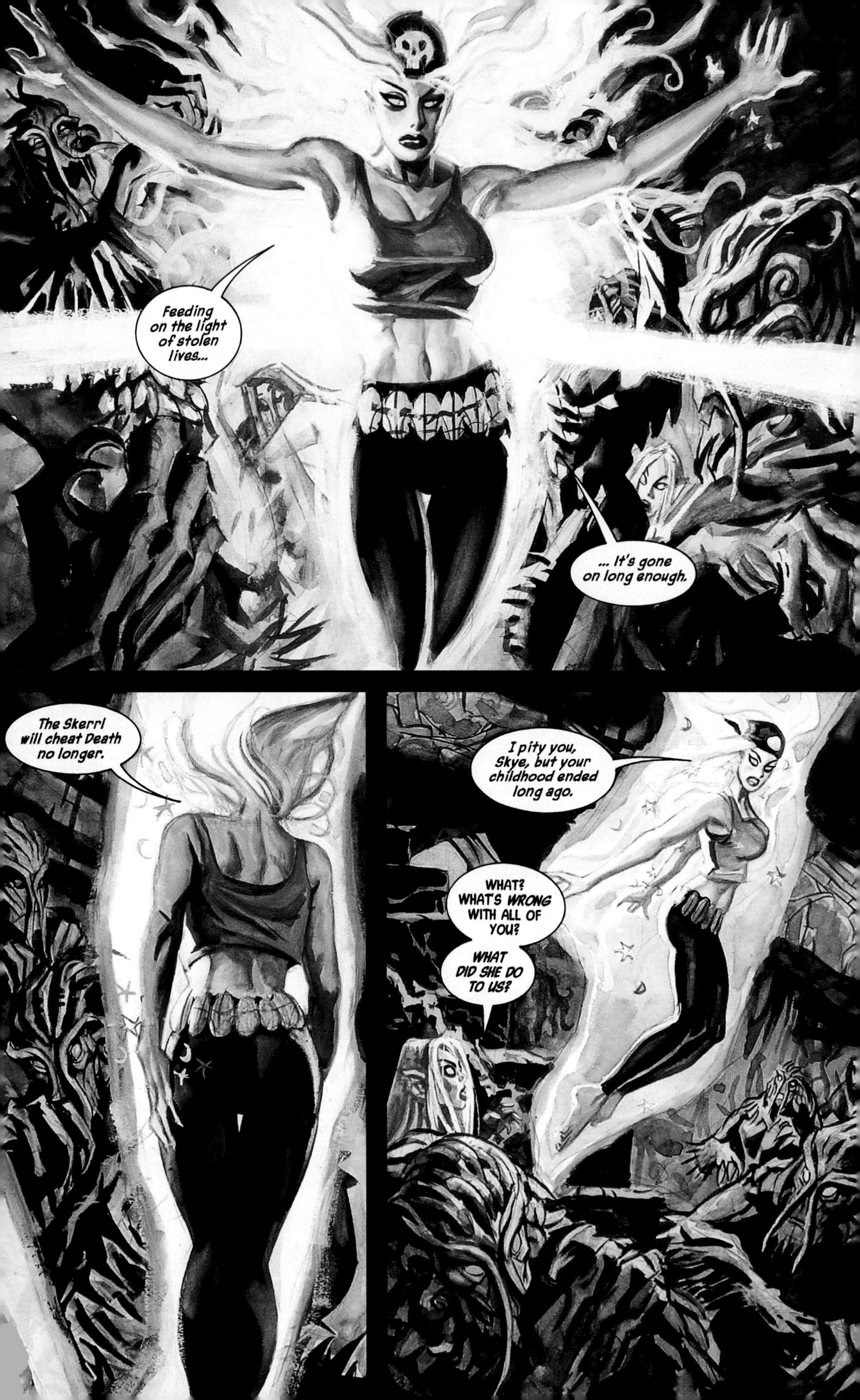
Feeding on the light of stolen lives...
... It's gone on long enough.
The Skerrl will cheat Death no longer.
I pity you, Skye, but your childhood ended long ago.
WHAT? WHAT'S *WRONG* WITH ALL OF YOU?
WHAT DID SHE DO TO US?

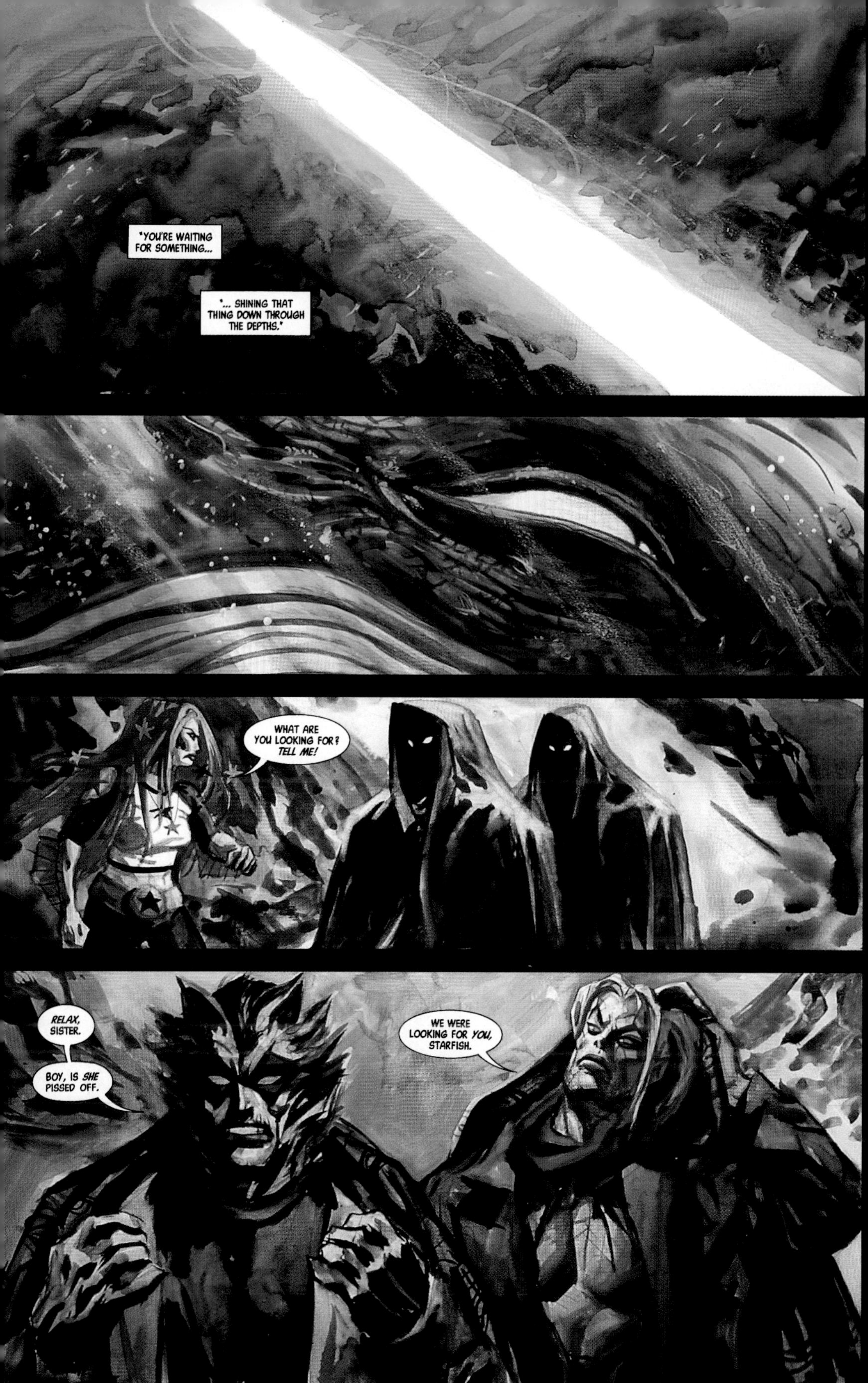
"YOU'RE WAITING FOR SOMETHING...
"... SHINING THAT THING DOWN THROUGH THE DEPTHS."
WHAT ARE YOU LOOKING FOR? TELL ME!
RELAX, SISTER.
BOY, IS SHE PISSED OFF.
WE WERE LOOKING FOR YOU, STARFISH.

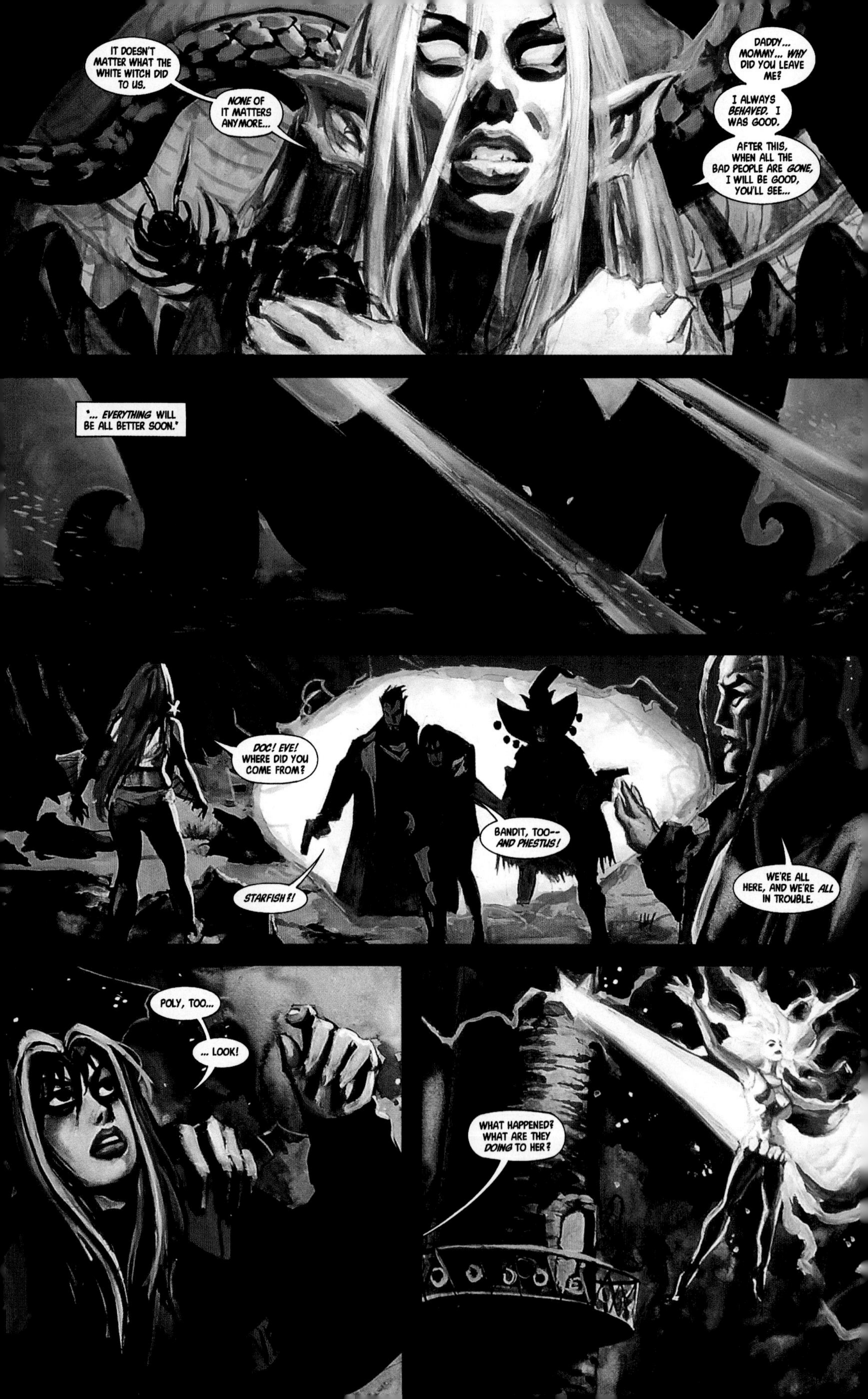
IT DOESN'T MATTER WHAT THE WHITE WITCH DID TO US.
NONE OF IT MATTERS ANYMORE...
DADDY... MOMMY... WHY DID YOU LEAVE ME?
I ALWAYS BEHAVED. I WAS GOOD.
AFTER THIS, WHEN ALL THE BAD PEOPLE ARE GONE, I WILL BE GOOD, YOU'LL SEE...
"... EVERYTHING WILL BE ALL BETTER SOON."
DOC! EVE! WHERE DID YOU COME FROM?
STARFISH?!
BANDIT, TOO-- AND PHESTUS!
WE'RE ALL HERE, AND WE'RE ALL IN TROUBLE.
POLY, TOO...
... LOOK!
WHAT HAPPENED? WHAT ARE THEY DOING TO HER?

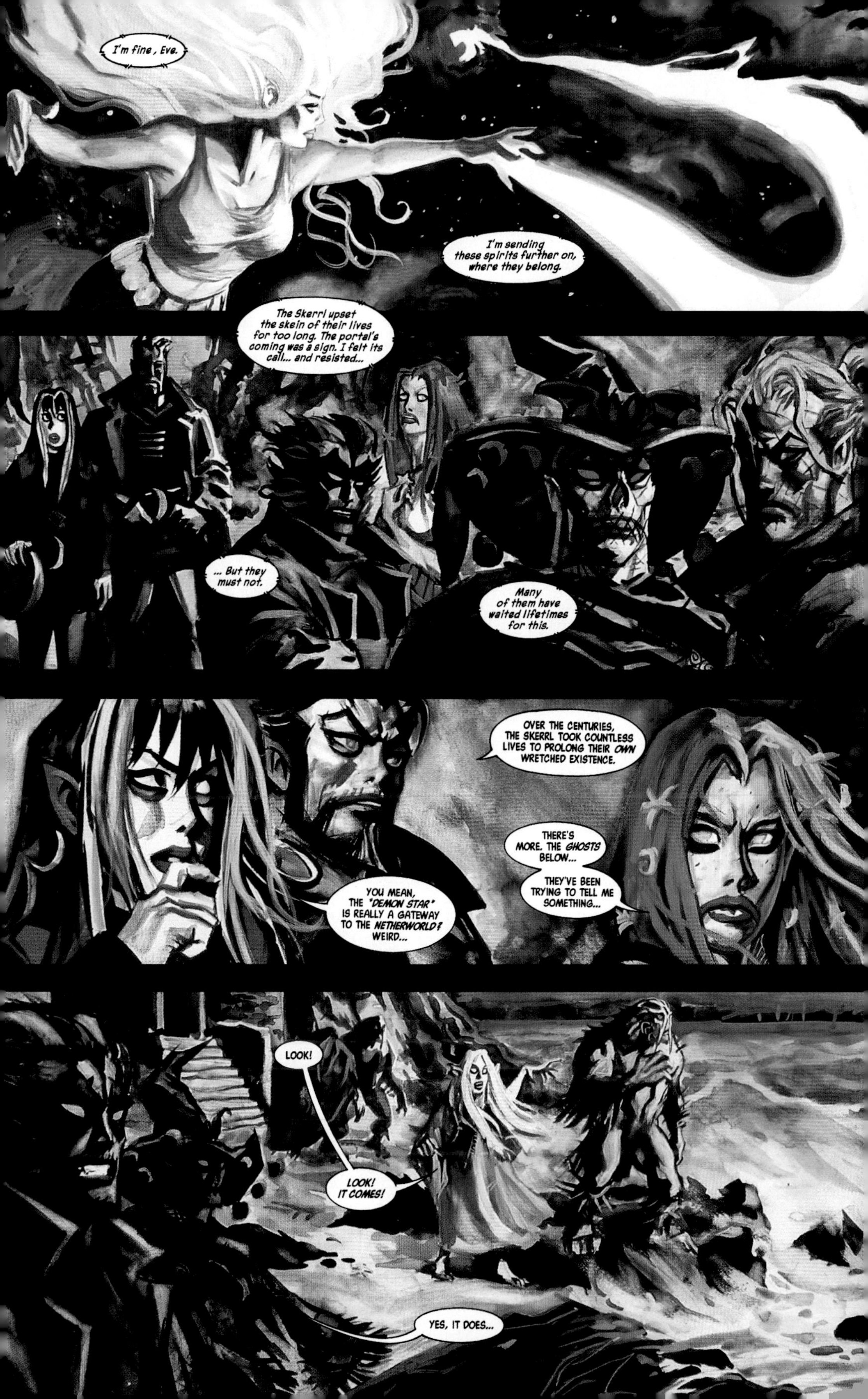
I'm fine, Eve.
I'm sending these spirits further on, where they belong.
The Skerrl upset the skein of their lives for too long. The portal's coming was a sign. I felt its call... and resisted...
... But they must not.
Many of them have waited lifetimes for this.
OVER THE CENTURIES, THE SKERRL TOOK COUNTLESS LIVES TO PROLONG THEIR OWN WRETCHED EXISTENCE.
THERE'S MORE. THE GHOSTS BELOW...
THEY'VE BEEN TRYING TO TELL ME SOMETHING...
YOU MEAN, THE "DEMON STAR" IS REALLY A GATEWAY TO THE NETHERWORLD? WEIRD...
LOOK!
LOOK! IT COMES!
YES, IT DOES...

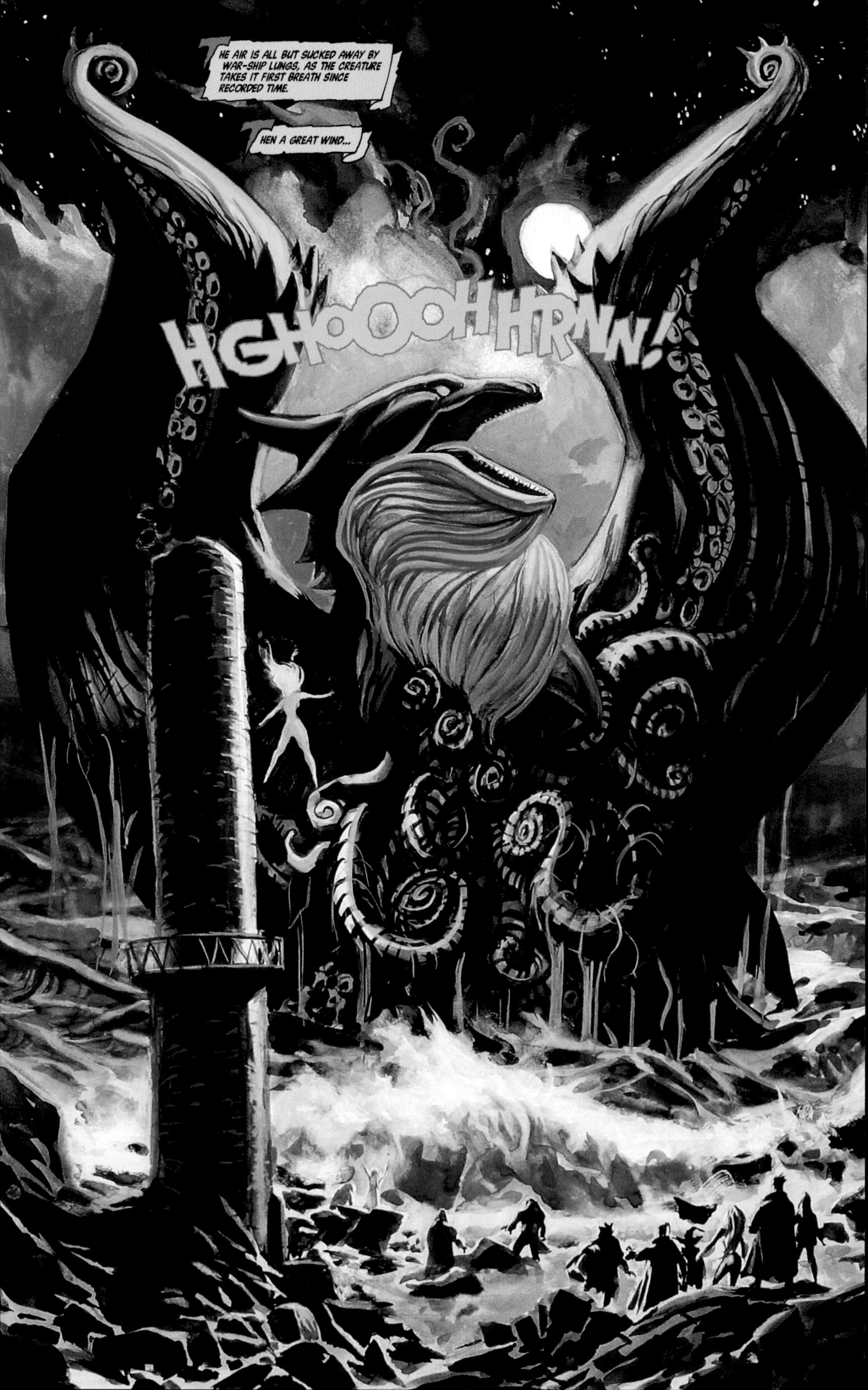
THE AIR IS ALL BUT SUCKED AWAY BY WAR-SHIP LUNGS, AS THE CREATURE TAKES IT FIRST BREATH SINCE RECORDED TIME.
THEN A GREAT WIND...
HGHOOOOH HRNN!

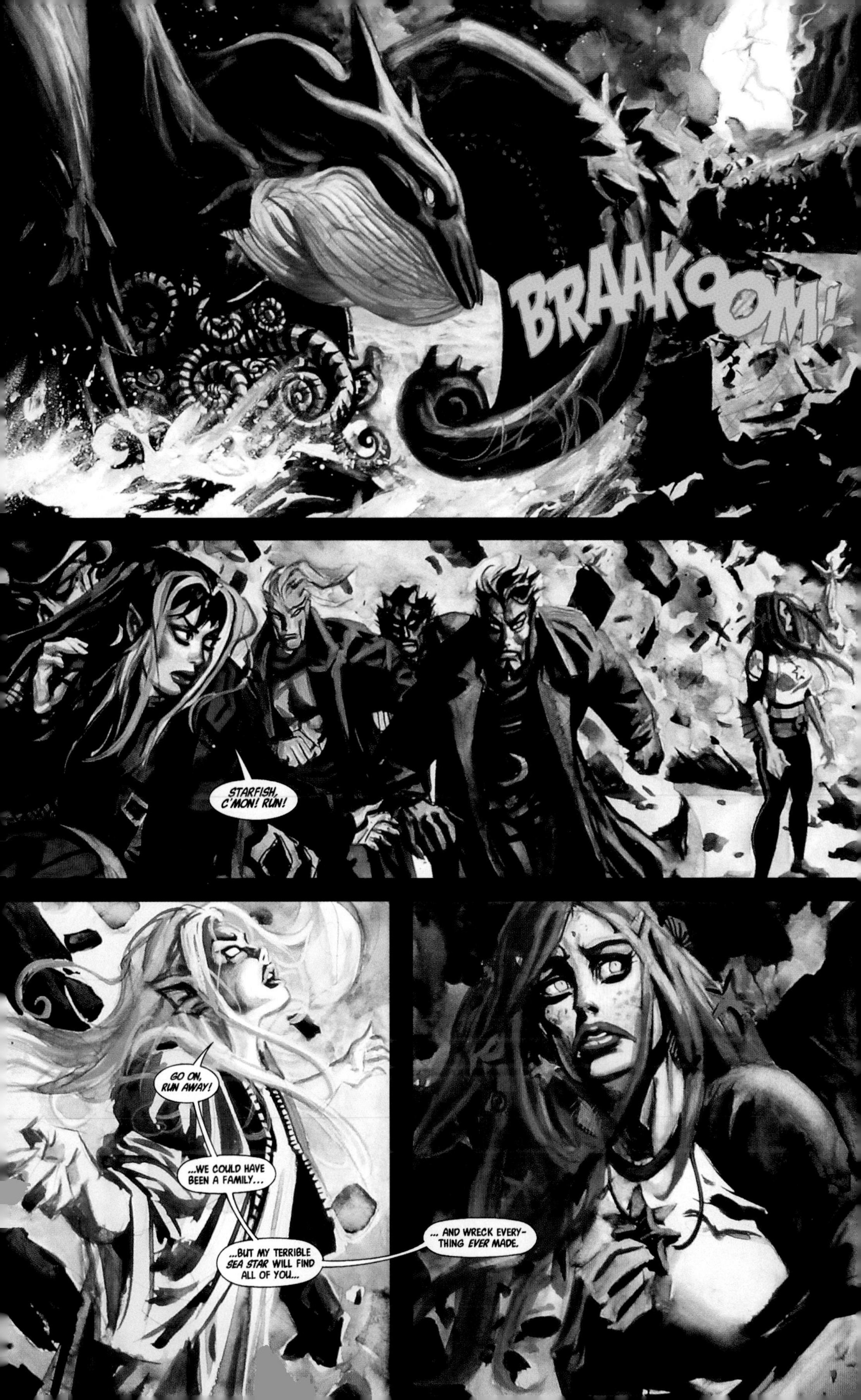
BRAAKOOM!
STARFISH, C'MON! RUN!
GO ON, RUN AWAY!
...WE COULD HAVE BEEN A FAMILY...
...BUT MY TERRIBLE SEA STAR WILL FIND ALL OF YOU...
... AND WRECK EVERY-THING EVER MADE.

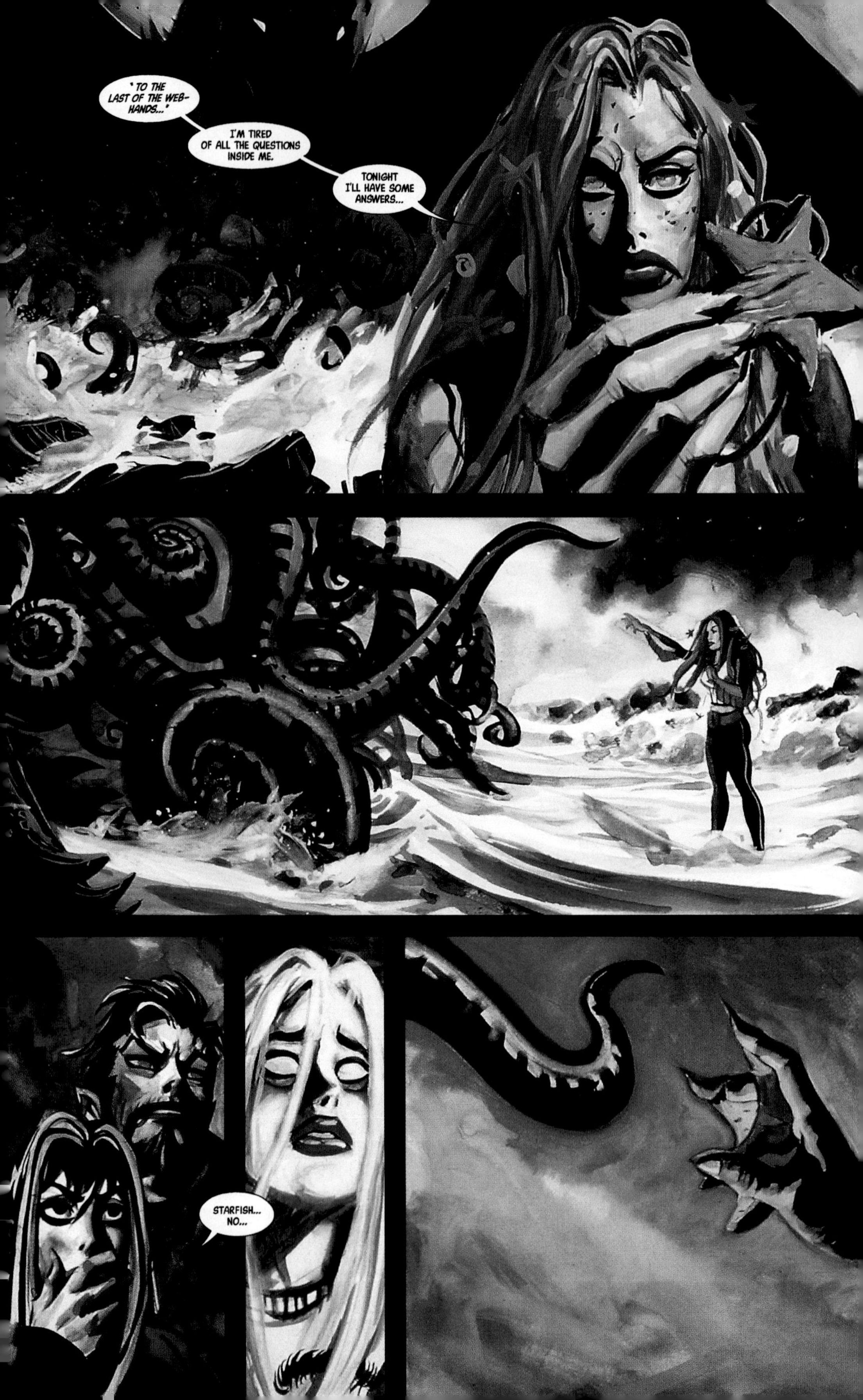
"TO THE LAST OF THE WEB-HANDS..."
I'M TIRED OF ALL THE QUESTIONS INSIDE ME.
TONIGHT I'LL HAVE SOME ANSWERS...
STARFISH... NO...

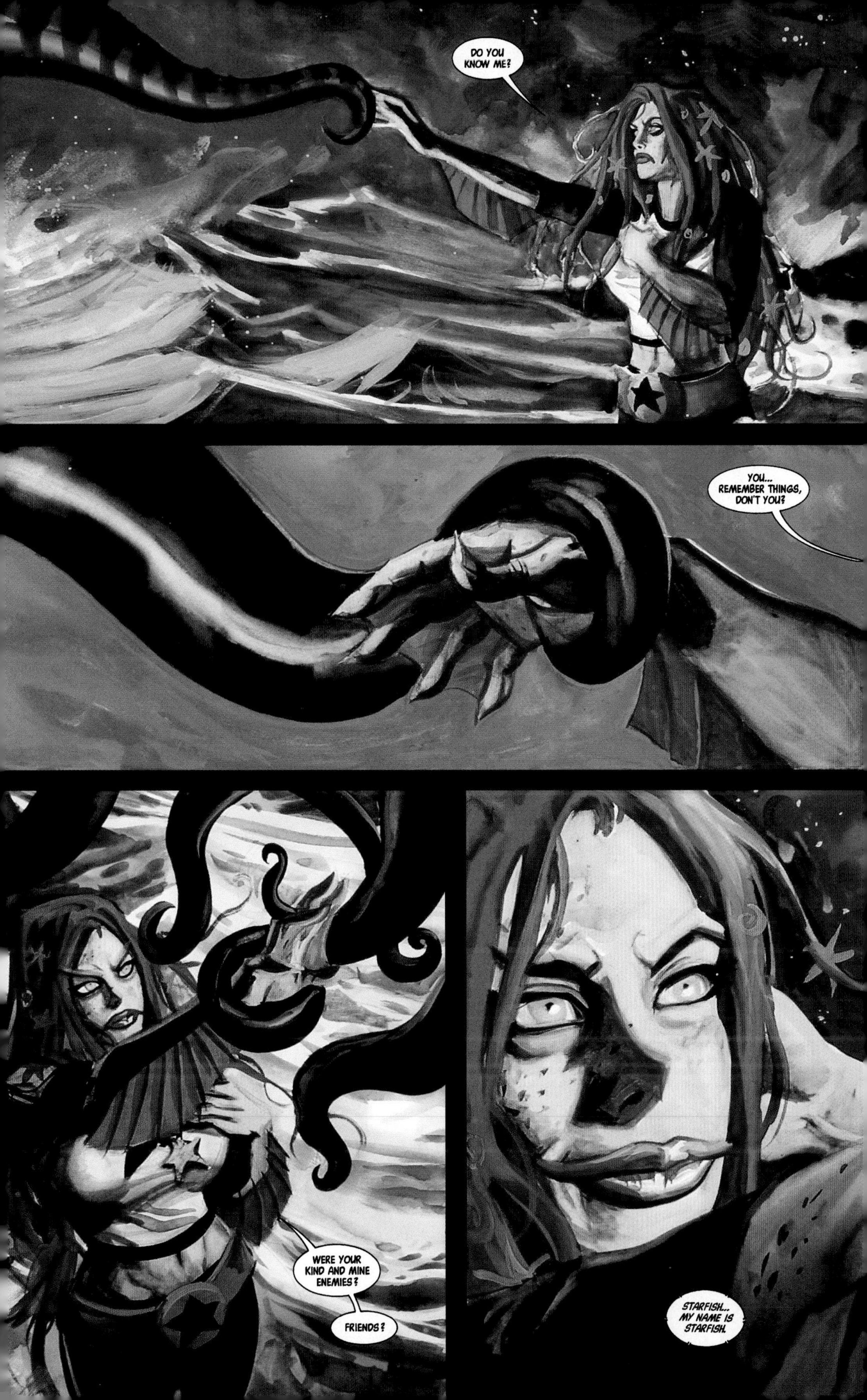
DO YOU KNOW ME?
YOU... REMEMBER THINGS, DON'T YOU?
WERE YOUR KIND AND MINE ENEMIES?
FRIENDS?
STARFISH... MY NAME IS STARFISH.

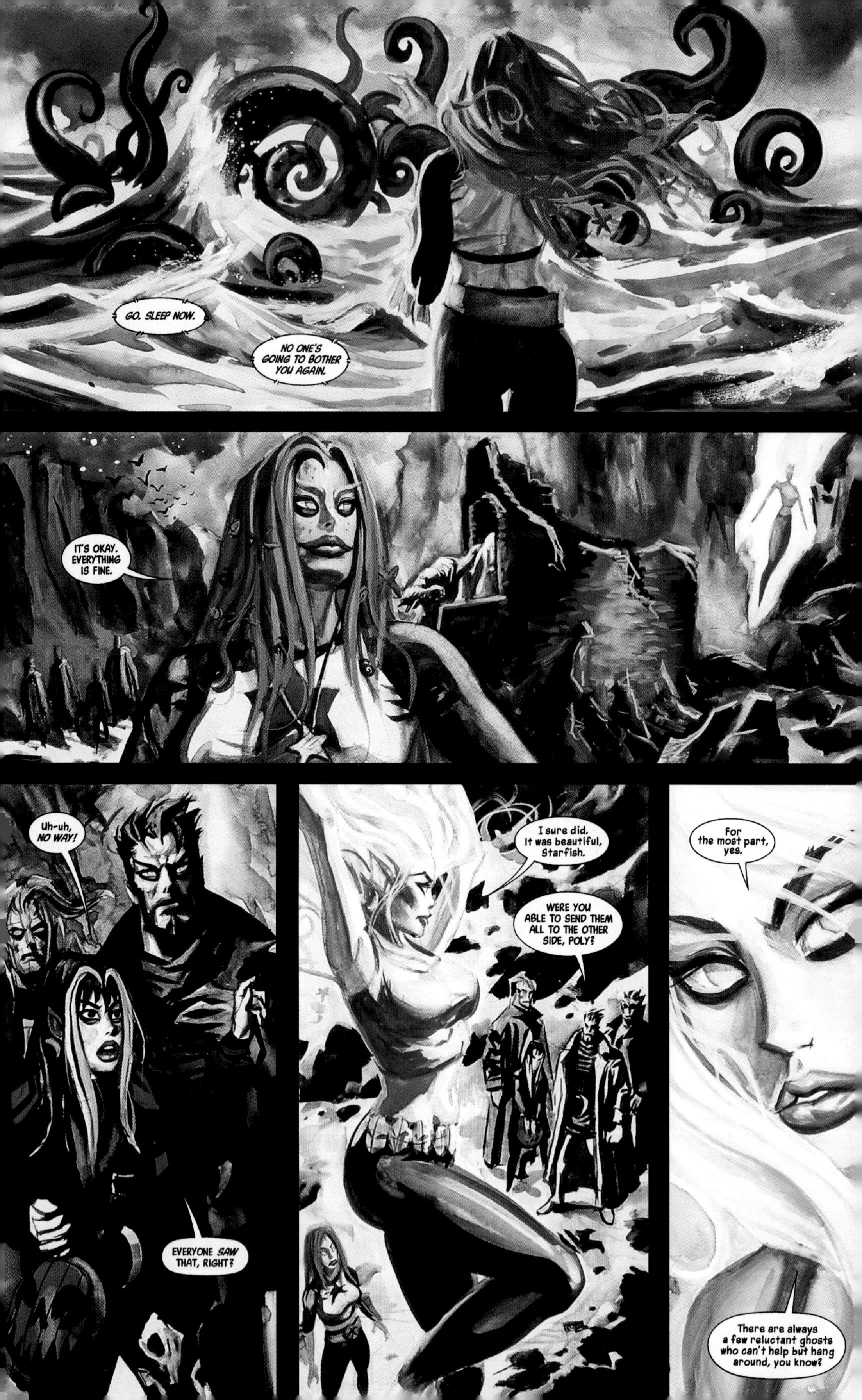
GO. SLEEP NOW.
NO ONE'S GOING TO BOTHER YOU AGAIN.
IT'S OKAY. EVERYTHING IS FINE.
Uh-uh, NO WAY!
EVERYONE SAW THAT, RIGHT?
WERE YOU ABLE TO SEND THEM ALL TO THE OTHER SIDE, POLY?
I sure did. It was beautiful, Starfish.
For the most part, yes.
There are always a few reluctant ghosts who can't help but hang around, you know?

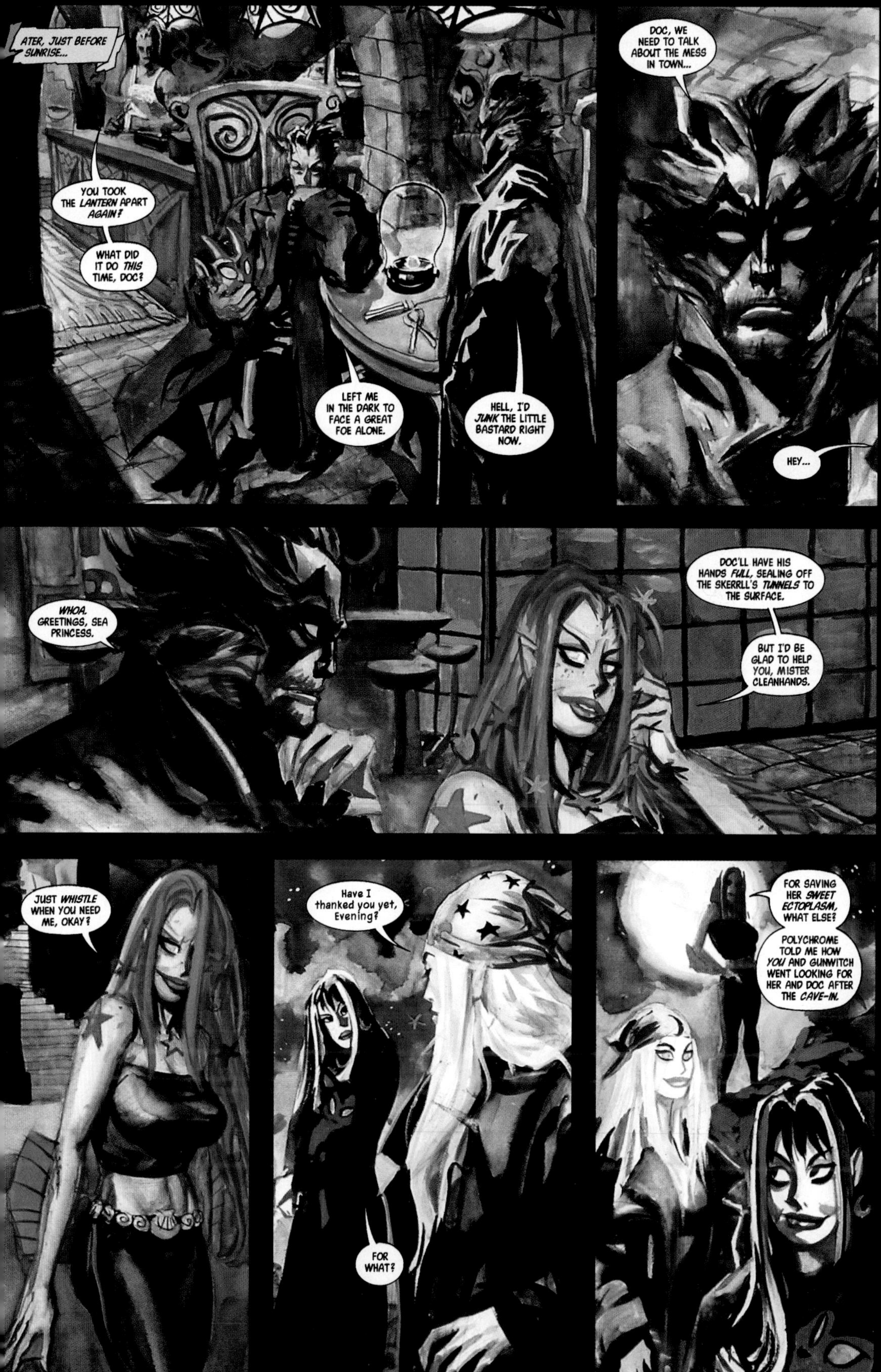
ATER, JUST BEFORE SUNRISE...
YOU TOOK THE LANTERN APART AGAIN?
WHAT DID IT DO THIS TIME, DOC?
LEFT ME IN THE DARK TO FACE A GREAT FOE ALONE.
HELL, I'D JUNK THE LITTLE BASTARD RIGHT NOW.
DOC, WE NEED TO TALK ABOUT THE MESS IN TOWN...
HEY...
WHOA. GREETINGS, SEA PRINCESS.
DOC'LL HAVE HIS HANDS FULL, SEALING OFF THE SKERRLL'S TUNNELS TO THE SURFACE.
BUT I'D BE GLAD TO HELP YOU, MISTER CLEANHANDS.
JUST WHISTLE WHEN YOU NEED ME, OKAY?
Have I thanked you yet, Evening?
FOR WHAT?
FOR SAVING HER SWEET ECTOPLASM, WHAT ELSE?
POLYCHROME TOLD ME HOW YOU AND GUNWITCH WENT LOOKING FOR HER AND DOC AFTER THE CAVE-IN.

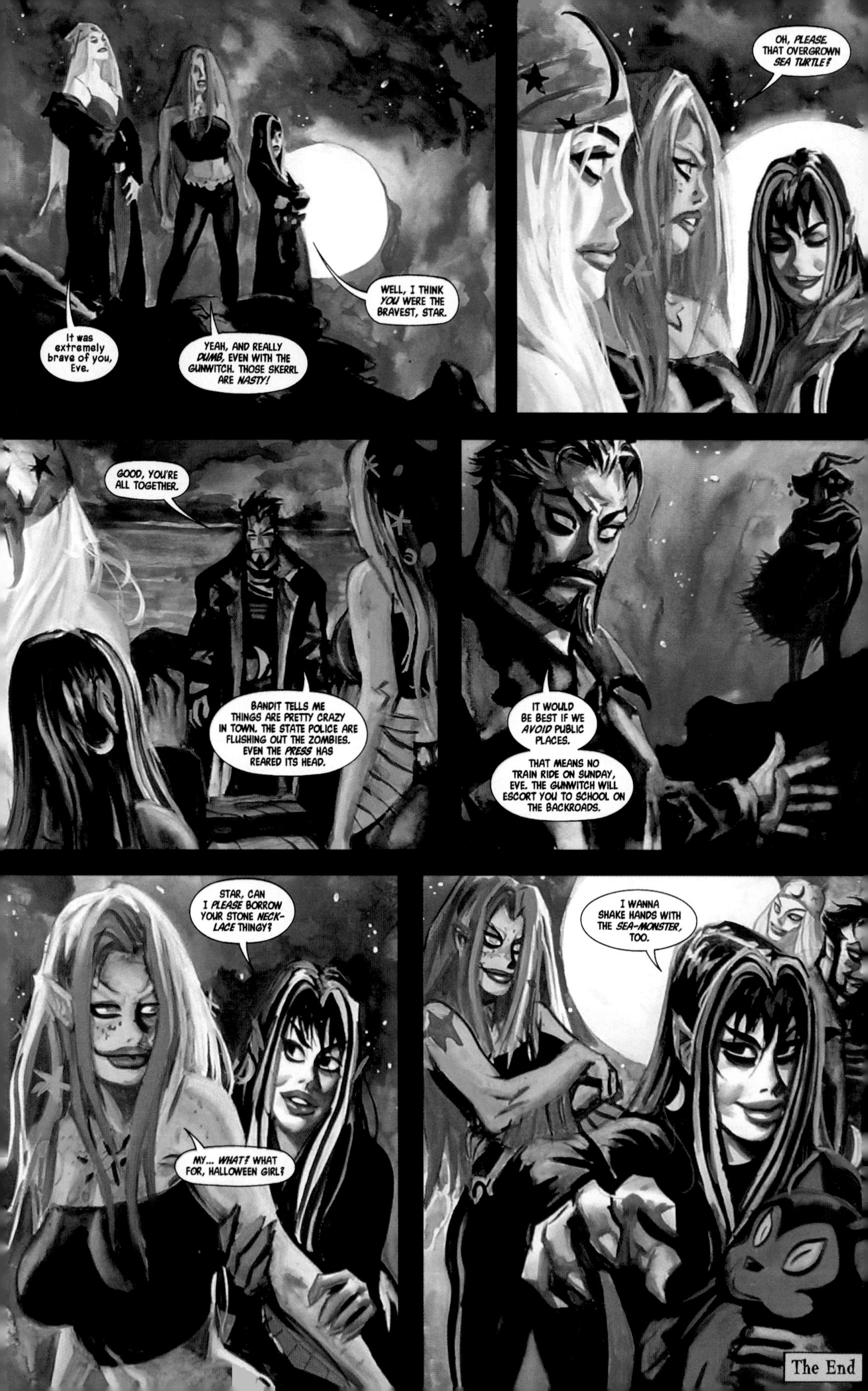
It was extremely brave of you, Eve.
YEAH, AND REALLY DUMB, EVEN WITH THE GUNWITCH. THOSE SKERRL ARE NASTY!
WELL, I THINK YOU WERE THE BRAVEST, STAR.
OH, PLEASE. THAT OVERGROWN SEA TURTLE?
GOOD, YOU'RE ALL TOGETHER.
BANDIT TELLS ME THINGS ARE PRETTY CRAZY IN TOWN. THE STATE POLICE ARE FLUSHING OUT THE ZOMBIES. EVEN THE PRESS HAS REARED ITS HEAD.
IT WOULD BE BEST IF WE AVOID PUBLIC PLACES.
THAT MEANS NO TRAIN RIDE ON SUNDAY, EVE. THE GUNWITCH WILL ESCORT YOU TO SCHOOL ON THE BACKROADS.
STAR, CAN I PLEASE BORROW YOUR STONE NECK-LACE THINGY?
MY... WHAT? WHAT FOR, HALLOWEEN GIRL?
I WANNA SHAKE HANDS WITH THE SEA-MONSTER, TOO.
The End

xxxxxx PRODUCTION GALLERY xxxxxx

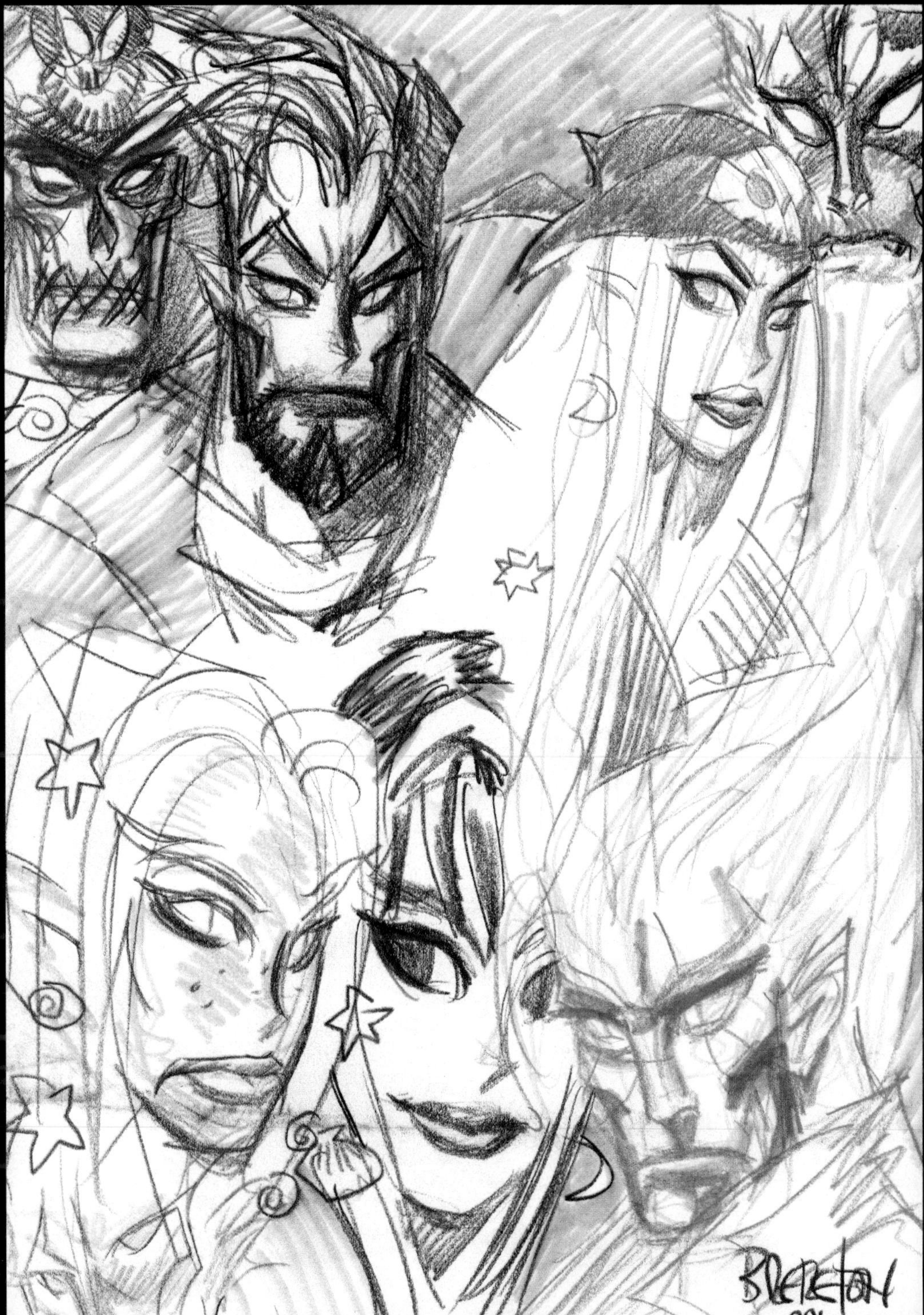
BRERETON
001

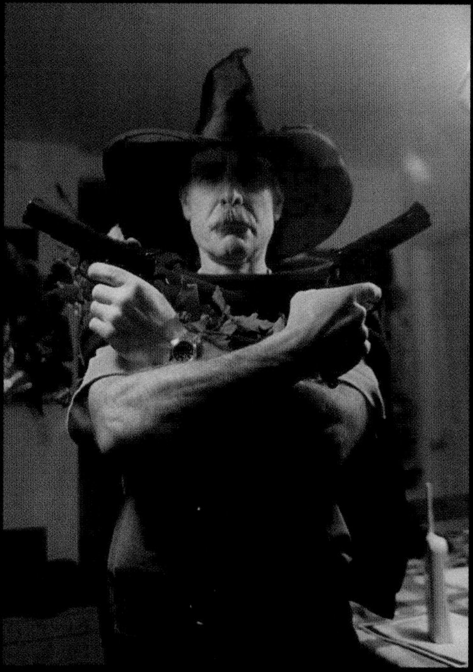

Above, George Brereton poses as The Gunwitch.

George Brereton as Doc Horror.

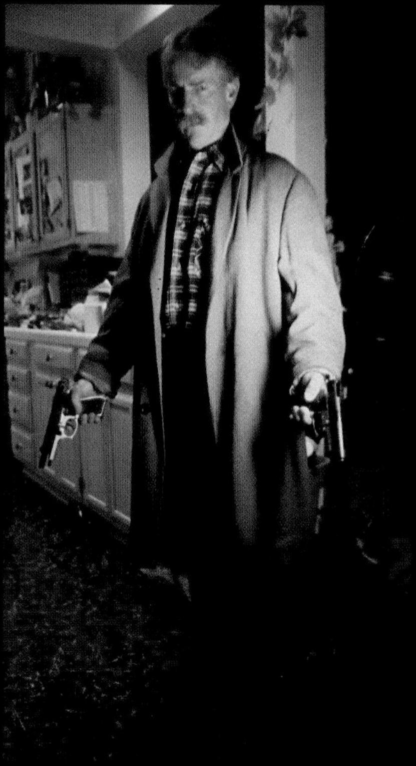

Below, George models as The Gunwitch.

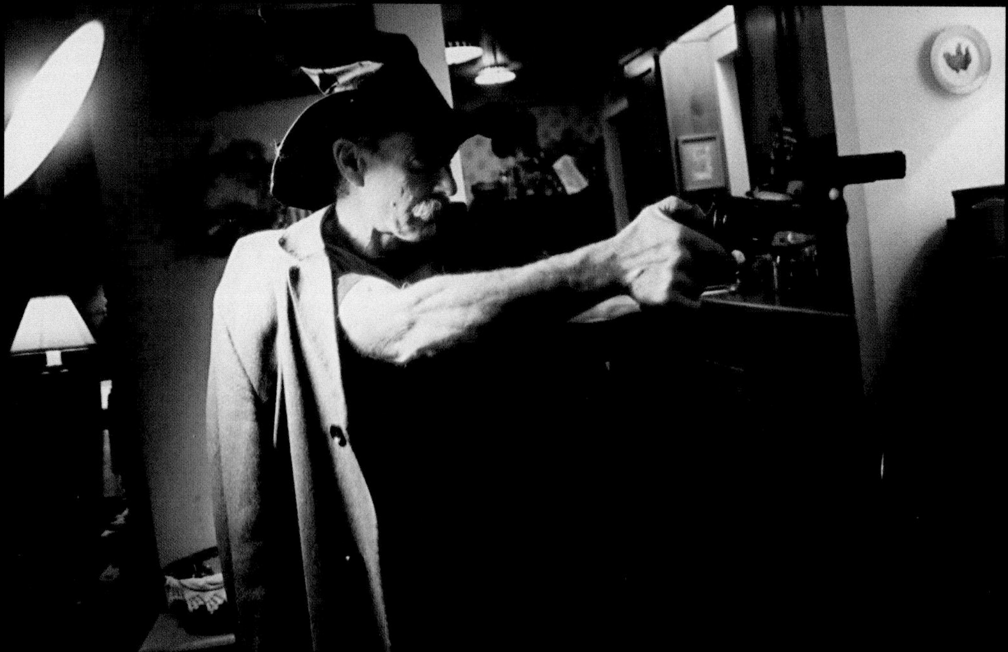

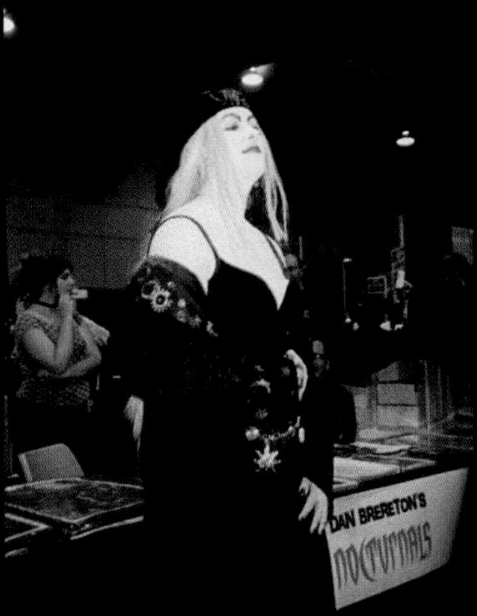
DAN BRERETON'S
NOCTURNALS

Jennifer Mencken dressed as Polychrome during the 2001 San Diego Comic Con.

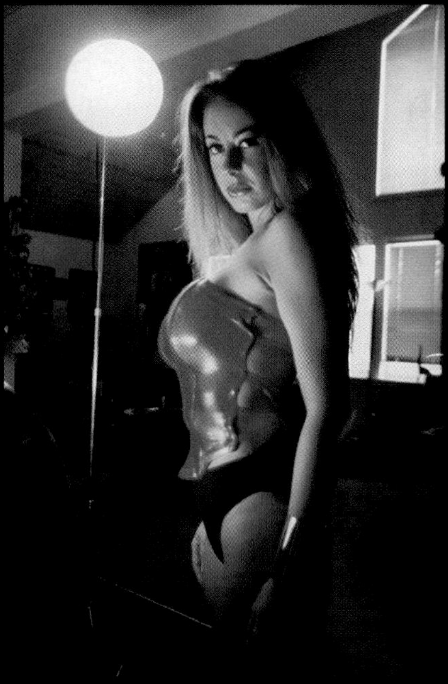

Diana Knight poses as Starfish on the cover of *The Dark Forever* #1.

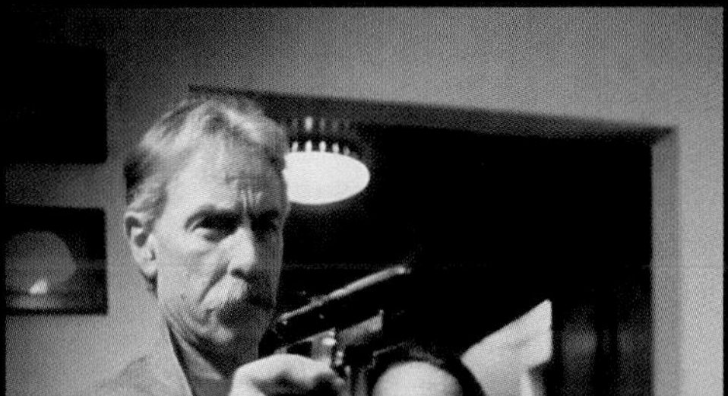

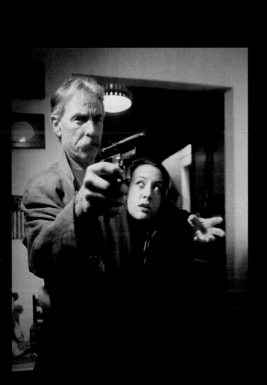

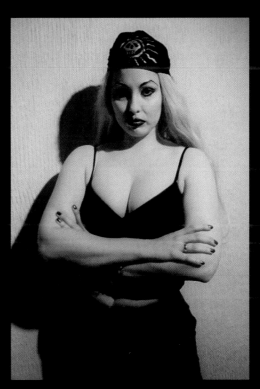

Lindsay with Grandpa George.

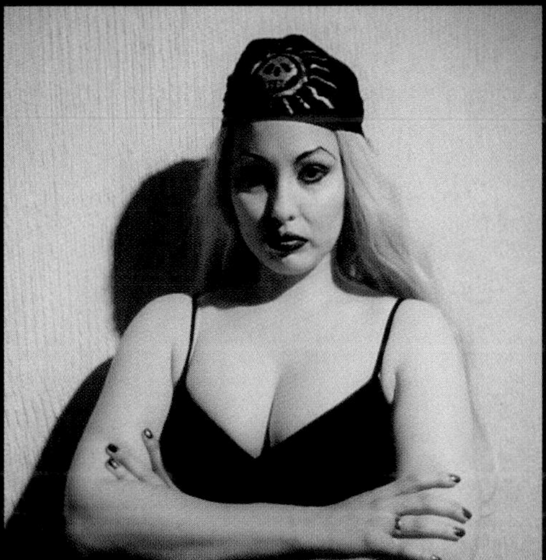

Clarissa models as Polychrome.

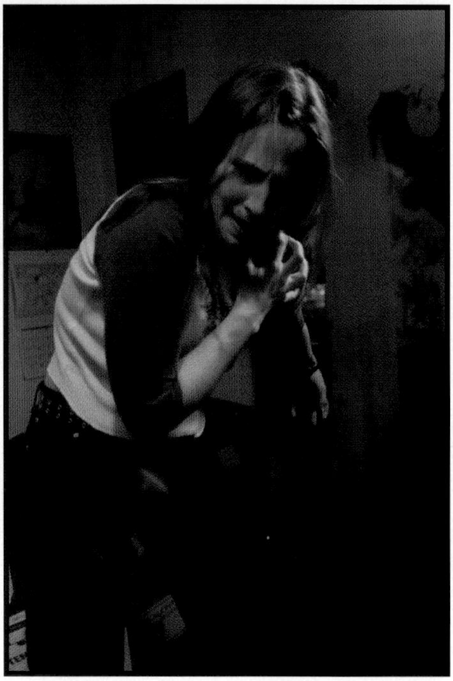

Dan's sister, Michele, creeps in as a Skerrl "Zombie."

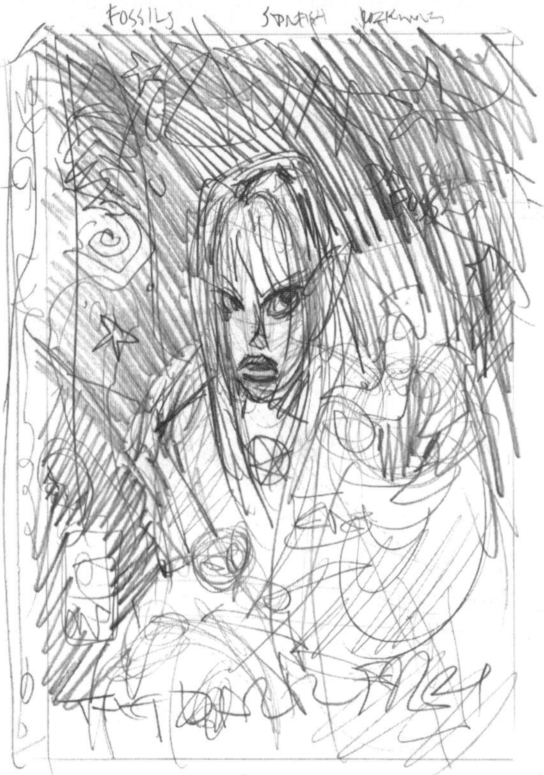

Above, an unused cover concept for *The Dark Forever* trade paperback.

Below, Michele poses as Polychrome.

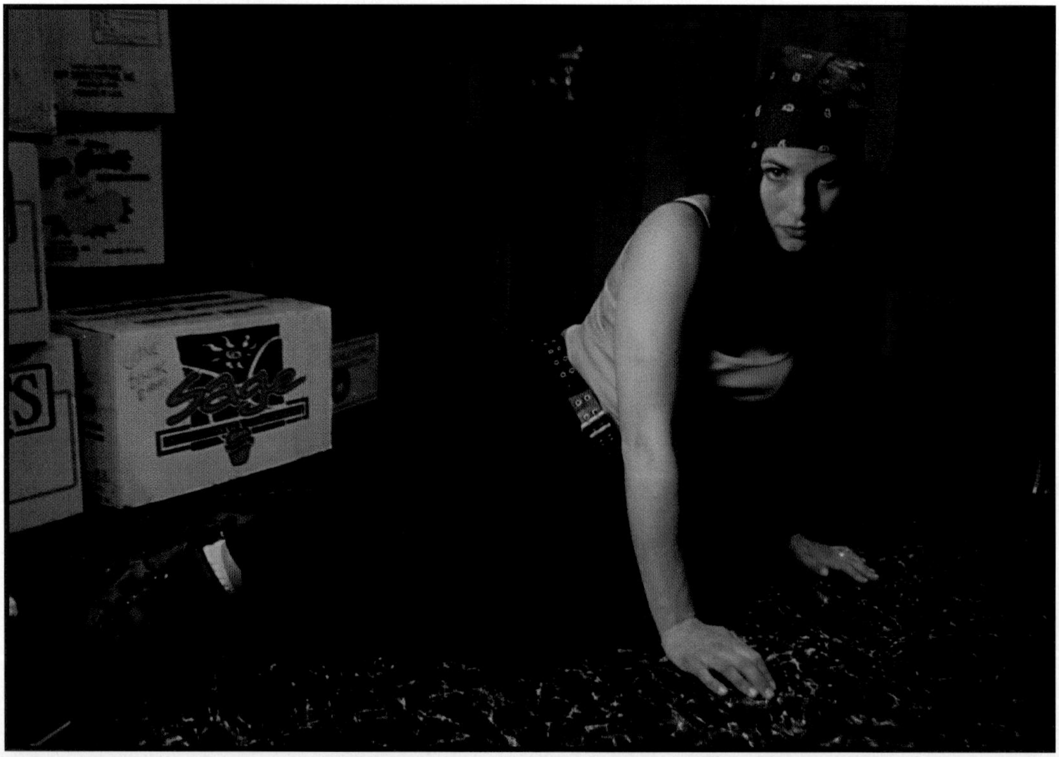

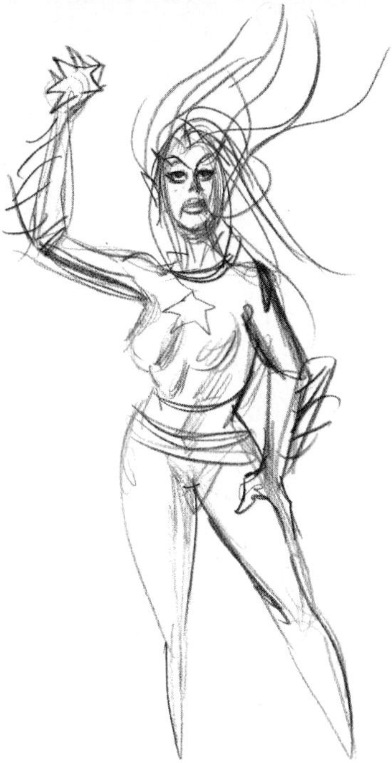

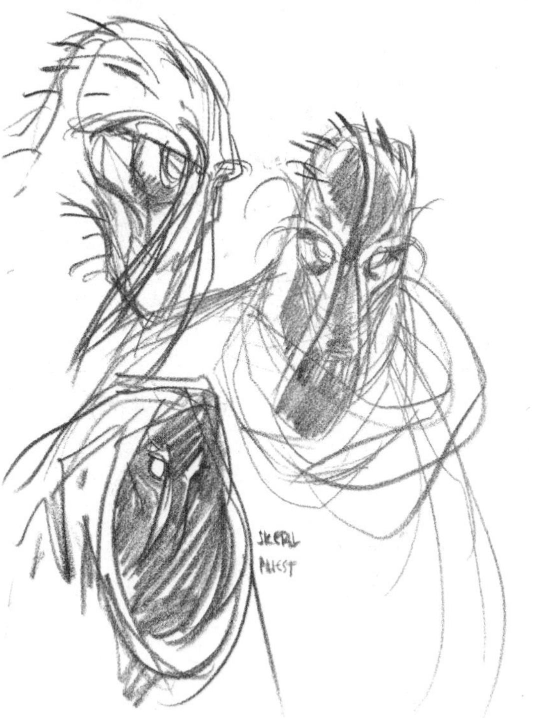
SKRULL
PRIEST

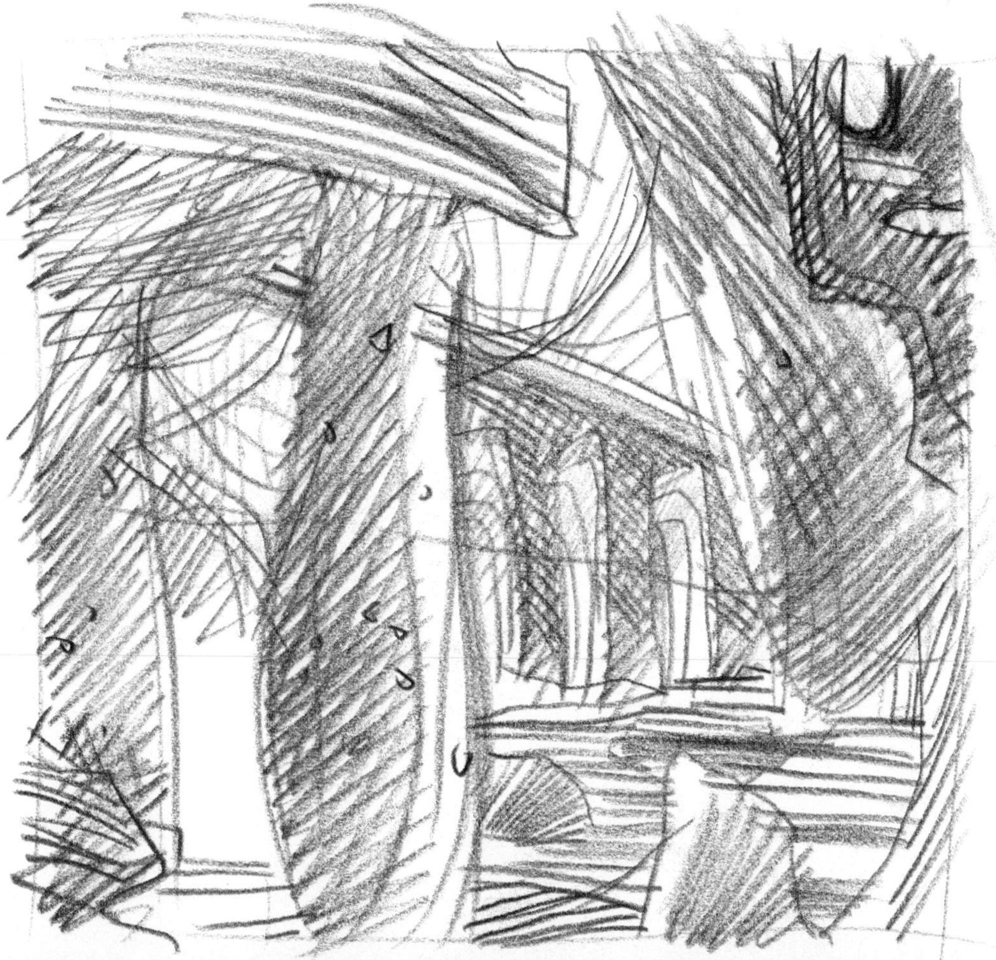

Below, Lindsay Brereton models.

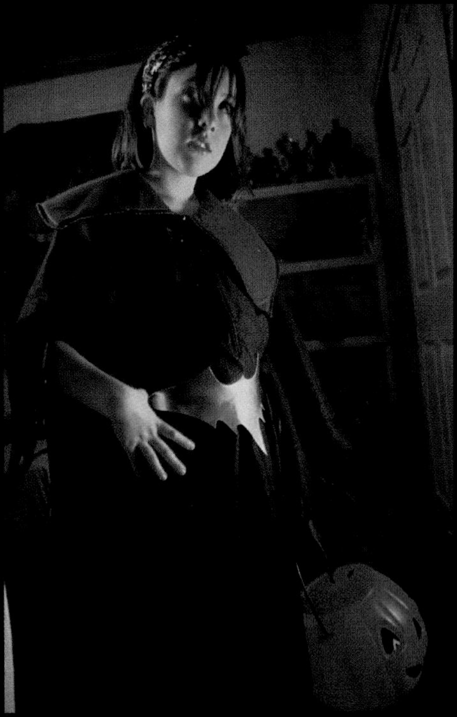

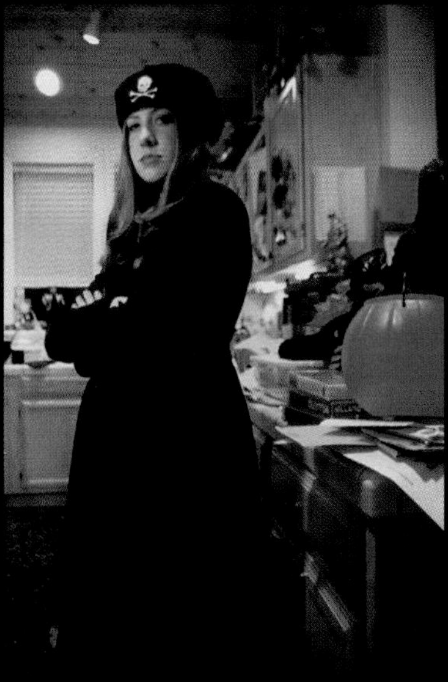

Pictured left, Lindsay dressed as Eve as seen in the *Witching Hour*, 1997.

Photo reference is an integral part of the working process for me. The vitality and presence of the model is key, as well as lighting and basic accuracy with the figure. The human component is a major element, as well: I don't know how Eve could have come into being without the inspiration my daughter Lindsay has brought to the character over the years.

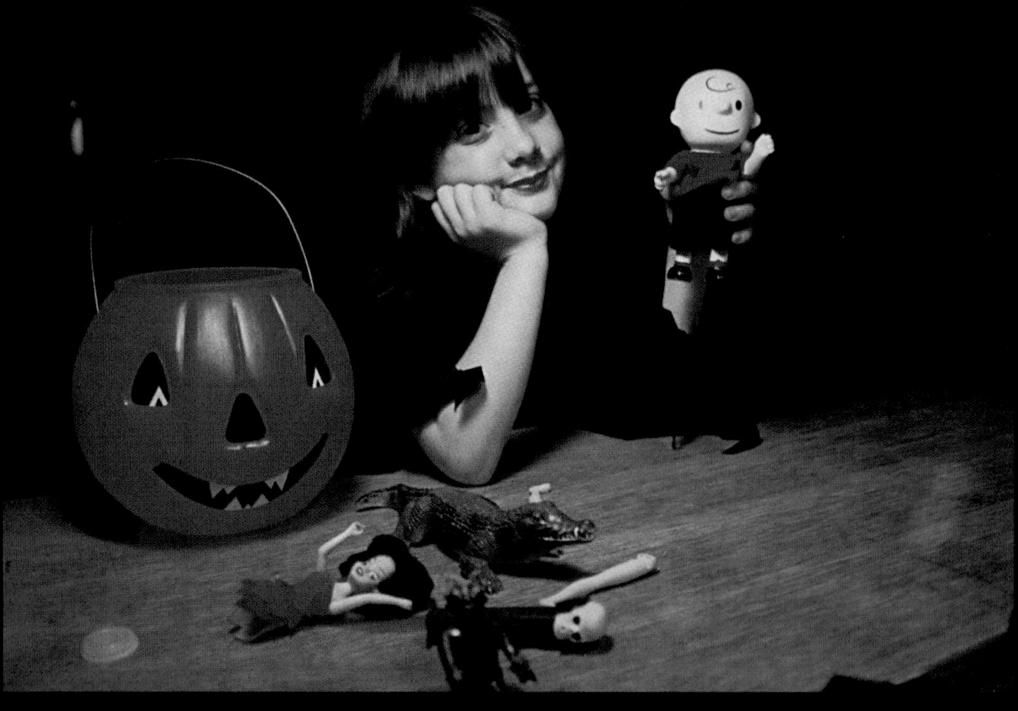

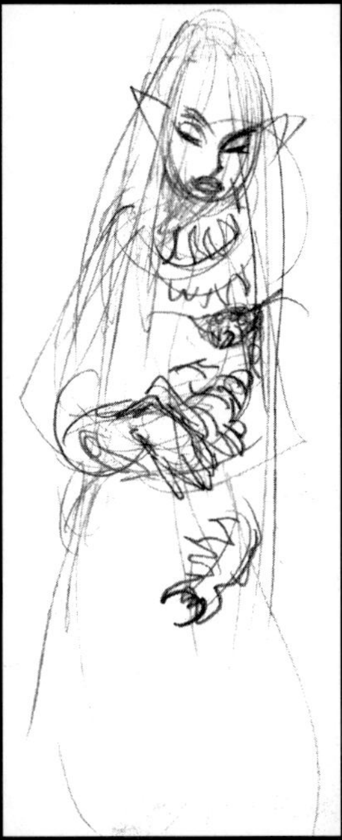

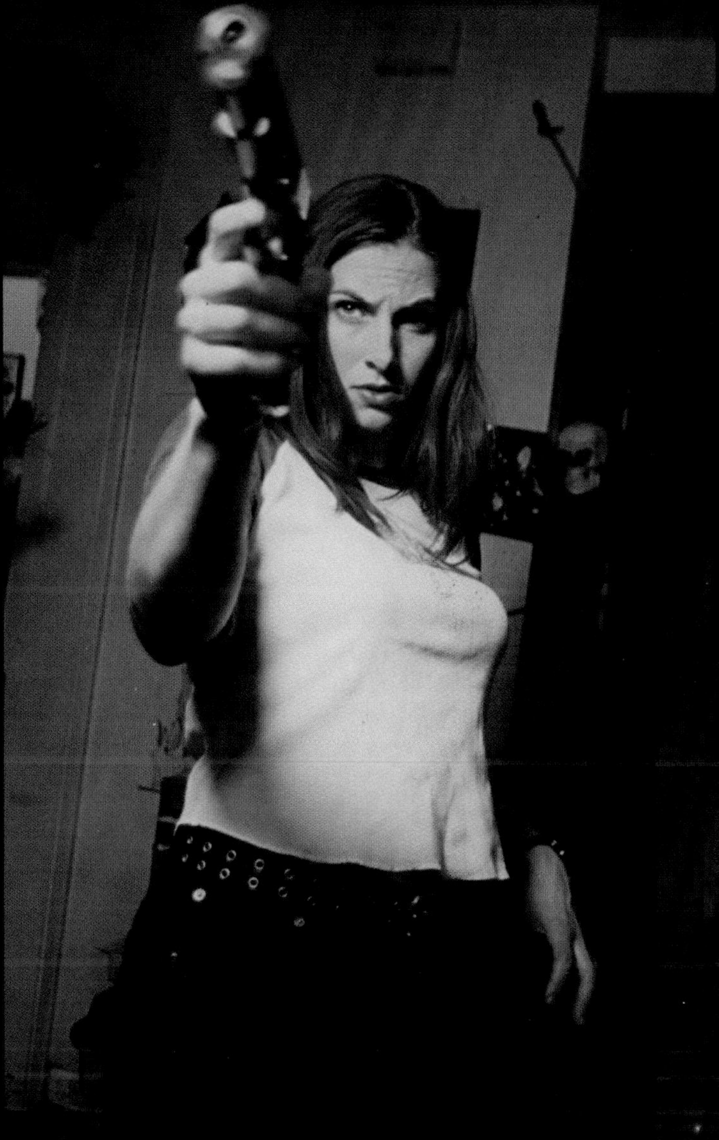

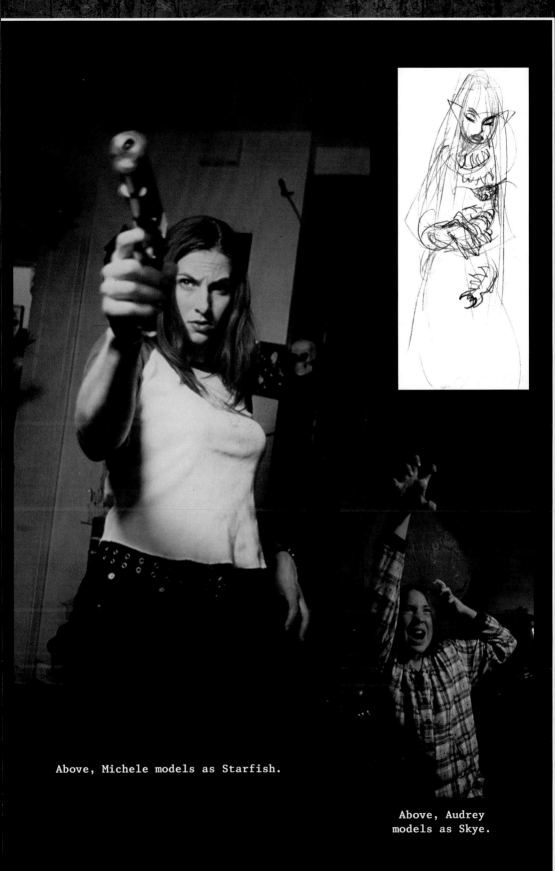

Above, Michele models as Starfish.

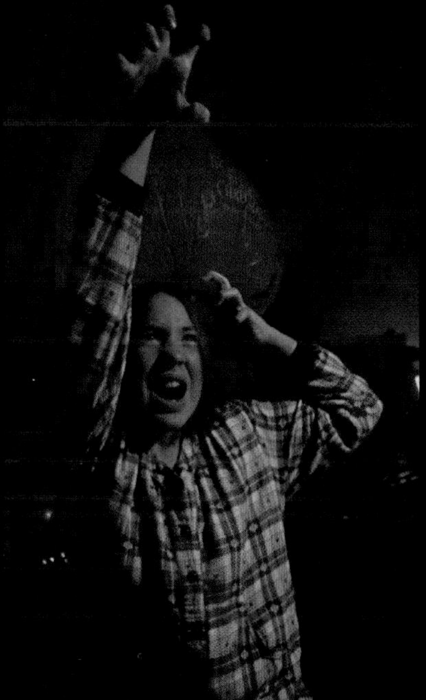

Above, Audrey
models as Skye.

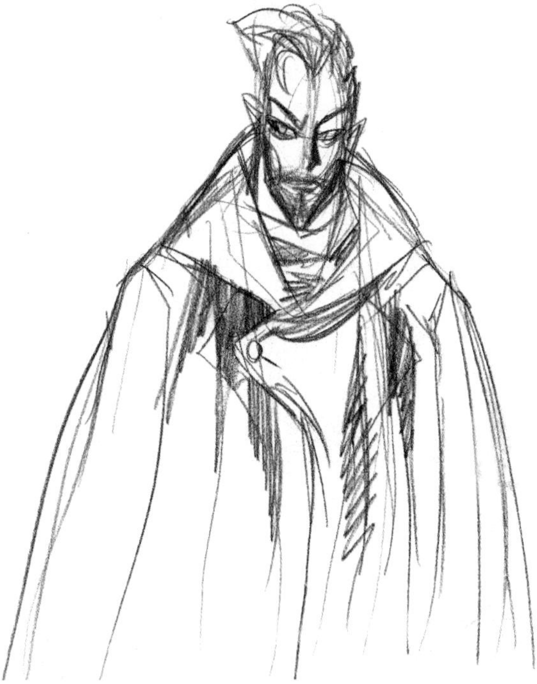

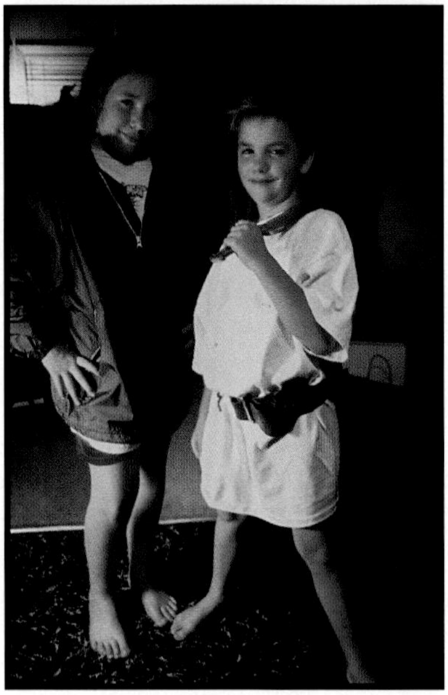

Above, Audrey and Hunter as Peeper & Ector, Eve's school chums.

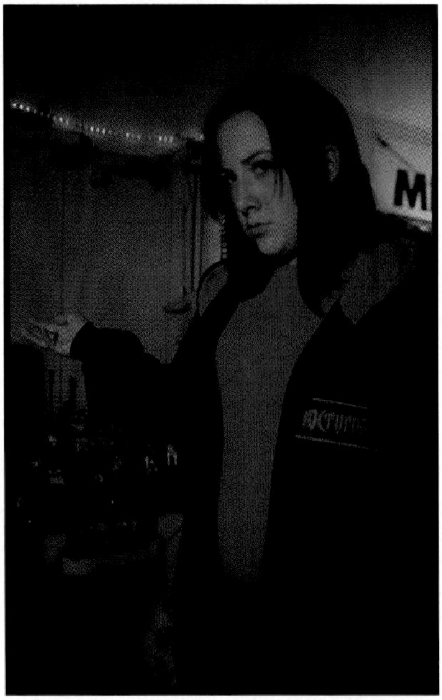

Lindsay as Eve, 2001.

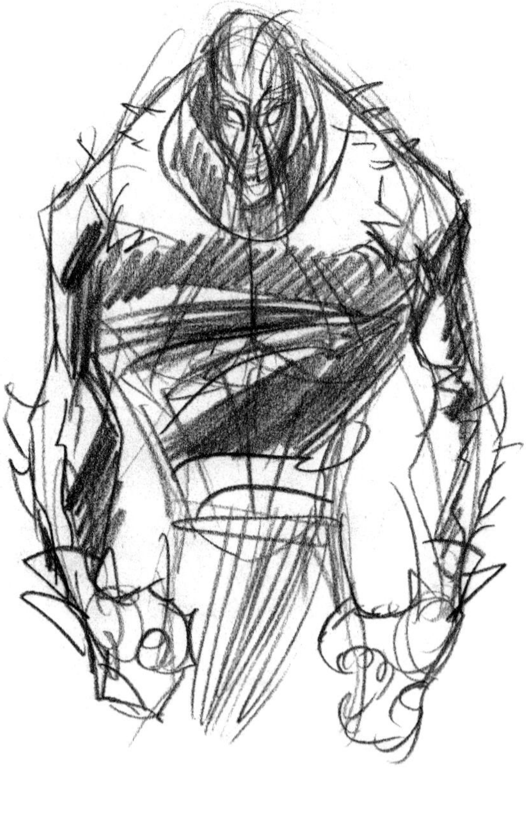

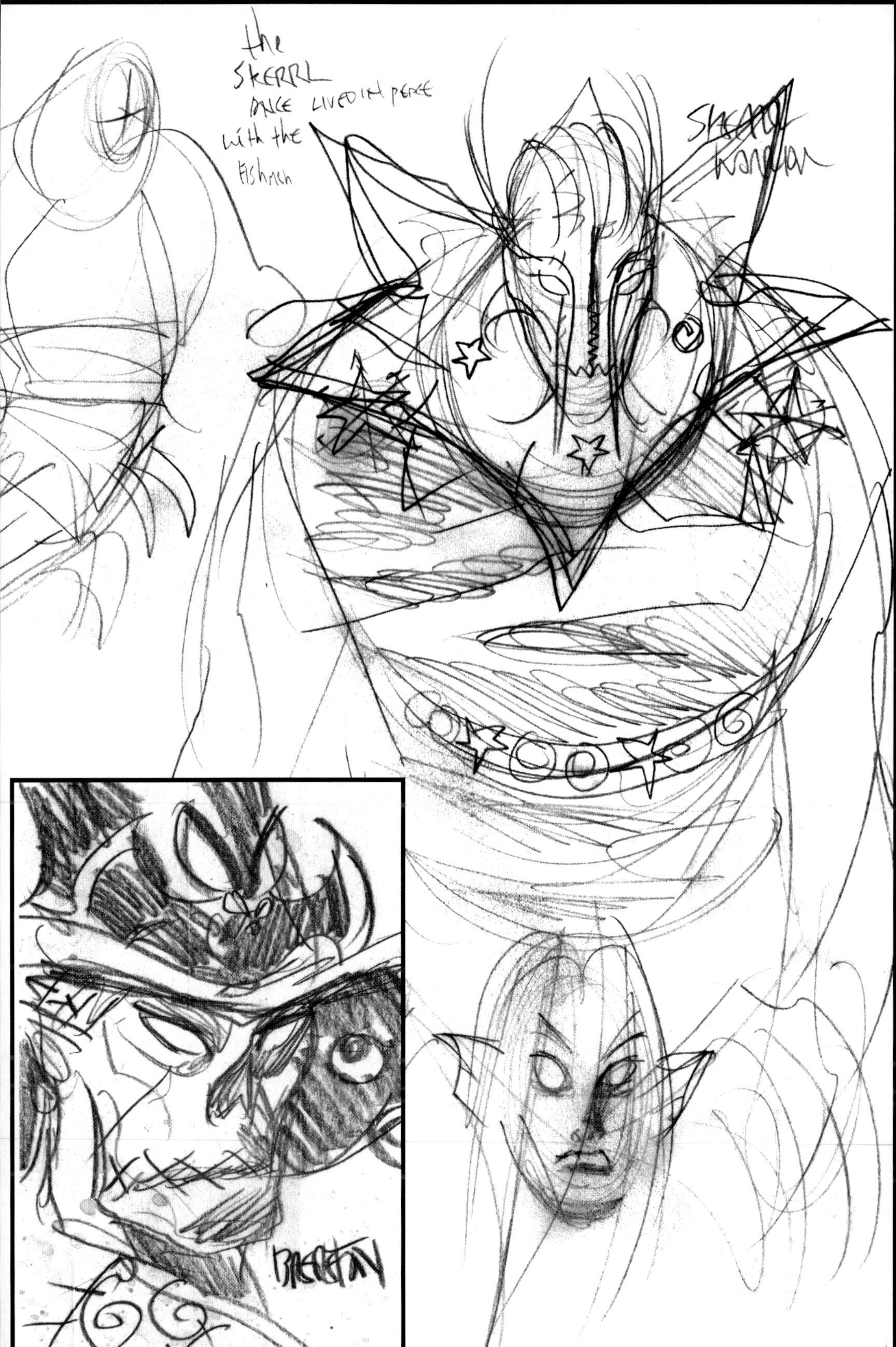
the SKERRL ONCE LIVED IN PEACE with the Fishmen
Skerrl warrior
BRERETON

xxxxxxxx AFTERWORD xxxxxxxx

Many years and publishers ago, when *Nocturnals* first premiered, I called my friend Dan Brereton to congratulate him on a job well done. Taking full advantage of our similar points in the comics field to contact a fellow pro, I wanted to glorify my opinion by sharing it directly with the creator of the work I was so enamored with. Luckily, Dan was receptive to my praise and allowed me to deliver my fan mail in person.

For myself as a sort of artist-creative type, I'm always impressed when someone takes on the whole job by themselves. Writing hasn't come naturally to me before, so I get inspiration in those who seem to take to it well on their first try.

I felt then as I do now—that Dan has accomplished a quality work with strong plotting and dialogue with that hard-boiled feel that I wouldn't even know where to begin to get. The careers of Dan and I have followed similar paths with us both premiering our first printed comics in 1989 (his was *Black Terror*, mine was *Terminator*—his was much better), and we both later went on to illustrate the major icons of DC and other publishers. As we both use watercolors to paint with and our friends and family to model, the process by which we work is probably the most similar of any two comics painters.

These similarities make us a good comparison to one another, but as far as creative paths taken, mine has been much more the established superhero icon pimping route, while Dan has dabbled his toes in the more hot and cold running waters of creator independence and new properties.

I look to guys like Dan with much admiration for charting a path into what I aspire to one day do. Dan's *Nocturnals* is an exciting pantheon of hybrid-genre characters that stand up well in the glut of colorful comics universes. I especially loved how Dan delivered a traditional 22-32 page format with painted illustrations to tease the reader that it would be possible to give that level of effort on a more regular basis.

I'm sure with Dan's ambition, as with mine, we didn't always wish for our styles to be seen as the more expensive and less frequent comics category. Painting comics is a pain in the ass to do, but we'd like to be measured against everybody else making comics equally. I think that Dan may help that case more than I do.

Having said that, though, I do have one big concern. It's the same concern I've had with Dan's work for years and it's something I've spoken with him about several times already. It's those damn fucked-up noses of his. Don't act like you don't know what I'm talking about, you've seen it in everything he does. Dan draws/paints these weird, little, turned-up skull-face noses on almost everybody. Now, notice that I said "almost," as clearly Dan shows that he can draw what a nose really looks like and paints many other characters with the full, normal deal.

So what is this fascination with disfigurement? Just about every character Dan's had in over 10 years looks like a Berni Wrightson Frankenstein monster. Usually with odd features in an artist's work you'll find it physically on the man himself, but Dan's got a perfectly normal nose! He still has yet to explain this bizarre love for exposed nasal cavities to me in a way that makes sense. I recommend that everyone corner him on this issue, pressuring him to reconsider his folly and end this nostril nightmare.

With much respect,
Alex Ross

Drawings Alex Ross did in pencil as studies for possible painted pin-ups.

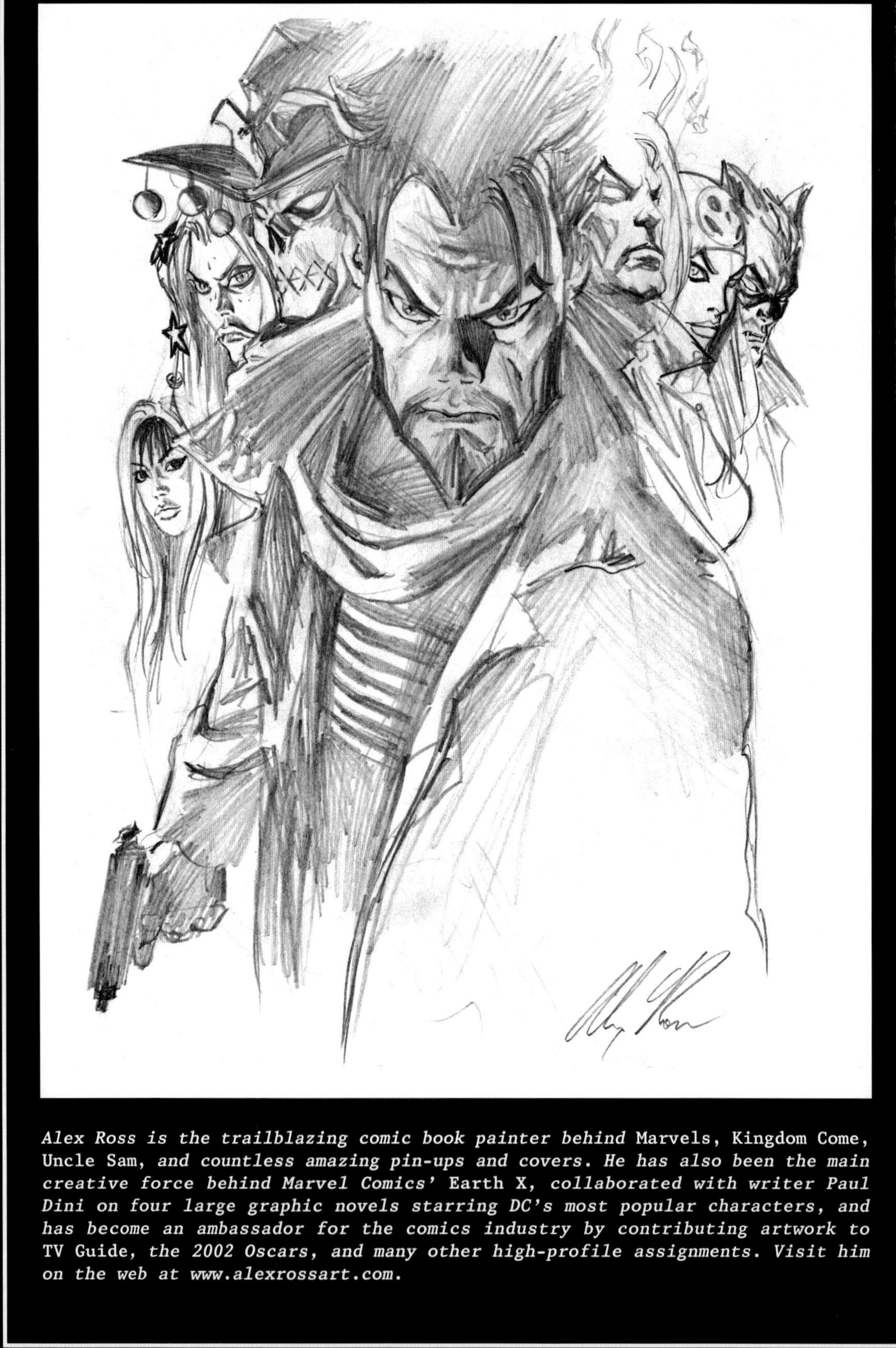

Alex Ross is the trailblazing comic book painter behind Marvels, Kingdom Come, Uncle Sam, *and countless amazing pin-ups and covers. He has also been the main creative force behind Marvel Comics'* Earth X, *collaborated with writer Paul Dini on four large graphic novels starring DC's most popular characters, and has become an ambassador for the comics industry by contributing artwork to* TV Guide, *the 2002 Oscars, and many other high-profile assignments. Visit him on the web at www.alexrossart.com.*

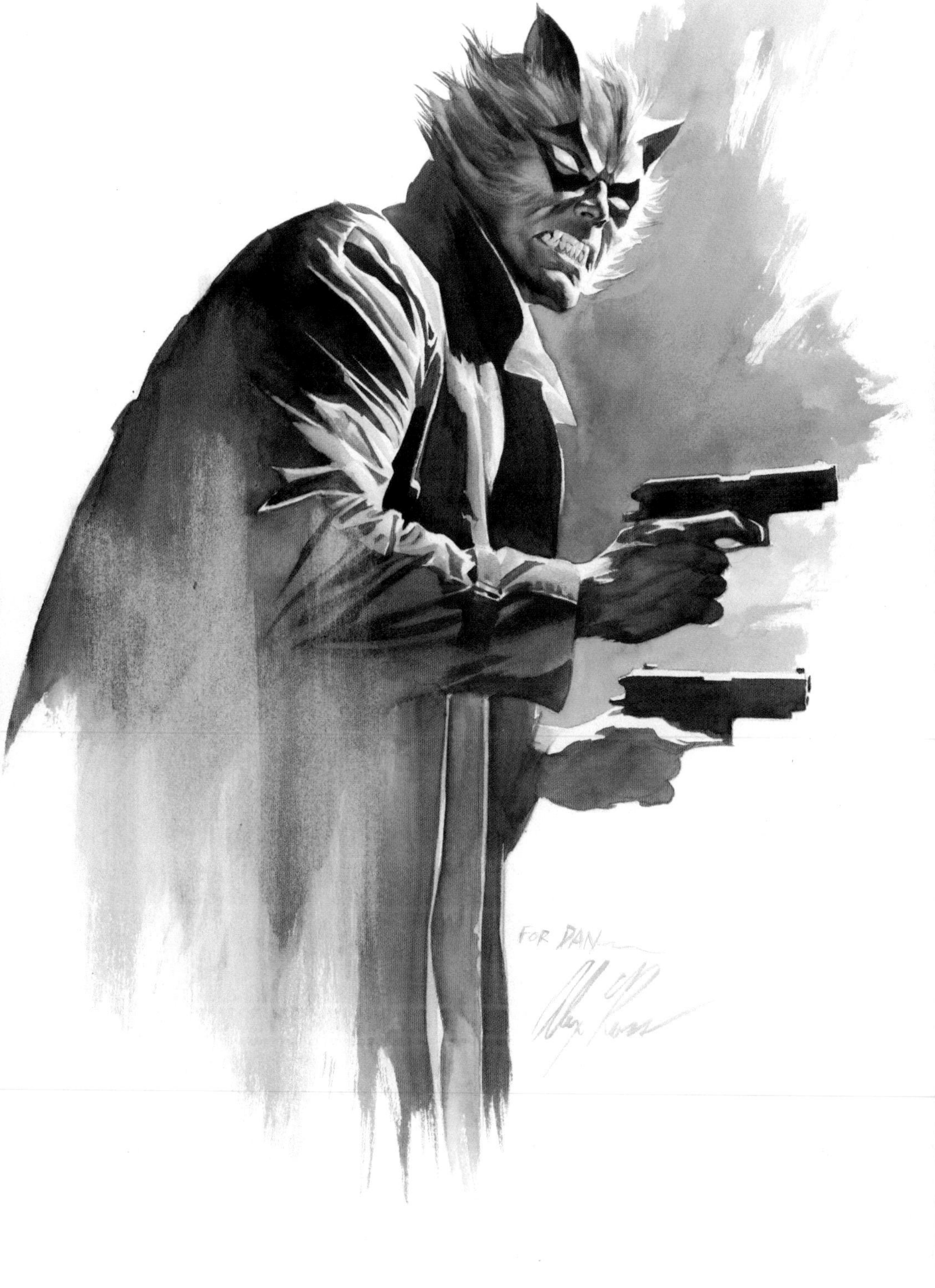
FOR DAN

Dan Brereton has been painting comics for fourteen years, writing them for seven, and reading and collecting them all his life. His works include *The Black Terror* (which won him the Russ Manning Most Promising Newcomer Award in 1990), *The Psycho*, *Dread*, *Legends of the World's Finest*, *Thrillkiller*, *Buffy The Vampire Slayer*, *JLA: Seven Caskets*, *Giantkiller*, *Nocturnals: Black Planet*, *The Gunwitch: Outskirts of Doom*, and many more. The Nocturnals were born out of his obsession with storytelling, motion pictures, monsters, crime fiction, Halloween, and the spirit of Fall. Dan lives with his children in the Sierra Nevada Mountains.

XXXXXXXXX THANK YOU'S XXXXXXXXX

I would like to first thank all of you who have taken the chance, picked up the books, stuck with them, been inspired by them, and urged me to keep them going. These stories are nothing without your readership.

I'd like to express my thanks and gratitude to my family: Mom and Dad, Lindsay, Audrey, Hunter, Michele, Levi and Matt—your support and inspiration have always been invaluable to me.

I'd also like to thank, for their various energies, contributions, support, and friendship, the following people: Beverly and Henry, Kelvin, David, Randy, Donna, Brian, David, Anh, Alex, Phil, Harris, Jamie, Joe, James, Keith, Steven, Jim, Sean, Bob, CB, Nicola, Steve, Ken, Clarissa, Jennifer, The Suttons, Kheang and Jo, Gregor, Justin, and certainly not last nor least, Chartruz.